# MAN'S DESTINY
# UNPLUGGED
## SEVEN AMAZING YEARS I SPENT LIVING WITH JESUS

*By*
ANGELA PORTER

*Man's Destiny Unplugged*
Copyright © 2021 by *Angela Porter*

All rights reserved. No part of this publication may be reproduced, distributed, or transmitted in any form or by any means, including photocopying, recording, or other electronic or mechanical methods, without the prior written permission of the author, except in the case of brief quotations embodied in critical reviews and certain other non-commercial uses permitted by copyright law.

ISBN
978-1-954932-42-5 (Paperback)
978-1-954932-41-8 (eBook)

# CONTENT

Chapter I
Growing Up As A Child .................................................. 1

Chapter II
Growing Up As A Teenager .............................................. 17

Chapter III
Life In The Army .......................................................... 35

Chapter IV
My Early Years In New York ........................................... 67

Chapter V
The Hell I Suffered From The Occult ........................... 79

Chapter VI
My Intense Search For Jesus And How He
Began Revealing Himself To Me .................................... 91

Chapter VII
My Journey From New York And Life In Naples ........ 101

Chapter VIII
My Move To West Palm Beach .................................... 111

Chapter IX
Hitting Rock Bottom .................................................. 119

Chapter X
How God Led Me From Danger To Safety ................ 129

Chapter XI
A New Phase—The Start Of A New Life .................... 177

Chapter XII
Our Move To Jamaica .................................................. 227

Chapter XIII
Our Journey Continues ............................................... 239

Chapter XIV
The Unfolding Of The End In Jamaica ........................245

Chapter XV
Leaving Jamaica Was The Best Thing .......................... 251

Chapter XVI
God's Supernatural Orchestration ............................... 261

Chapter XVII
The Unfolding Of The Unexpected That
Almost Crushed Me .................................................267

Chapter XVIII
The Departure I Was Not Prepared For ........................ 279

Chapter XIX
The Revealing Of Jesus ............................................... 287

# CHAPTER I

# GROWING UP AS A CHILD

I was born and raised in a place called Hillside. Hillside is in the parish of St. Thomas. It was, and still is, a little district of about four hundred people, at the back end of the northeastern part of Jamaica. You had to be intentional if you are going to Hillside because it does not lead to anywhere—you go there and then you leave. This was where my journey began.

I had a happy and lively childhood. There were girls and boys that I played with. There were the neighbors' kids that I played hide-and-seek and cricket (played with a bat and a ball) with. We fashioned our bats from coconut fronds, and we used fruits as balls—generally, sour oranges.

At evenings, we all gathered at the river and bathed. During the day, we explored our communities. We generally left home and ventured out to the surrounding hills to see what was out there. We found mangoes, locusts (a small fruit with a pit), pear (avocados), guavas, cashews, etc. We sought, found and enjoyed these fruits as well as the adventure that just being out there provided. We sought the cashews primarily for the fruit, which we ate at the moment we found them. The nuts were reserved to be taken home to be roasted.

These were days of innocence. We had no television sets, and we did not have many reasons to get out of Hillside. As I mentioned earlier, Hillside was not a district that you passed through on your way to anywhere—you had to go there. We knew nothing of missing kids or kidnapping, so there was nothing to be afraid of. We also were not aware of pedophiles and rape. Our knowledge of boys only extended to a girl liking a boy or vice versa.

When we returned home from our adventures at evening, dinner would already be prepared, and our parents were not worried. As far as they knew, they had no reason to. Hillside was a child's paradise. We grew and flourished. There were no self-esteem issues. We were all children, and we were free.

Mondays through Fridays, we attended school—basic school and primary school. They were the only two schools in Hillside. For much of my childhood, I knew the person who was in charge of the basic school. Her name was Ms. Brown. I had been to her home at least twice. She was the sole teacher of the basic school.

The principal of the primary school was a woman named Mrs. Ferrar. There were two other teachers working at the primary school. This was the school I attended. For reasons not known to me, I did not attend the basic school.

I recall on the first day I went to primary school, I felt a bit intimidated. Some of my classmates attended the basic school and were friends from there. They also appeared to be academically prepared at the level they were. I did not have that preparatory tutoring.

There was a girl named Lura and another named Meredith. Lura's mother, I learned, worked with Social Security. I did not know about Meredith's. In any event, they were friends and they made it known in all they did. They were self-assured and confident. I did not know those words at that time, but looking back, that's the way it seems now. I recall wondering, after realizing that Lura lived just across the fence from school, if she was so cocky because she lived within such close proximity. By Hillside's standard, I lived far away from school.

By all accounts, Mrs. Ferrar, the principal, was the most affluent in Hillside. She, of course, was the principal. Additionally, her husband owned a gas station in Willow Grove—a town approximately two and a half miles from Hillside. She had no biological children, but she had three nieces living with her. The girls' mothers were in America and England. They, too, were self-assured, but I attributed that to their aunt being headmistress, as the title was back then, of the school and also that they were rich. I did not know Mr. Ferrar. However, I would see his vehicle come and go because the main road in and out of Hillside ran past my home. Of course, in Hillside, all the adults knew what was going on in other people's lives—good or bad. It was that type of close-knit town where information flowed. So, of course, I knew who drove what.

So I entered first grade feeling that I had a bit of disadvantage, even though I did not know what that meant at that time. We, the first graders, were blessed, however, to have a teacher by the name of Ms. Rens. She was married to a fourth cousin of mine. At that time, I knew nothing of that family connection. The Renses lived by the Hillside square and had a big white house with a wraparound veranda. That was where Ms. Rens lived. She liked me from the start, and that bolstered my confidence. I cannot remember how my transformation in learning began, but I started learning fast, and soon, I became *brighter* than my classmates, including Lura and Meredith. I had a thirst for learning then, and I still do to this day. I eventually was accepted in Lura and Meredith's circle. I continued to be a fast learner, and I was thriving.

In the mornings we had *devotion*. Devotion was the first order of school business each day. All the children gathered, and the principal or one of the teachers moderated. We sang songs and read the Bible. It was at devotion in Hillside Primary that I learned the song "All Things Bright and Beautiful the Lord God Made Them All," as well as other God-glorifying songs. In the evenings, the blackboards were pushed to the sides so that all the students could see the moderator at the top end of the building. The school was a large open space, divided in classes partitioned by blackboards. The principal's office was in a separate room. At 4:30 p.m., the bell rang, and it did not matter what we were doing; we had to hurriedly put everything away and get ready for evening devotion. The blackboards were immediately pushed to the side, and we all stood. I recall one of the evening songs we sang was, "Now the Day is Over." We also sang the national anthem, "Jamaica, Land we Love." It was there, at Hillside Primary, that I really started learning about God.

One day, I heard that Mrs. Rens was going to be leaving. I remember thinking that if that is true, it will be bad for me. I really liked her and felt a sense of attachment to her. I was also thriving under her tutelage. At that time, in Hillside, a child would not ask an adult certain questions. If we did, we were considered rude, *not knowing our place*. We were supposed to wait until we were told. On occasions, though, we overheard the adults talking about things that they did not want us to hear about. If we did hear, we were expected not to repeat what we heard. If we did repeat it, we would be spanked On this particular Friday, as I recall, we went outside expecting our normal time of games—holding hands, singing songs and repeating our multiplication tables. This Friday, however, was different. Ms. Rens was not feeling well. I later learned that she may have been pregnant. Anyway, she announced that she was going to be leaving. Immediately, I started feeling quite sick. I believe I or some other child asked her why she was leaving. I was wondering if she did not like us anymore. We were told that her husband was being transferred, by his job, to another country in the West Indies. I began crying. Others cried too. We all loved and admired Ms. Rens. She was a loving and caring teacher, who made us all feel special. I felt like I belonged to her, and I think most of the other children felt the same way. She made her announcement; we cried and then we started to sing. It was on that day Ms. Rens taught us the song:

> When you come to the end of a perfect day, and you sit alone with your thoughts, when the chimes ring out with a carol gay and your friends will have to part. Well, this is the end of a perfect day, near the end of a journey too, but it leaves a hope that is big and strong and a wish that is kind and true. For memories have painted this perfect day with colors that never fade, and you find at the end of a perfect day, the soul of a friend you have made.

I was no more than nine years old when we learned and sang that song with and for Ms. Rens, but I have never forgotten it.

I remember Ms. Rens's parting encouragement, after hugging each of us, "Keep doing well." I never forgot those words, though, consciously, I never thought of them. I went on to do very well, in the years to come, at Hillside Primary.

When the school had what it termed *Open Day*—a day when each child's achievements were recognized—our parents and other well-wishers came to school for the occasion. First and second place were announced for each subject, and prizes were awarded. For consecutive years, except for arts and craft, I placed first in every subject. I was quite pleased, and my mother beamed with pride; Papa was gone to work. He worked as headman and bookkeeper for certain properties, and I do not recall him ever taking a day off. He was a dedicated worker.

I would later tell people that not having excelled in arts and craft at Hillside Primary, somehow, hampered my future ability to draw or do well in anything that was arts and craft related. Years later, while attending Willow Grove Secondary School, I failed to get one hundred percent in a final exam in biology because the teacher said that I did not draw the heart correctly, although I labeled it perfectly. My inability to excel in arts and craft was haunting me.

At some point, during this period of my early life, Papa got a job at Copper's Hill. Copper's Hill was east of Danvers Pen and was also located in St. Thomas. His job required him to oversee a property. It was a large property consisting mainly of bananas. There were also some chickens in two large buildings. The owner of the property was Mr. Pengelley. He lived in Kingston, and he visited the property each Friday to pay the workers and to take away bananas and eggs. There was a decent house on the property, and this was where we lived.

Copper's Hill was primarily a farming community. There was a grocery store, but there were not many other places of public convenience that I can remember. There was a man called Mr. Sivier. He was my father's boss. He had a wife and a number of children, mainly boys. He came by our home often. He had a big broad nose, and the texture of his face was bumpy and rough. Almost from the beginning, I did not like Mr. Sivier. I believe I expressed my feelings to my parents. In any event, the Siviers became our good friends, and, soon, we were going to their home on Sunday nights for church services. Mrs. Sivier conducted these services. On Sunday afternoons, we attended Sunday school at the Watsons.

We walked to school at Danvers Pen. Danvers Pen was approximately six miles from Copper's Hill. Papa had a bike, and there was a man in the area with a pickup van. His name was Mr. King. He went to Danvers Pen often. He had a son called Delroy. Delroy had bow legs and was friendly and pleasant. We became friends with Delroy. Each morning, we tried to be ready at seven o'clock in order to get a ride from Delroy's dad. We succeeded often, but on occasions we missed the ride, and when we did, we had to walk to school. We also got a ride home from school with Delroy's father, but many times, we had to walk. It was on one such occasion, while walking home, that I met the Watsons. There were two of us, and they stopped to give us a ride.

They invited us to Sunday school at their home. Mr. Watson had many acres of cane and bananas. They also had a lovely home. The biggest in Copper's Hill. He also had a fine car of that era. They had no children.

On the first Sunday that we were going to the Watsons, we got dressed, walked about two miles, trotted up a hill track of red dirt, which was a shortcut to their home. I was impressed with the yard— benches, fruit trees, flowering plants, etc. The house was two levels and was beautiful. I announced our presence, and Mrs. Watson came outside. She welcomed us to her home, and she began teaching us about Jesus, while we sat on the benches. We did this many Sundays, enjoyed it and looked forward to going.

One school morning, we missed Delroy's dad, and while a group of us was walking to school, we saw a man. Thinking back, he must have looked crazy because my recollection is that we all started running. To evade him, we ran into a nearby cane field, and he pursued us. Some successfully made their way through the cane field to the other side of the road. We ran in different directions. I was behind, and I saw the man, his hand held high, with a machete about to come down on my sister, Pat. Suddenly, courage welded up in me, and I pounced on the man. The machete fell to the ground, and I said, "Run Pat, run!"

Pat started running with me following behind. Soon, we too were on the other side of the road. Either we outran the man or he gave up chasing us, but we saw him no more. We continued on our way to school. I do not remember what that day at school, for me, was like, but I do remember feeling scared about going home that evening, and I promised myself that I would not miss Delroy's father. Delroy must have told his dad about the incident because for many days afterward, Delroy's dad waited for us, even when we were a bit late coming down from our home in the mornings or leaving school in the evenings.

Life at Danvers Pen School continued. We learned our multiplication tables as well as other things, and I did very well at learning them. Dad continued being Headman at Mr. Pengelley's property, and we continued attending church at the Siviers'. One day, while at home, Pat and I went down to a stream, just across the road from our house. We heard a fluttering sound. We looked in the direction of the sound and saw a large multicolored bug, on its back in the water, coming toward us. We quickly gathered up the remaining dishes and took off running in the direction of home. Upon getting home, we told our parents about the bug. I do not recall that we ever went down to the stream again.

One day, I was in the house with my mother. Dad came home from the direction of the Siviers' house. He was visibly upset and told us that he was being terminated. I do not remember if that was the word he used. I knew, however, that Papa was no longer going to be working for Mr. Pengelley, and we were going to be returning to Hillside. I cannot remember if I was glad or sad. The people, most of whom I encountered at Copper's Hill, were strange to me as a child, and the walk to school was long. Apart from the Grants, there were no other playmates. The homes were far apart, and there was not much for kids to do, but I did enjoy walking through the banana field on Mr. Pengelley's property, from time to time, picking ripe bananas off the bunches. It was also fun to go in the coops and pick up eggs, freshly laid by the hens. Apart from that, the place was spooky.

From a child, I was very protective of my family members—male and female. Instinctively, as my father left to go out after making the announcement, I followed close behind. Some distance between where we lived and the Siviers' home, my father saw and got into an argument with Mr. Sivier. I recall Papa telling Mr. Sivier that he was a liar.

I believe Mr. Sivier, realizing that Mr. Pengelley was extremely fond of my father, was jealous. Mr. Pengelley was saying favorable things about my father. For example, he said that the property was producing much more since my father took over. Since Mr. Sivier was the man between my dad and Mr. Pengelley, Mr. Sivier could say what he wanted without my dad knowing what was said.

I never learned what the lie was. I knew that my father never took anything that was not allowed from the property. The argument continued, however, and I remember distinctly that my father told Mr. Sivier, "My kids will not eat stone for bread, but if they do, their blood will be on your shoulders."

I do not remember what Mr. Sivier's reaction was, but I was never more proud of my dad than at that moment, and even though I did not know what the future held for us, I felt ten feet tall. I assumed that the rebuke came from the Bible. I latched on to it, and I felt, at that moment, that we were in God's hands, and I knew it was going to be okay. Nevertheless, I was quite upset that the people who had us in their house every Sunday night, when I would rather be home in bed or preparing for school the next morning, would do this to us. I never trusted them, but I realized my mother was very committed even if her heart may not have been fully in it. My mother was a pleaser.

For a long time, afterward, that was the only saying I knew and could quote from the Bible. I was so proud of my dad, and because I thought that what he told Mr. Sivier was from the Bible, indeed, I felt a close connection with God and knew he would indeed see us through. We returned to Hillside. I do not recall any details of the move.

We did move into a different house than the one we left when we went to Copper's Hill, and this one was my parents'. I returned to Hillside Primary after being away for two years. I continued to do well in school. On holidays, I continued to explore the outskirts and surrounding areas and swim with my cousins and neighbors in the river along with other activities.

One Friday of each month, I voluntarily skipped school and went to the field with my parents. The field was situated in the mountain area. My parents farmed there. We took pots, plates, etc., and while my dad and brothers were farming, I cooked with my mother and sisters. We picked things from the field and cooked them right there. It was like a picnic, as we all sat around and ate the freshly harvested delicious foods. I loved learning, and I loved school, but I always looked forward to those days when we went to the field. We returned home in the evenings feeling a sense of accomplishment and joy.

I also loved exploring, and I was adventurous. On occasions, I woke up early, in the mornings, and I left home before anyone else awoke. As a child, I, generally, did this to get to a certain mango tree or pear tree before anyone else did.

One morning, I woke up quite early and went off to a mango tree, a little way from home. I walked down the street, and I turned into a lane beside Ms. Jane's house. Ms. Jane was an old lady that lived alone. There were a number of tombs of deceased family members, directly by the lane, in front of her house. I walked on, in the dark, to the Number Eleven mango tree. It was a large mango tree, situated in an area surrounded by houses but not particularly close to any. The mangoes ripen and then fell to the ground. There were times when we, the children in Hillside, went directly from school at lunchtime, or after school in the evenings, to the mango tree. It was all about who got there first, and so when we were dismissed, we made our way there.

When I got to the tree, it was still dark. There was some moonlight, and I was able to find some mangoes. As I continued looking for more mangoes, I heard some sounds, as if someone was walking on dried sticks and leaves. I continued to look. The wind blew, and more mangoes fell. I then scrambled to that location and picked them up.

I was satisfied with my effort and decided to leave. As I was walking away, I thought I heard footsteps behind me. I looked behind but did not see anyone. I hastened my steps. As I got closer to Ms. Jane's house, the steps became clearer. I looked behind, and, this time, I saw two pink slippers, resembling a pair of ballet shoes, with the back broken down. I also heard a cackling sort of sound, but I did not see anyone. The pair of slippers was moving towards me, as if worn by an invisible person. I ran past Ms. Jane's house and out into the street. As I entered the street, I heard a distinct woman's voice, laughing, and the slippers returning to the direction from which they came. I believe that was the last time I went to the Number Eleven mango tree by myself.

On many levels, Hillside was an innocent place. In my years there, I was aware of only two acts of violence. In one instance, a man was accused of killing another man at a place called George Peace. I believe it had to do with an issue involving their cows. I do not know if that is accurate, but that is the story that went around. The victim was not from Hillside. I do not believe anyone at Hillside knew him. The police investigation, however, led to the murderer being a man from Hillside. That was novel and, I dare say, unheard of for the people of Hillside. Murder was simply not something that was associated with Hillside. There was nothing there that pointed in that direction. The man was arrested, tried, found guilty and sent to prison.

On another occasion, a little boy was killed. The report was that two men had a quarrel, and one of them threw a stone. The little boy was in the wrong place at the wrong time and was hit. There was a back and forth as to who threw the stone. Eventually, it started going around in Hillside that it was a particular individual. The information got to the police in Willow Grove, and he was arrested. He spent a few years in prison before he was released. Some thought he got off *light*. Others said that because the police were not fully sure who threw the stone, the sentence was somewhat lenient. The little boy was related to the Renses, and they were distant relatives of my family.

One Saturday evening, my mother sent me to buy some groceries at the Campbells' shop. That was the main grocer in the district. It was about 5:30 p.m. The sun was still shining. As I passed by a plot of land belonging to the dead boy's grandparents, I saw the little, brown- complexion boy, with curly hair, looking at me from a Tangerine tree, while he shook it gaily and laughed with me. He appeared to have been enjoying himself. I stood there for a while looking at the boy and laughing back at him. I do not know how long I was there. I was about ten years old. It suddenly occurred to me that it was Matthew, and he was dead. I then ran all the way to the store.

I purchased the groceries, at Mrs. Campbell's store, placed them in two bags, put the bags on the floor and just stood there. It got dark, and I continued standing there. My parents did not come looking for me. The explanation could be because Hillside was a harmless place, they thought that there was no need for concern. I continued to stand there for a very long time.

There was a bar attached to the grocery store. A man named Paul was in the bar. He traveled to and from the USA. Sometime between eight and nine o'clock, I heard Paul say he was going to Dolly. Mr. Dolly, as he was called, lived in England for many years. I do not know if he originally lived in Hillside, but he returned there to live, and he opened a pub. It was there that Paul said he was going. The pub was located to the north of my home, separated by a gully. When I heard him say that, I immediately took my bags up and started following behind. He walked past the road leading to Mr. Dolly's pub, and I followed. He went directly to my gate, and then he turned back. I believe that Paul, seeing me standing there for so long, assumed that I was afraid of something and decided to walk me home. There was no *thank- you* because he did not say a word. I was, however, very thankful. When I got home, I related the incident to my parents. I do not know if they believed me. I never heard anyone say they had a similar experience, and I do not remember if I told anyone else.

Mr. Campbell later hanged himself at a plot of land on a hill that they owned, just south of where I lived. It was rumored that he borrowed some money, gambled it away and was unable to repay it. His wife, it was said, had no knowledge of the loan or his gambling habits.

She was, understandably, so ashamed that she migrated to America. I do not know if she ever returned to Hillside for a visit.

A woman named Ms. Zeth, who also lived in Hillside, died tragically. She was married. She did not live very far from my home— about a five-minute walk down the road. She had a beautiful daughter named Anna. Ms. Zeth also had two sons. One Saturday, Ms. Zeth's husband reported that she left home, to go to the field, that Saturday morning and had not returned at dusk that evening. I think he said he went looking for her but did not see her. Ms. Zeth was quite fat.

When we heard about it, I followed my dad down to the crossroads where Ms. Zeth may have traveled—to her field—and to which she would have to return. The police were summoned, and they came. This was a big deal for the people of Hillside. These were not everyday occurrences. A search party, including the police, went in search of her. Later, about an hour, we heard that they had found her, but she was dead. She was found with a machete protruding from one side of her body to the next side of her body. The police theorized that she may have slipped, while walking with the machete, rolled down the hill and fell on the machete, at which point it plunged into her. I do not remember what her husband's reaction to the news was. Some months later, on a moonshine night, my sister, Pat, and I were outside our backyard looking at the stars. I heard Pat say, "Look, look, Ms. Zeth." To my utter dismay, there was a woman in full white and of the same size, walking just like Ms. Zeth and going in the opposite direction of her home. Quite afraid, we ran inside and went to bed.

The first time that I saw two adults who almost got into a fight, in Hillside, involved my brother, Carlton, who was a police officer in Kingston and was visiting us in Hillside for the weekend. It was customary for Hillside folk to get dressed up on Sundays and congregate at the square. And so, on this Sunday, we went out to the square. My brother got into an argument with a childhood friend. I do not know what the nature of the argument was, but it got quite heated. My brother had his service revolver on him, and that scared me. Though my brother was never an aggressive person, the other man, was at a distance from him, and he had a stone in his hand. Just as the man seemed ready to throw the stone, I got in front of my brother and said, "You're going to have to hit me if you throw it." I remember the man saying words to the effect, "You must be glad your sister is there." That diffused the argument, and both men went their way. I do not know if they ever spoke again.

My dad had some goats. On occasions he would take the goats to the hill and let them graze there. At evening, he or one of my brothers would get the goats. This particular evening, it appeared that the goats were making their way down before someone had a chance to get them. My brother, Dane, went to get the goats and came back home with the news that a large ram goat, of ours, was eating some grass at the side of the road of a man's property, and the man took a knife and slit the ram's throat, killing it.

My dad was very upset that evening, and I became very upset, as well. It was a very sad evening for my family. The senselessness of the act and the obvious mean-spiritedness made the whole thing very hard to comprehend. I remember consoling my dad while totally despising the man who committed this unnecessary and, I thought, most evil act. I do not know what became of that man.

On a more personal note, I was a sort of tomboy. It was fashionable, when I was a kid, for us girls to climb trees. One day, while in my early teens, I left home and went down to a neighbor's property with the intention of climbing an ackee tree. I got the neighbor's permission to do so. I proceeded to climb the tree, and I got up in it. It was a big tree and had big roots protruding out of the ground. I do not recall how it happened, whether a limb broke or my hands just got loose, but a short time after getting up in the tree, I was involuntarily on my way down. I was falling face up, and I remembered thinking that I'm going to break my back. At that moment, I felt as if someone flipped me into a sitting position during the fall. When I hit the ground, I was on my buttocks rather than my back. I was unable to move for a while, and so I just sat there thinking that God had sent an angel to rescue me. After thirty minutes, I felt well enough to get up. I got up and started moving. It was difficult to walk at first, but I pressed along in the direction of home. By the time I got home,

I was pretty much okay. I was sure that an angel caught me, flipped me up and broke the fall. I fell from a great height on the huge root of the tree, and I was fine within an hour. I told my mother what happened, once I got home. I believe that was when my tree climbing ended as well as my tomboy syndrome.

Another time, we went swimming at the river. Going swimming at the river was part of our childhood. We also bathed there on a regular basis. This day in question, we went to a deep part of the river to swim. I was a good swimmer. However, at a certain point, I started going down and coming up. It appeared there was a bit of current there. I was with my cousins, my brother and others. As I was going up and down, and could not seem to get out, I was getting tired, and I thought that I was going to drown. Just then, my cousin looked in my direction, saw me, and they rescued me. My nostrils burned, while I lied on the gravel and tried to regain my strength. I am convinced that God caused my cousin to turn in my direction at that crucial moment.

When I was fourteen years old, I washed my uniform—a tunic along with the belt—and placed them on the clothes line at home. When I went to remove them from the line, the belt was missing. I needed my belt. School rules demanded that the belt be worn. I was very concerned, and I prayed, that night, and asked God, "Please let me find my belt." I then went to sleep.

While I was asleep that night, I dreamed that I should go outside, and there I would find my belt on a pepper tree. I got up at that point—about 2:00 a.m.—and went outside, and there, on the pepper tree, was my belt. I learned at that moment that Jesus hears and answers prayers. At age sixteen, while a student at Willow Grove Secondary School, we were sitting the Jamaica Certificate Examination (JSC). The JSC required that you sit for these examinations by taking individual subjects. I applied to take seven subjects, including English and mathematics. I was not particularly strong in math. Part of the reason was that I had a love for English and, by all accounts, was very good at it. My English teacher was Ms. Giggs, and my math teacher was Mr. Giggs. They were wife and husband. I always did my English assignment in Mr. Giggs's class, and he was not very amused by it. I continued this behavior, however, resulting in him standing by my desk, during his class, or constantly coming to my desk to be sure that I was doing *his* work and not *Vera's*. Vera, of course, was Ms. Giggs.

I arrived at school, on the day of exam, ready to sit my seven subjects. As the instructor, presiding over the exam, started handing out the exam papers and giving us the necessary instructions, it occurred to me that I did not study much and was, therefore, not feeling very confident. The thought came to me to pray. I remembered the prayer that I prayed when my belt went missing, and here I was again in a situation where I needed to do well. I wanted to do it for me; additionally, I wanted my parents, especially Papa, to be proud of me. Papa was a very knowledgeable and intelligent man. Education meant much to him. He had a saying—you could call it an adage—which he said almost daily, "Knowledge is power." I did not want to let him down. Papa was once called to the principal's office, and he defended me. He was a man of integrity, and he believed in honesty. He disciplined us when necessary, but he did not allow anyone to take advantage of us, so if we were right, Papa would say so right there, regardless of who the person was. He was not afraid to speak truth when a situation necessitated it. And so, for my success and my parents' pleasure, I bowed my head and prayed. I took the exam, and that was that.

One Monday morning, I was walking in the direction of the principal's office. Upon arriving at school each morning, if time allowed, I first went to the girls' bathroom to freshen up. This was one such morning. The bathroom was in the vicinity of the principal's office. Just outside her office, around a corner, there was a bulletin board, inside a cabinet, where important announcements were posted. As I approached that location, I saw Mr. Giggs, Ms. Bowmer, the principal, and a few others, facing the cabinet and looking intently at something in it. They seemed quite pleased with what they were looking at. Mr. Giggs informed me, even before I had a chance to see for myself, that the JSC results were out and I had passed *all* seven, including mathematics.

They seemed quite surprised. I was too because I even got a few with distinction—meaning a very high pass. Mr. Giggs was most pleased with my math performance.

I realized, on that day, that Jesus had, again, come through for me, when I desperately needed him to. I had not set out to please my math teacher and the principal, but they were quite pleased. I was most eager to get home and tell Papa and Mother the good news, and they were very happy when I told them.

# CHAPTER
# II

# GROWING UP AS A TEENAGER

There were two churches in Hillside, the Methodist church and the Church of God of Prophecy. The more affluent attended the Methodist and all the others, who so wished, attended the Church of God of Prophecy. It appeared, in Hillside, that the church one attended was determined more on the basis of class rather than a set of beliefs. We attended the Church of God of Prophecy. I do not remember exactly when I started going to church. Reverend Graham, the area administrator, visited the Church of God of Prophecy when they had *revival*. These were usually a week-long series of meetings, and many people from outside Hillside attended. The tempo of the services was also heightened. They sang lively hymns and choruses and beat the tambourines. The preaching was different from what it would normally be. This seemed to have been because these preachers from outside Hillside had more experience with preaching. Whatever the real reason, all I knew was that it was not the same.

These were exciting times for families in Hillside—those who were not members of the Methodist church. My mom finished dinner early. We finished our school homework, washed the dishes and asked if we were allowed to go along. Mother generally said, "Yes."

When we arrived at the church, the songs would have started, and there was usually an air of excitement. Even those who were not very interested in church-going, usually the men, could be seen in good numbers, standing on the outside looking in. We went inside, found a seat, close to the back of the church, and sat there. Mother, it appeared, preferred to sit closer to the front. Maybe, she did not want to be distracted by the crowd on the outside. Mother enjoyed the singing and clapping. At times, she could be seen dancing and really enjoying the songs. The service continued, and I sat at the back, with my friends, talking and singing along, as well. We were also having a good time. This was the sort of event that Mother and our female neighbors discussed and agreed to attend. Therefore, my friends were there, too. It was an occasion to get out of the house at nights. My parents were strict and, because there were no street lights, we were not allowed to go out and about freely at nights as we did during the daytime.

Mother spent much of her days seeing to the things of the home—washing, cooking and seeing to our welfare. When we attended Hillside Primary School, we went home for lunch, almost daily, and Mother always had something cooked ready for us. In the early days, there was no electricity in Hillside. We had no television, no refrigerator, or any of those modern amenities. We did have an icebox, and a truck came by often selling blocks of ice. We purchased a twenty-five or fifty block and placed it in the icebox. Mother placed meats and other perishable things in the icebox. Mother's entertainment was limited to stopping by the neighbors' homes or one of those neighbors stopping by us. They talked about what was going on in Hillside, at that time, or anything of interest they may have heard on the radio, usually a newsworthy item. It gave me great pleasure, therefore, to see my mother enjoying herself.

Mother had a very happy look on her face when she was having a good time. This gave me much happiness, and I thought, even as a child, that she deserved to be happy. On occasions, Mother also visited her brother's home. We went along and, while the adults talked, my siblings and I played with our cousins. We played games—hide- and- seek and ring games. On the nights when the moon shone, those games were most enjoyable. At other times, we used a torch provided by my uncle. The kids were never allowed to be a part of the adults' discussions. There were also times when we visited with the neighbor, living closest to us, and a similar format ensued.

My dad was not as sociable. He did not visit other people's homes. He opted to remain home and read or listen to the radio. He never went to sleep until we were safely back home. Papa's social activities were limited to stopping off at Willow Grove, on some Fridays after work, and having a beer, or some other alcoholic drink, with his brother, Levy, who lived in Willow Grove. Sometimes, Papa went to Mr. Dolly's pub or another bar at a place called George Hall. I never knew my father to have had any friends. His brother visited our home, on a regular basis, and they talked. Papa spoke to other men, apart from his drinking associates, if they visited our home. At the time of Papa's death, my eldest brother said that a man named Radnor was our father's friend. My brother, therefore, wanted Radnor to eulogize our father. I knew nothing of that friendship. My dad visited Radnor's bar, but I never heard of a friendship between them. I told my brother, "No," and at our father's funeral, I did the eulogy.

One night, after the preaching ended at the revival, there was an altar call. My mother went forward and made the decision to follow Jesus. I do not think my father was very pleased with this decision, but my mother would not be deterred. My mother immediately started, as I recall, behaving like a Christian. On another night, when the altar call was given, I went forward, and I, too, decided to follow Jesus. I do not remember if I told Papa. Mother was now a Christian. Mother would be going to church, often, and I would go with her.

There was a visible change in my mother. In the past, when my dad got into an argument with her, Mother responded and argued with my father, even telling him that he was miserable. This was a general feeling among us children, as well. We thought our father, with all his good qualities, was miserable. Now, however, Mother would not respond to our father when he tried to argue with her. There were other changes as well. As kids, we thought Mother was also miserable. It might have been the frequent bickering with my dad and fussing with us about what needed to be done, was not done, or was not done properly—which I guess was not according to the way she wanted it done. Mother was now more accommodating. She appeared to have got more patient. She was not, by any means, perfect, but one could see that she was really trying, and there were a lot of positive changes in her.

For me, my Christian walk, at that point, was not that easy. I encouraged my friends Evita, Beata and Donette to become Christians. They did not seem ready to make that decision. We continued to be friends. There were not many choices, and we had been friends for a long time. As younger kids, we explored our environs together—we bathed at the gully and at the river together; we went to school together, and we were accustomed to visiting each other's homes. I was a teenager, and a normal one, so there was the consideration, too, of boys, and there were some cute and handsome boys in Hillside.

I went to church regularly and was liking every moment of it. I threw myself into the church environment. Under the guidance and tutelage of Mr. and Mrs. Lane, I started to read the Bible. Mr. and Mrs. Lane were the caretakers in Hillside for the Church of God of Prophecy. They also acted as the local pastors, though, they never gave themselves any titles. They were simply known as Brother—and Sister Lane. They liked me a lot, and I both loved and respected them. I helped them to clean the church, and I performed other such duties, as were required. I loved God then, and I do even more now. I remembered the prayers he answered when I needed those things so desperately. I also believed in my heart that it was the right way for me.

There was also a young woman called Emelda. She lived with and was raised by her aunt. She was not very outgoing. I recall, as a child, that she was not interested in having me or anyone else for a friend. Emelda became saved too. She may have made her decision the very night I made mine. Emelda was very serious about her Christian walk. She was a lot more serious than I was. She wanted me to be as serious as she was, and she made that effort to reach out to me. Emelda and I became close church sisters. On Saturday evenings, she called across the *divide*—a gully that separated our plots of land—to find out if I was ready to go to church. We went and joined with Mr. and Mrs. Lane to prepare the church for Sunday morning services.

There was a pastor, living outside Hillside, who was responsible for the Church of God of Prophecy in Hillside. Her name was Mrs. Barclay. We called her Reverend Barclay. She lived in the Morant Bay area at a place called Lyssons. She was very fond of Emelda. Emelda visited her often and, after a while, she took Emelda to live with her.

Emelda had a cousin named Sean. Sean was always a very skinny boy. It was Sean's mother whom Emelda lived with. I do not recall when Sean decided to follow Jesus. I do remember that Mr. and Mrs. Lane gave all of us, children, Bible verses to study. At Wednesday night services, we recited the Bible verses. Once, they assigned the books of the Bible. We were to study them in order and then we would recite them at a particular time. Sean was very competitive as was I.

The day arrived for us to recite the books, as they are in the Bible. This was a competition, and a prize was going to be awarded. I do not recall how many of us, kids, were there, and I do not remember if Emelda was there, but I do remember that Sean and I were standing close to each other, and at the sound of "Start" we did.

We could hear each other, and the goal was to finish first, while accurately reciting each book in order. At the end, Sean was convinced that he finished first. Whether he truly thought that, or was just being his competitive self, I do not know. Mr. and Mrs. Lane were the final deciding votes and so, while others applauded and cheered our efforts, they pronounced me the winner, and Sean had to settle for second place. Sean and I taught Sunday school. The groups we taught sat close together. There were times when Sean told me something I taught the kids was not correct. We resolved those differences in an amicable way, and there was no animosity.

I do not remember the event that led to my departure from the church environment and my close involvement with the direction in which God was taking me.

In 1975, I turned sixteen. Hillside was still a remote district and had no visible changes from earlier years. I was, however, a normal teenager and was a self-willed one at that. I decided I was going to have a sweet sixteen birthday party. I went ahead and printed, I believe, fifty invitations. The venue for the party was going to be Mr. Dolly's pub. He had a large enough room attached to the bar. He had a generator and a juke box. You had to put 10cent into the juke box, choose the song you wished to hear, press that tab and the selection played. We had no television. We were not privy to magazines, etc., at home. I am not quite sure how a sixteen-year-old girl from the boondocks of Hillside came to know about sweet sixteen, but I did, and I was running with it. Two weeks after printing the invitations, I was at the church.

Reverend Barclay was also there. I cannot remember if my mother was baptized at this point. Rev. Barclay was talking to me about getting baptized. I was telling her about my sweet sixteen party and the plans I had made and was continuing to make. She encouraged me to scrap the plans for the party and almost convinced me. I told her that I would think about it, and I did. I wanted to do what was right in the eyes of Jesus, but I was really strong-willed and that caused me to be determined. The more I thought about it, the more I wanted to do it. After all, I reasoned, I already told my friends, and the plans were underway. I decided to proceed with the party, and on the specified date, the party went on. There was a birthday cake, and, of course, the juke box was playing. For reasons I never bothered to evaluate, after the fact, my sweet sixteen birthday party turned out to be a lot less than I thought it would be. Rev. Barclay and the Lanes were right. I was wrong.

Church was never the same after that for me. I did not get baptized, and I started drifting. My mother continued her Christian walk, while I returned to activities with my friends. Those activities were many and varied. Let me omit those details and suffice to say that when I walked away from Jesus, it took me down a path I had not planned to go and to places I wish I had not gone. This one, I will tell you; at the age of seventeen, after graduating from Willow Grove Secondary School, where I was successful in passing seven JSC subjects after praying to Jesus and asking for his help, I got a job with the government of Jamaica in an area called JAMAL (The Jamaica Movement for the Advancement of Literacy). It required me to travel to Cedar Valley, where I taught adults to read. It was far from home, but it was not difficult getting transportation there. I was required to go there three days per week— Mondays, Wednesdays and Fridays. The other two days, I worked at the JAMAL office in Morant Bay, assisting the secretary or filling in for her on the days when she was off. Her name was Sadye.

I would soon learn that having some knowledge of sweet sixteen does not prepare you for the world out there. I was a young and bright woman, academically, and I was full of life. I had, what many termed, a *bouncy* personality. I had snow-white teeth and was always laughing. I laughed easily, was feisty and always stood my ground. I was a happy, young woman.

Sadye seemed to like me; I asked her how to find certain places in Morant Bay, and she directed me or accompanied me. She lived in Morant Bay, walking distance to the office. She was much older than I was and looked very well. She mainly wore pants. I believe, during those years, gabardine fabric was the rage. Sadye had gabardine pants of various colors, and she was fond of head wraps. I do not recall ever seeing her hair. She was accustomed to wearing head wraps in colors that matched her slacks. So, if she wore a pair of light yellow slacks, she also wore a light yellow head wrap. She had an uncanny knack of getting the shade of color, of her head wrap, to exactly match that of her slacks. I do not know if they were custom-made. We never discussed clothes in such details. I complimented her, regularly, and on one occasion, I told her, "You must have quite a wardrobe."

Looking back, had I been a wiser and a more prepared young woman, for a world outside of Hillside, I may have observed certain telltale signs, but I did not. I recall, on a particular occasion, I was reprimanded by the office administrator. Surprisingly, I do not remember her name, but she was in charge of that whole region. The Morant Bay office was the only JAMAL office in St. Thomas, and every complaint landed on her desk, and she had the final say. I do not recall if the incident I am about to reference was the time she took the opportunity to point it out to me, but she did.

Her office was located in the middle of the building, and she was the only one that occupied it. I normally arrived at the JAMAL office in the mornings, on the days that I was not required to go to Cedar Valley. I also went there on certain Fridays to collect my pay. Whenever I went there, it was customary for me to go to her office and say, "Good morning," before proceeding to other things. This particular day, I was summoned to her office. I did not think it was a normal request to do something around the office, which on occasions she assigned. I think the way in which I was summoned, suggested otherwise.

I went into her office, and she levelled an accusation at me. I honestly do not remember what I was accused of, but I recall distinctly that she did not tell me who told her what she was accusing me of. Because I was accustomed to standing up for myself, I challenged her that if she was going to accuse me, she had an obligation to inform me of her source. She refused. I believe I told her that I was going to report her to her superior. That may have been when she told me *she* was it. I think she further informed me that I could contact the Ministry of Education, which she knew was virtually impossible, especially the low-level unknown I was. I thought, if and since she was my last resort, there was no place to make a redress of complaint, and I dismissed the matter. I also thought, based on what was said and how it was said, at the time, it had to have been Sadye. Sadye was the secretary. Sadye was the person with whom I had close association, and Sadye was the one going in and out of her office. I did not say anything to Sadye, but I decided I would be very careful. I was now deliberate about getting to the office early, when I went there and also made sure I got to Cedar Valley very early, as well. I was now so early that, on occasions, I got to the office and had to wait outside until someone got there to open up—again, I do not recall what she accused me of, but I was not going to take any chances. The accusation, by the way, was an outright lie, and it made me realize that someone was against me and was trying to *set me up,* as the saying goes.

I recall, when I accepted the position, the administrator told me I did not have to be at Cedar Valley early because the people—the adult students—would not turn up early. They generally showed up at approximately eleven o'clock in the mornings, long after I had already got there. Now, however, I was getting there a lot earlier than before. I was sitting there, for long periods of time, with nothing to do than just wait for them to show up. The waiting got so bad that I begged them to come earlier, and most of them did. Outside of that episode, the administrator was generally friendly and kind to me. At one point, she commended me on the job I was doing in Cedar Valley. I do not know who told her, but I believe it may have been the field officer for the Cedar Valley area, who dropped in a few times while class was in session. It was true; I was doing a good job and was enjoying it. The people were learning, and I think they had hope for a brighter future. I was very careful in all that I did, including my interactions and dealings with Sadye. There was no confrontation, but I am sure she noticed the difference in my actions. *Did I say I was naïve?* Having been suspicious of Sadye, I should have been on my p's and q's. I was really trying to be, but one day, Sadye invited me to spend the weekend with her. Instead of being cautious, I immediately thought things to the effect that since Sadye is well dressed, she must have a nice home; she can teach me some *hip* things. She can show me more of Morant Bay and its environs, and things along that line that a naïve seventeen- year-old young woman would think. On the basis of those thoughts, I accepted her invitation. I was working and was allowed to make certain decisions regarding my welfare. As a result, I simply informed my parents that I was going to spend the weekend with a friend. They did not object. My parents, especially my father, were very protective of us. He was also a stern disciplinarian. He was extremely fair as to how he administered discipline. Mother was the nurturing parent. Papa was the disciplinarian. When we did something wrong, he warned us twice. On the third occasion, however, he would beat, spank and flog us. These were the words used to describe what my dad did when he disciplined us physically. He had a thick belt. It looked a bit like rubber, but I think the common consensus was that it was leather. It always hung on a nail right outside my parents' room. Papa returned to that spot, time and time again, and took that very belt and spanked us. Though there were eleven of us, who, at some point, as children, were spanked by that belt, no one has ever removed it.

Papa always gave us three lashings, after his earlier two warnings, but that was all he needed to. We felt the sting of those lashes way into the night. Depending on who was being spanked, we all felt sorry for that sibling, though, we never uttered a word. Papa worked during the days and came home in the evenings. Mother was the nurturer, but if we stepped over her boundaries, she told Papa, once he got home and had time to cool off. She never told us what those boundaries were, but as children, we knew when they were crossed, and so after each crossing of her boundaries, she generally said, "I'm going to tell Macelino." My father's name was *Marcelino*, but, for some reason, Mother always dropped the *r*.

The weekend that I decided to spend with Sadye was one on which I was being paid, and I went to the JAMAL office that Friday morning. I took some clothes and left them at the office with Sadye. That evening, I did not go home, to my house, as was customary; instead, I went to Sadye's. When I arrived at her house, her behavior did not seem as welcoming as the invitation she extended. I was shown to her guest room. We had some conversations, but there was not that level of camaraderie that one expects of a host. I remember thinking how far removed she seemed. I do not remember how the remainder of that Friday evening was spent, but I do remember thinking, on that Saturday morning, that something sinister seemed to have appeared in her persona. I was toying with the idea of telling her that I was going to leave, but I never got around to doing so.

After breakfast, at approximately ten o'clock, a knock was heard at the door, and Sadye opened it. There was a young man, of between my age and the early twenties, standing there. She introduced me and told me to go with him. When I inquired as to why and where, she gave me a perfectly reasonable explanation, as it appeared at that time, and so I did not think there was any reason to be afraid or be distrustful.

I followed the young man, as he made his way through the streets of Morant Bay. After a while, we entered a building. The details are vague, right now, but I recall that there was a makeshift bed, and that animal, in human form, came on to me. I resisted him, but I did not win that battle. As long as the day was, as I recall, that beast had his way with me. At one point, I protested and wanted to leave, and, as if possessed by a devil, he took an ice pick and threatened to stab me in the head. He seemed very intent on carrying out the threat, and I was very scared. Later that day, a young man came by, who appeared to be his friend, and he introduced me as his girl. I remember thinking how dare he think that Sadye had a right to give me to him and wondered what they were up to. While the other young man was there, he continued to threaten to stab me in the head with the ice pick. He was menacing enough, for me to believe he was going to carry out his threat, and so, as at other times when I was in trouble, I began to pray. Shortly, thereafter, his friend told him to put the ice pick down and at some point he did. I started thinking what a crazy thing I had done. I had gone to this woman's home, without my parents knowing who I was with or where I was. I decided I needed to go see my mother. I made up a story, as to why I needed to go in the direction of Hillside, and he bought my story and decided to go. There is a river, that runs past Hillside, called Johnson River. I told him about the river and suggested that we walk along the river's path. It was where we often bathed, and it was also where my mother and some of her fellow moms washed our clothes. He and I started walking, along the river, going in the direction of Hillside. It was approximately ten miles away, and there, as I had hoped, was Mother. I was very glad to be alive after what I went through and was very glad to see my mother.

I greeted Mother and introduced this animal, even managing to smile, while not letting my mother know that I was being held against my will. I was a hostage, due, in part, to my stupidity. I do not remember all that happened after that, but, on that day, I went back to Morant Bay. I remember showing up, once more, at Sadye's house to ask for my clothes. She asked me to come in, but I refused and insisted that she gave my clothes to me. She did, and I left. I never saw Sadye again. I had not really thought about this awful experience since that time. I never told Mother or anyone else about it, and I do not remember if this was the incident that led to my departure from JAMAL.

Life continued, as a teenager, in Hillside. I hung out with my friends, went to parties, got in an out of a few relationships with boys, talked back to Mother, when I disagreed with her and talked behind my father's back, when I felt the need to do so. Papa, at times, talked about himself, in glowing terms. He was very well-read and was very intelligent. My father drank socially; he could never be considered an abuser of alcohol or one who, remotely, had a drinking problem. On Fridays, which was, as I recall, the only day that Papa drank, he came home somewhere between 10:00 p.m. and midnight. He sat in the living room, while everyone in the house, including Mother, was asleep and talked for long periods. He talked about current events, what was wrong with the youth, Hillside, the world, church people, etc. Sometimes, I became awake, lied there and listened to Papa discuss, with himself, all these issues. I thought, as a teenager, that I agreed with him on most things. He did not speak very loudly. I believe he was always considerate of the fact that we were asleep. The house was not very big, however, and so I heard when I was awake. I never heard Papa speak of anyone, in a disparaging manner. I believe everyone who knew my parents and who knew us—their offspring—would agree that they raised us well. The fruit of their labor is evident today. None of us has ever come up against the law.

The administrator for the Church of God of Prophecy for the region, including Hillside, was Reverend Graham. He did not live in Hillside, and he visited extremely rarely. His visits could be termed sporadic. He came by, on some nights, when there were revivals in Hillside, which were few and far between. He, however, attended *convention* at Willow Grove, yearly. Convention was a time when all the Churches of God of Prophecy attended a designated location, to fellowship and share the vision of the Church for the coming year. It was lively, and it generally lasted for a week. The *good* or anointed preachers preached there. The attendees enjoyed lively worship services, ate together, met new people and were exposed to different ways of doing things. We, children, never went to those conventions, but Mother always looked forward to going. This was a high point for her and therefore a big deal. Not all members of the Hillside church went, but all those who were financially able did. The Lanes always went. This was a high point for them too, and being the caretakers of the Hillside church, they had a higher status than Mother and would be more recognized.

We were not by any means rich or well-to-do, as some would term it, but Papa always worked. I do not remember a time, before his retirement, that Papa did not have a job. Each Friday, he gave each of us some *pocket money*. It was not a lot, but we were thankful to have our own money to spend for *sweetie* (candy) and other such things. It made us independent, and we did not have to feel as though we were any less privileged than our neighbor or friends, even, though, we had less material possessions than many.

Papa also taught us not to have, what he called, *inferiority complex*. This was something he constantly spoke about and wanted to be sure that we understood. To that end, he provided for us, as a family and individually, and gave us what we needed, as best he was able to afford. He made Christmas very special for us, and we always looked forward to it. We went to bed on Christmas Eve and woke up Christmas morning with much excitement. I believe it was this attempt, to keep us from feeling deprived, why my father always did what he could, to enable Mother to attend the conventions.

Papa had a Honda 50 bike that he rode to work. When Mother needed to go shopping at Willow Grove, he took her on it as well. After shopping, Mother generally took a route taxi home. One day, after Mother returned from Willow Grove, I asked her how her day went. She told me that a car ran over her foot. I was very concerned, and it took me a few days to realize that Mother was joking. She had a sense of humor, and when she laughed, she could really enjoy a good laugh. I do not recall what year it was, but Papa took Mother on the bike to convention. Mother, not being a woman of the world, had not been exposed to fun things like bike rides. Before my dad got his bike, Mother had never ridden on a bike. Mother, sitting on the back of the bike, clung to my father, as if for dear life. Reverend Graham saw Mother on the bike and made a derogatory comment.

The way my father told it, was that when Elder Graham saw Mother on the back of the bike, he made a comment that was most unbecoming, as far as my father was concerned. My father, not one to back down, made his displeasure, about the comment, known then and there. Knowing how proper my mother was, and never one for confrontations, I can only imagine the embarrassment she must have felt. I do not remember if this incident happened when my father brought my mother to the convention in the morning or when he picked her up in the night. In any event, Papa was so miffed that he spoke openly about it once they got home that night. Papa and Mother were not accustomed to telling us, children, of such matters, but, this time, he made an exception. I do not remember what my reaction was or how I felt. It is likely that I may have been neutral. Papa had a valid point. However, as a teenager who, just over a year ago, was very active in church and the things of Jesus, I did not know what my feelings were.

Reverend Graham had, in the past, preached against Christians wearing jewelry. He also thought they should not wear wedding bands. My mother, wanting to obey Reverend Graham, decided that she was going to stop wearing her wedding band. That was too much for my father. He was having none of it and told my mother so. My mother, being a new Christian, did not want to be thought of as being disobedient and may have told Reverend Graham that my father would not allow this. I do not know if this was communicated to Reverend Graham directly or through the Lanes or some other, but it caused a rift between my father and Reverend Graham, and there was that lingering tension.

One Friday night, shortly after that incident, Papa went out drinking, as usual, and he returned at his usual time. One thing was different, though, Papa was not talking, in his usual tone, about the matters he discussed in the past. He was not overly loud, but you could tell he was incensed, and he tore into Reverend Graham. He said that Reverend Graham was way out of order to interfere with him riding *his* wife to the convention. I fully agreed with Papa, as I lied there listening. He did not know I was awake and was listening. He made some comments about the church, as a whole, and then proceeded to talk about Reverend Graham's hypocrisy. He said that Reverend Graham was always wearing his gold watch, while wanting my mother to remove her wedding band, which was a symbol of his fidelity to her. I do not know whether the fact that my father was talking about Reverend Graham affected my mother's sensibilities, or if, indeed, my father was being loud or a little of both. My mother got out of her room and stood at a doorway between the living room, where my father was and an adjoining room and said these words, "Porter, every

Friday you drink and you come in here and make all this noise waking up the children. Why do you have to behave like that? Cannot you do better than that?"

In the past, when my mother had the occasion to speak to my father about anything, that she thought she needed to address, my father gently pleaded his case by saying, "Gwendy, cannot or do not you see x or y?" There were many such times I can remember when my father was heard making his case. My mother could go on and on about a thing and so anything my father could do to stave off an argument, he did. Sometimes, my mother continued arguing but not for very long. This Friday night, my father got very upset. He thought my mother was taking the side of Reverend Graham and was being unfair to him because he was not a Christian. He said that he always defended and protected my mother, and my mother needed to agree that Reverend Graham totally *past his place*.

My mother replied, "He was wrong, yes, to interfere with you carrying me on the back of the bike, but you do not have to go on like that." My mother made no more concessions. That was not helpful, and my father became irate, meaning, his voice got louder. I got up and went out there and tried to calm the situation. My father, not realizing that I was awake, for much of the time, started explaining to me. A few other siblings got up, came out rubbing their eyes, and said that they wanted to sleep. Mother went back to her room; we went back to ours and soon Papa was calm. I fell asleep and did not hear when Papa retired to bed. The following day was quiet. There was no mention of the inconvenience and that minor commotion the night before.

My mother's name was Gwendolyn Porter. She was affectionately called Ms. Gwendy or simply Gwendy by her close friends. Some of the neighborhood kids addressed her as Ms. Gwendy or Mrs. Porter, depending on who they were. My mother and father got into constant bickering that never amounted to much more than just bickering. There were times when they had a few heated arguments. My mom could be heard saying, "You see, you, Porter, you no good you know," and Papa could be heard saying something to the effect, "Gwendy, why do you have to be carrying on like that?"

We went about our normal course performing our various duties around the home. Those arguments eventually died down. At such times, a female neighbor and friend of my mother generally stopped by our house to offer her usual comment. She always said, "I heard you and Porter arguing this morning." This was her lead-in for my mother to begin telling her what started the argument. My mother's response, generally, was, "Cho, Porter too miserable, you hear." It always appeared that things went back to normal after the tempers flared.

The truth be told, as kids, we thought both our parents were miserable. As teenagers, we said that to our mother, whenever she went on, at length, about something we did or did not do. Papa never went on about things we did. He simply spoke to us about why it was wrong to do it. Although we thought he, too, was miserable, we dared not say that to our father's face. He could be heard from, time to time, saying, "I know you children think I am miserable, but . . ."

Papa was a good person and a very good father, but he was human. He often spoke about his good points, and he had many. So, from time to time, Papa praised himself. Because Papa could spank us, and there was nothing we could do about it, while he spoke at times, I would go off somewhere so that he could not hear me and I would say, "self- praise." I drew out the "praise" as in *praaaise*. One such time, I was in a room, Papa was talking and I was saying *self-praise*. He came after me, and I ran. Papa often said, "Self-praise is no recommendation." It was this saying, in a tongue-in-cheek way, I was throwing in my father's direction.

I had started becoming a rebellious teenager. I began talking back to my mother, when she spoke. One day, I argued with my mother. I do not recall what sparked the argument—but my mother was up in the yard, and I was below. Our property was like a two-level house. There was the lower level—very fruited, along with other produce, and there was also a pig pen down there—and the upper level—the house, some fruit trees, shrubs, a coop with chickens, as well as various other plants. I was at the lower level arguing with my mother. I behaved badly. I had no reason to have spoken to my mother the way I did. When I was finished, I was ashamed. I was so embarrassed that when my friend came by, later that day, I could not look her in the face. When I was arguing with my mother, she said, "Do you not know that God will judge you?" I believe, it was not long after my mother said that that I stopped. I remember feeling as though a ton of bricks had hit me when she said it. Of all the things my mother said, that day, this is still the one that I remember. I do not remember if I prayed for forgiveness that night; maybe, I was too ashamed.

A few days, after recovering from my embarrassing conduct of arguing with my mother, Mother and I were back on course. She told me that, on that day, when my neighbor, who was also my friend, came by, she went into my room. I went and checked my clothes, and I discovered that she had taken some of my *good* clothes. My good clothes were those reserved for more formal occasions. I was livid. She did not ask permission, and I did not want anyone, who was not a sibling, wearing my clothes. In no small way, I told her so, and, from that time, our friendship waned.

One Saturday night, they were having a party in Hillside. My older sister, Pat, told me to ask our father if we could go. Our father asked a few questions and then he said a stern *no*. I do not know what it was that we did not understand about our father's response, but when my father and mother had retired to their room, Pat thought that we should steal out and go. Well, no form of stealing is good. An older brother, the second child of eleven, saw us there and told our father. That was the first time I had defied my father.

We were teenagers, now, and we were rebelling against authority. This was not sitting well with my father. He waited until the following night when we were snuggly in bed. He knew there was no easy way out; we would have to fight our way past him, to get through the door he entered, or try to unlock the other door, which led to the outside. My father was very upset. It was the first time we had disobeyed him, and he may have seen that through a few lenses. He may have thought he no longer had control over us, we no longer respected him, or that we needed to be reminded that he could still spank us—and spanked us he did. He took the usual belt, came in and bore down on us. We were trapped. Pat stood on the bed and flailed her hands, in an attempt to ward off the blows, but to no avail. It appeared, Papa had worked out, in his mind, how he was going to carry this out, and he was being most effective. We screamed and writhed, but Papa continued. A little later, Mother approached and begged for us telling Papa, "Porter, that's enough." He threw a couple more blows, as if to show Mother, too, that he was still in control and then he stopped.

After that spanking, our father gave us, things began to change. Papa was no longer as strict, and we were allowed to go, pretty much, anywhere we wanted. It was now left to our discretion. We tried to make wise choices, but the outcome was not always what we anticipated. There are certainly some choices I would not make, if given the choice to do it all over again.

# CHAPTER
# III

# LIFE IN THE ARMY

After JAMAL, I wanted something to do. I did not communicate this to anyone, including my friends. After all, we were all hanging out, living at our parents' homes and going and coming. One day, Donette, one of my friends, took a page from a local newspaper to show it to me. It was either from *The Jamaican Gleaner* or *The Star*. In it was an advertisement for women soldiers. This was a new phenomenon. I knew absolutely nothing about the Jamaica Defence Force, but I had the academic qualifications they were asking for, and I applied in 1977. One of the requirements was that applicants should be no younger than eighteen years old. I was seventeen years old, and would be eighteen in a few months, so I decided that I would go forth with the application, on faith. I wrote a letter, took it to the post office and mailed it. A few weeks later, I received a response asking me to come in for testing, etc. I was excited to receive the letter and immediately began making preparations to go.

Because I was a tomboy, of sorts, in my early teens, I did not believe that this was going to be a challenge for me. I had low afro, at that time. I was dressed in a pair of blue overalls. I received my parents' blessings, on the day I went, and I left early, that morning. I arrived at Up Park

Camp, South Camp Road, Kingston, on time. I was given a written test, a medical examination, and I had an interview. I returned home to await the results. Soon, the letter came, informing me that I was accepted, and I should report to Up Park Camp on a specific day in March 1977. This was going to be the beginning of training. The day of departure came. I wished my parents, my siblings and my eldest niece a sad good-bye. I was off to a different phase of my life. I was leaving Hillside behind. I was apprehensive but excited, looking forward to the challenges that lay ahead.

I arrived at Up Park Camp early, that March morning. We were directed to a building, and a senior non-commissioned officer instructed a male soldier of a lower rank to give to us certain articles of clothing—solid green khaki shirts and pants, socks, black boots, dark blue beret, white polo-type blouses, white sneakers, blue skirts and other articles of clothing. We were also given a green canvas bag that was called a kit bag. Once we received our allotted supply, we were directed to put everything in our kit bag. The next order of business, on our schedule, was breakfast. We were shown to the "other ranks" mess hall. The *other ranks* are those soldiers who are non-commissioned officers. Their ranks range from lance corporal to warrant officer.

We were the second "intake" of women in the Jamaica Defence Force. *Intake* is just another way of saying batch or group, but that was the choice of word the army used. When we arrived at the mess hall, one might have concluded that the male soldiers had not seen women, on Up Park Camp, before. They seemed giddy with excitement. We were new recruits, however. We, therefore, ignored their excitement and continued to follow the instructions we were given. We took an aluminum rectangular-type container, and we formed a line. It was an assembly-line type format, in that, we moved along the various dishes that were being served, told the server what we wanted, and he dished it for us. At that point, it did not appear that any of the women, from the first intake, was assigned to the other-ranks mess hall.

After receiving our meal, we sat and ate. There were tables and chairs, arranged in a manner, as one would expect to find in a dining room. After we finished our meal, we were told to "muster." Whenever you congregate, by order of anyone in the army, it is called *muster*. The Jamaica Defence Force (JDF) had a coast guard, an air wing or air force, a service battalion, and the infantry (fighting soldiers)—regardless of where you were assigned, you were simply considered to be in the army. After we mustered, we were directed to a convoy of trucks. These were big, green open-back trucks, and they were very high off the ground. I was not deterred by that. Once we were told to get in, I climbed up; we all climbed in, made ourselves comfortable, and, soon, we were off to New Castle. It was a novel experience riding in an army truck, while wearing "civilian" clothes. Those are any type of clothes not issued by the army. We did not communicate with each other. However, while traveling through Kingston and seeing the people looking at us, we gave approving glances at each other. Many people may not have been aware that women were now in the army, and this appeared as exciting and novel an experience for them, as it was for us. As they looked, in what appeared to be amazement, and grinned, we grinned back at them and waved. And, thus, we continued through the streets of Kingston.

We were traveling through a less busy and less populated area of Kingston. Soon, the road became narrower and steeper. It got steeper and steeper, as the journey progressed. We were forced to hold on, to prevent us from sliding on the wooden bench-like seats. It was also getting colder and colder. Dressed in my overalls and tank top, I began feeling quite chilly and wished I had worn something else. I had thought that the overalls were most appropriate for the occasion. I had always prided myself on dressing for the occasion. Since the soldiers wore green khaki, I reasoned, I was going to wear blue overalls. Although it was chilly, I felt that my attire was well-suited, and based on the way some of my fellow recruits looked at me, I believed they approved. Eventually, after about a two-hour ride, up the steep and winding slopes, we arrived at New Castle square.

Because we had to be holding on, for so long, in order to not slide back, as well as the constant laborious huff of the truck's engine, we were happy to arrive at New Castle. It was a large square. There were some buildings around the square and a couple of large canons on one side of it. Sometime later, we were approached by three male corporals. They gave us an extremely warm welcome. They told us that our residences were farther up, in the hills.

New Castle sits high, in the St. Andrew hills, above Kingston. So high, it gets very chilly at nights, though, Kingston is pretty much always hot. After the initial wait at the square, a few Land Rovers— green open back jeeps with canvas over the top—came and transported us to what would become our new home, for three months. We arrived there and were shown to our rooms. There were two of us in my room, a young woman named Sabina and I. Sabina was a good roommate. I cannot recall anything she did that was upsetting. I was the youngest in our intake, and constant mention was made of it. I recall, when the third intake arrived, after more than a year of our graduation, some of my intake members, jokingly, told me that I was no longer the youngest. My sister, Marva, was a teacher at Port Antonio Secondary School. I visited her in Port Antonio, on occasions. When I received my acceptance to the army, I visited her, and she gave me some money to shop. I was not sure what was needed, while on training in New Castle, and so I shopped for what I liked. There was a long, flowing, floor-length red and white sheer night gown that I liked. It was beautiful. The fabric was light-weight, and the red and white alternated in the design. I wore that night gown on the first night. Sabina's night dress was more conservative. I remember, clearly, how she complimented mine, and I could see that she really meant it. There was no jealousy, and she really made me feel lovely and special.

The corporals, who met us at the square, visited our home in the evenings. They, generally, stayed until early in the night. Bedtime was set at a certain hour, and there were a few women, from the first intake, who were living with us, to keep order and to guide us. They also assisted in training us. We depended on them for guidance. They were extremely professional, kind and helpful, and we liked them. That was the general consensus. Berisford was strict, but she was also more like a mother figure. McAlroy was strict. She approached her army duties with a sense of urgency. On the inside of her, though, was a big, silly kid, and she laughed raucously, at times. That laugh would keep us liking her.

We were allowed a few days to get acquainted with the place, each other and to sort things out. In the evenings and mornings, the Land Rovers came to the residence to get us. We packed into them, and they took us down to the square for our meals. When we were all finished, they took us back home. The residences were about a mile from the square. The way up was steep. The residence I was in was very nice. There were nice lockers and wardrobes and lovely, dark-colored, long strips of wood flooring. The drapes were very nice. I remember saying to someone how very nice the home was, and I was told they were used by officers on their vacations, weekends, and possibly rented to other vacationers, when not in use. I did not doubt that; they seemed most fitting. I also remember thinking that my fancy nightgown was well suited for the ambiance. All the women dressed very nicely. One got the feeling, that everyone was putting on her best, at all times, and I was very thankful that Marva assisted in making me feel right at home. I always thought I owed her a debt of gratitude.

I believe it was on a Monday when we began training. As usual, the jeeps picked us up at the residences and brought us down to the square. We ate breakfast, after which we were given an orientation. We went to the various buildings and were told what was done at each. Some were used as classrooms, for teaching the theoretical aspects of the army. We visited the armory, where all the guns were kept. There were many long and short guns, and I was amazed and fascinated. I did not recall ever seeing a real gun before. I learned that the long ones were rifles, and the short ones were called pistols.

We were taught how to conduct ourselves as new recruits. We were to salute the officers whenever we saw one, even if he or she was wearing civilian clothes. We were to respond, "Yes, sir," to male officers and "Yes, ma'am," (short for madam) to the females. For others, corporals, sergeants, warrant officers, we were to say, "Yes, corporal," etc. Privates were the only ones we could be familiar with. Failure to do so would bring us a charge of "insubordination."

It was an instructive and productive day. I asked if we, women, would be trained to use the guns, as well. The male soldier replied, "Yes." I was elated. I did not know his rank, and I really did not care. I was looking forward to training. I was very motivated. At the end of the day, we had dinner and were driven home.

That night, we were instructed by Berisford and McAlroy to prepare our clothes for training. Our outfit was white blouse, blue skirt, blue shorts, white socks and white sneakers. We also wore a blue beret. Now that training would begin, we were told that Berisford and McAlroy were lance corporals. A lance corporal can be considered half of a corporal. It is the first rank one is promoted to in the army. We also learned that one cannot be a trainer without, at a minimum, having the rank of lance corporal. Being a private is not considered a rank, per se. Everyone who graduates, at New Castle, automatically becomes a private. Lance corporal rank is a one-bar chevron—indicated by a white V-shaped piece of cloth sewn on the left or right arm of the person's uniform.

We had begun to get curious about the way things worked in the army. We tried to evaluate the lance corporals' every move. We had no knowledge of how a lance corporal was supposed to act, what he or she should know or anything else. We theorized, among ourselves, that they may have been promoted because the army needed women, from the earlier intake, to guide us. I do not know why we thought that. Maybe, our curiosity was getting the better of us. Regardless, we were now required to address them as Lance Corporal Berisford and Lance Corporal McAlroy. We immediately fell into line and complied.

They may have realized that this form of address was making the home-front overly regimented and formal and that the camaraderie we all enjoyed, the past few days, had changed. They told us, while we were at the residence, we could continue to address them as Berisford and McAlroy, but when we returned to Up Park Camp, we should be sure to return to the formalities.

Training began, and I was enjoying it. We went to training on Mondays through Fridays. On the weekends, we did our laundry and took care of other personal matters. I did well in the physical training. We learned to slow march, left turn, right turn and salute. The sun shone down brightly on us on the square, and it was hot. There was nothing to break the noon-time sun directly over us. We marched and marched. Marching was important because the chief of staff and other high-ranked officers of the Jamaica Defence Force attended graduation. Relatives, friends and well-wishers also attended.

We were trained, primarily, by the men, but Berisford and McAlroy were always there. Since women were new to the army, they were not fully equipped to train us. Classes were instructive and informative. I learned much, and Sabina and I sat close together. We were doing well. I was particularly excited when it came time for weapons training. Rifle training was done separately from pistols. We went to the armory, and we signed for the weapons. There was a separate column for the type of weapon, magazine and number of rounds. We were instructed, individually, how to clean, breakdown and assemble a rifle. They also taught us how to insert the magazine and apply the safety latch. We were not allowed to shoot the weapons at New Castle.

Three months came and went, and it was time to demonstrate what we were taught. We were given written tests, and I excelled at those. It went around to the trainers and my fellow trainees that I scored highest on the written tests.

Graduation day arrived, and the always mundane-looking square was now transformed into Hollywood's version of the Oscars. There were green official cars, similar to limousines but not as long as stretch limos. They had colorful flags on both sides of the front of the cars. The officers wore wrinkle-free khakis with epaulettes of gold stars and other symbols. Their brown, velvet-looking, peak caps had colorful ribbons around them. It was evident, that they were the top brass of the army, although we did not know what all that meant.

We all recognized the chief of staff. He stood out; his car had more flags than the others, and when his driver opened and closed the door, to allow him to exit from the back seat, one clearly saw the level of importance, distinguishing him from all the others.

Many people attended the graduation, and they were all well dressed. For the very first time, we were dressed in our "ceremonial" dress. The design of the outfit was a blouse and skirt with a belt. The belt had a gold-like buckle on the front. The outfit was made from brown material, a similar fabric to that of the top brass of the JDF, just a bit lighter in shade. The design of the blouse was short sleeves with a collar and epaulettes on both sides. They were smart looking. We wore black laced up shoes with stockings. We also wore our blue beret. On this occasion, however, we had a gold-looking pin, in the shape of a crown, stuck directly in the center, at the front of the beret, and the beret was broken to the right side. We marched, saluted and did various formations. The chief of staff gave the main address. Other officers spoke. There were congratulations, and, finally, it was over. We were now privates.

I did not see my parents until the ceremony was over. While everything was going on, I thought about them. I was careful not to fidget or to try and look around to see if I saw them. I did not want to get in trouble. Messing up in the army was always a big deal, but if you are going to, you would be well advised not to do so when the chief of staff or a commanding officer was present. It was said that such action does not reflect on you, the individual, but rather on the instructor or instructors, as the case may be. Accordingly, the instructors informed us that if we made them look bad, it would not be good for us.

After the festivities were over, we were told to "fall out." At this point, we were free to leave the formation and attend to our personal affairs. I looked around and saw my parents. I do not remember all the members of my family who were present, but I recall that my nieces, Shalanda and Deneen, were there. They looked tired, bored and hungry. Food was prepared for the guests. I arranged for my family to have something to eat. They were happy to see me, and I was very happy to see them. They said that they arrived a little late but early enough to see the parade, and they enjoyed it. They were extremely proud of me. I was not allowed to go home with them. Instead, we returned to Up Park Camp.

We were happy to be back in Kingston with all its lights and variety of activities. Once inside Up Park Camp, the drivers stopped outside the gate of a fenced building. This was the women's barracks, and it became our new home. We climbed down from the back of the trucks and Land Rovers and took out our kit bags and other belongings. Lance Corporal Berisford and McAlroy climbed out from the front. The most senior rank generally sits in the front of the vehicle. They, too, took their belongings from out the vehicles. We mustered, and we were led inside the building by the lance corporals.

It was a long building with a veranda that ran the full length of it. It was made of concrete and had concrete flooring. The floor was grey, smooth and very shiny. The shine on the floor was akin to that of a tiled floor but without the partitions. It was a rectangular shaped floor. We walked across the veranda into the enclosed part of the building. At the front section, closest to the gate, was a room. That was the lance corporals' room. At the other end, were the bathrooms. The rest of the building was our living space. It was an open space. Lockers and single beds were lined along the walls. They were alternately placed, a bed then a locker, and this formation continued for the full length of the space on both sides.

Each of us was assigned a bed and a locker. I was hoping Sabina would be next to me, since we were roommates in New Castle. That was not to be. Sabina, I learned, was sent to "Int." *Int.* is short for Intelligence Unit. That was where the army's version of the spies lived and worked. I did not know what the qualifications were for working at Int. When I asked a few questions, I was told very little. They did not like being asked questions, and they were very secretive. I spent five years in the army, and

I never knew what they did. They wore civilian clothes, drove around in unmarked cars, and pretended as if the only person who was, remotely, on their level was the chief of staff. In any event, I wondered why Sabina was chosen for Int. and not me or, at least, the both of us. After all, I was as good, academically, and Sabina and I were similar both in personality and mannerisms.

The little I heard of Int., made it attractive to me, since they wore civilian clothes to work and drove around all day in fancy cars. I was told by someone that I was actually considered for Int., but the officer commanding the Women's Unit said I talked too much. I honestly did not know what she was alluding to. I have always enjoyed a good laugh, when I thought something was funny, and I have always believed in principles, but a tattletale I was not. It was good to receive that information. It meant that I could focus on the present and not daydream or fantasize about Int. There were approximately five members from my intake who were chosen for Int. Three of them came by the women's barracks often. It was good to see them. They were always well dressed, and they looked happy. Sabina was one of the three, and she always stopped by me, initially, to say hello, and we carried on a bit of small talk.

In the barracks, I was placed directly beside a young woman named Duchant. I never got along with her. Next in line was the oldest member of the intake, who was very helpful in assisting everyone in New Castle, who needed a little help with her drills. There were twin beds, grey blankets, white sheets and white pillow cases. The sheets and pillow cases were lily white and were always well laundered. The blanket was to cover the entire bed and then tucked neatly under the mattress. Emphasis was placed on *neatly*.

There was a special way to make the tuck at the bottom end of the bed. All the beds had to look the same. The lance corporals and, at times, the women officers inspected the beds daily. If anything was out of order, we would be punished. I struggled, at first, to do it right. I was assisted by others until I learned to do it perfectly. Many of the others struggled as well, but, eventually, they, too, learned to do it perfectly.

It was time to assign us to the various units in the army. Crooks and I were assigned to 1JR, working as clerks in the Orderly Room. 1JR was an infantry or fighting battalion. We were the only two females assigned to the infantry regiment. The Women's Unit came under the stewardship of the Support Services battalion. It had an officer commanding, who was a woman, but she reported to the commanding officer of the Support Services battalion, who was a male. It was a bit tricky working with the infantry battalion, while being administered by the Support Services battalion.

Sergeant Rudall was in charge of the Orderly Room, his brother was a lance corporal and second in command there. Crooks and I were privates, and we worked as clerks. I did not know the Rudalls before the day I started working at the Orderly Room, but I was a classmate of their sister, Alicia, at Willow Grove Secondary School. She was a very bright student, academically, and I was interested in learning what she was doing with her life at that juncture. There was a striking resemblance among the Rudalls—tall, slim and brown complexion. I do not remember what he told me she was doing, but she was working somewhere.

The commanding officer, who was the top guy in the regiment, sat in the interior of the building housing the Orderly Room. His name was Colonel Rennock. There was a side door from his office to the Orderly Room. The adjutant, who acted as the commanding officer's top aide, sat in an office in front of his. The Orderly Room maintained order, as implied in the name. Records for the soldiers in the regiment were held there. Vacation, pay raises, promotions, etc., were handled there. It was also where officers and soldiers in the regiment came to answer disciplinary matters called "charges." A soldier is charged if he or she disobeys a written or oral rule or command given by someone who is of a rank senior to his or hers. Within the regiment, there are companies— Alpha, Bravo, Charlie, Delta and so on. The various companies are governed by officers commanding, usually of the rank of major. There were captains, lieutenants and second lieutenants, who were other commissioned officers, working under the officer commanding to govern all the other soldiers in that company.

The officers came to the Orderly Room often. At the end of the day, when the officers and other ranks not on duty went home, an officer was required to be on duty at the battalion headquarters. This was the Orderly Room, and that officer was referred to as the orderly officer. As a result, they came, primarily, to see if and when they were scheduled. Crooks and I did some of the typing. They were aware of this and asked us, on occasions, if we saw any information about them going to the chief of staff. The information they were seeking was primarily related to promotions, but if they got in any trouble, they were also curious to know whether the matter stopped at the commanding officer's desk or if he sent the information to the JDF headquarters, which was where the chief of staff's office was.

Colonel Rennock liked Crooks and I. I think it was just a fascination of having women in his Orderly Room, after years of having only men. He seemed to have had a special fondness for me. He always called me to his office to get something or to take something to him. It is normal procedure for the commanding officer to call the orderly sergeant, make whatever request of him and then have him delegate that assignment. Colonel Rennock no longer observed such protocols. He was the commanding officer of the regiment, therefore, he could do whatever he pleased. He called me to his office often, spoke to me at length and also took the time to joke with me. He once said something that I did not think was funny, and I told him so. Throughout Crooks' and my tenure at the Orderly Room, he continued to be very cordial to both of us.

I believe Sergeant Rudall was unnerved by the fact that the commanding officer was being overly accommodating, friendly and nice to us. This was unheard of in the army. There is a charge for "insubordination." A senior rank was not to be or to seem to be friendly with a soldier of a junior rank. Crooks and I broke that wide open. The men, not allowed that privilege, would be heard to say, "The army mash up." That was their way of showing dissent, to what was happening, regarding the officers relating to us in the friendly manner that they did. Colonel Rennock did not seem to care about such things. I do not believe those protests ever got to his ears. The adjutant was likewise very friendly with us, and soon, all the officers in the regiment were also friendly with us. There was a Major Rollason who took us to a private shooting range, off Mountain View Avenue in Kingston, to train Crooks and me to shoot a pistol. We were enjoying our assignment at the Orderly Room.

Sergeant Rudall, in Crooks' and my estimation, was not fair. When it came to assigning Orderly Room duty clerk, he assigned us on the days when his brother did not want to work. I believe that the fact that we were very well-liked and got along, in a *familiar* way, with the officers was not helpful to us. He began finding faults, forcing me, one day, to ask him to please stop picking on me. He was furious and threatened to charge me. I went into Colonel Rennock's office sulking. He asked me what was wrong, and I told him Sergeant Rudall had charged me or was going to charge me. He called Sergeant Rudall into his office, and when Sergeant Rudall came out, there was no more talk of charging me. Sergeant Rudall was always strict, almost seeming harsh at times. When he supposedly laughed, the only indication was a glitter in his eyes.

We joined the regiment somewhere around July 1977, immediately after graduating from training in New Castle. We then, after about a month, were removed for some days to undergo field training at Moneague camp. Moneague is an outpost of the army located in St. Ann, not far from Ocho Rios. All the women from my intake, except for those assigned to Int., were required to go.

We dressed in green combat suits, including green flapper hats and laced up black boots. We loaded onto the trucks and Land Rovers. The women officers and the lance corporals, from the first intake, rode in the Land Rovers. This time, the idea was not such a novel one—riding in the back of the trucks. We had done it at least twice before. However, this was the first time we were wearing the green combat suits—we wore our ceremonial dress to work.

We all chatted and laughed. We were all assigned to units, and we all lived in the same barracks, but this was the first time we were leaving Up Park Camp as a group since graduating, so we felt a sense of freedom. Added to that, the officers and lance corporals were not in the trucks, therefore, we did not have to be concerned about addressing anyone by rank. I was simply Porter and Crooks was simply Crooks and so on. We chatted and giggled, as all young women are accustomed to doing when they get together, and we had a very good time. Soon, we arrived at Moneague.

There were no swanky buildings in Moneague. It was really a place for soldiers—male soldiers. We were housed in tents. The day we arrived, we were sent out in groups. We were given maps, and we had to find a certain point on the map. Each group was sent to a different point. The officers knew whether or not we succeeded because they were going to be waiting for us at those destination points. This was part of the reason they came along to Moneague. They were driven to their locations by Land Rovers, while we walked to the various assigned points.

It was a test of endurance for us. We walked for miles over hilly, grassy terrains. We had no food and no water. We were still in our combat suits, and the temperature was very hot. Fortunately for my group, we went through places where there were some orange trees with oranges on them. We picked and we ate. We walked and walked and walked. Soon, we were exhausted. We were shown where we were on the map and where we needed to end, but we did not understand how to read the map, and we got off track. After what seemed like many endless hours, we met up with our officer, Second Lieutenant Coppen. I do not remember if they came to meet us or if we eventually completed the assigned path, but it was a very difficult assignment, and when we met up with them, we told them just that and asked how could they send us all that way without water and food. Second Lieutenant Coppen was considered, by all, to be cool. She was not upset that we seemed to have questioned her authority. As I recall, she was seemingly apologetic and told us we should have been back a long time before. She said that we went a much farther distance than we needed to. We went way off the path. The other groups had long been back and were already sent back to Camp at Moneague to be fed. When we finally got there, everyone related her experience and wanted to know what took us that long to get back.

We spent the rest of the evening getting settled in, but that night, we were taken to an open field with no amenities. We had lanterns, however, and we spent all night in the open field. We alternated keeping watch while the others slept. Early the following morning, we were awakened and told to muster, in order to return to Moneague. We returned to Up Park Camp later that day. The next day, we again went out dressed in combat suits. However, this time we went to Twickenham Park. That was the official site where the army trained its soldiers to shoot weapons.

We arrived at Twickenham Park at approximately nine o'clock that morning. A number of male soldiers were awaiting our arrival. They were the instructors for weapons training. We were instructed to get up on some dirt hills, which they called mounds, firmly grip the butt of the rifle in our right shoulder, if right handed, size up the target, pull the trigger back and shoot. As the round left the barrel of the rifle, it jerked causing us to miss the target completely or get far away from the center. With practice, we got better. We spent that whole day shooting, and I did not mind at all. I loved target practice. Soon, I became very comfortable with using the rifle. It did not jerk as much, and before we left the range, I hit a few bull's-eye. We returned to the range the following day, and by day's end, we were all patting ourselves on the back, very satisfied and proud of our achievements, as markswomen.

We returned to Up Park Camp and to our units. Colonel Rennock was happy to have us back. I think Sgt. Rudall was sad that we were back. Things continued as they did before that brief respite. It was customary for the battalions to have a Christmas party sometime in December. The regiment had its own band, and they played at those parties. At other times, they played at large parades, at the funerals of the fallen and other social occasions. When there were functions at Jamaica House and Kings House, where the prime minister and governor general resided, respectively, they played at those functions as well.

Jamaica was a colony of Great Britain until August 1962, when it became independent. The Queen is, therefore, represented on the island by the governor general, appointed by the Crown on the advice of the Jamaican prime minister.

It was time for the regiment's Christmas party. Since Crooks and I worked at the battalion's headquarters, we were invited by the adjutant. I wore a blue denim skirt suit. The top was a vest, and I wore a merino-type yellow blouse on the inside. I also wore a blue denim-like canvas pair of shoes with a tan cord-like bottom that had a tan lace that wrapped around to my knees.

We arrived at the party. It was held at the regiment's band location. The mess hall was cleared and situated for dancing. The adjutant was Lieutenant Raul Sommers. He invited Crooks and I to sit beside him. Soon, Colonel Rennock arrived, and he too sat beside us. Dinner was soon served.

The waiters came to our table, and Crooks and I asked them for chicken, as did the officers. The meals arrived, and we began to eat. We were somewhat shy and unsure as to how to behave in the presence of the colonel and the adjutant, in this more formal setting. They were eating, and we were picking at our food. They were, no doubt, aware that we were somewhat self-conscious, and they appeared to be watching us. Not long after we started picking at the chicken, I heard Lieutenant Sommers say, "It is okay, you know, to eat chicken with your hands." We responded with a chuckle, and a short while later, Crooks and I felt emancipated, and we were happily eating the chicken with our hands. We finished our dinner, and the waiters cleared our table. We received very special attention because we were in the company of the commanding officer and the adjutant.

Shortly after dinner, as we sat there talking while continuing to enjoy the band, the chief of staff drove in. His driver stopped, and he got out of the car. He came over to where we were and asked Lieutenant Sommers to, "Please move over."

It sounded like a command said in a very nice tone of voice. I was sitting next to Lieutenant Sommers. Lieutenant Sommers, visibly surprised, quickly moved over. The chief of staff sat down beside me. He asked my name, how was dinner and was I enjoying myself.

His name was Major General Glen, and that was one for the JDF history books. Shortly thereafter, he invited me for a dance. I accepted. We proceeded to the dance area. At those parties, the soldiers were allowed to invite their significant others, and there were a good deal of them dancing on the dance floor. It was a large hall, but the moment the chief of staff and I entered, they all stopped dancing, and they cleared away and stood around the sides of the room. I do not recall what type of music was playing, but the chief of staff held me close in a waltz.

The soldiers were stunned, and it was clearly seen on their faces. We danced to that song, and we danced to another, though, in my case, not enthusiastically. I felt that we were depriving the other ranks. It was their party, and they had a right to be enjoying themselves. After all, they were allowed that opportunity only once per year, while the officers were always having parties at the officers' mess to which other ranks were not invited, and as a private, I did not feel comfortable in the arms of the highest ranking member of the JDF.

The chief of staff asked me if I wanted to stop dancing or if I was tired. I politely responded, "Yes." We left the hall, and as we did so, I looked back to see if the soldiers had reclaimed the floor. No one could be seen. It appeared that they were waiting for us to leave so that they could. They had never seen anything like that. It was, indeed, a most significant departure from the norm to which they were accustomed— for them to see the commanding officer and adjutant of the regiment associating with us on the level they did, but to see a private dancing in a waltz with the chief of staff of the JDF was too much, too soon, for them. Now, I thought, they must be saying, *The army really mashed up.* We went back and sat where we were before.

The chief of staff was going to another party in Beverly Hills. He asked me to come along. I protested a bit and then agreed. Habbens, the chief of staff's driver, drove us there. Beverly Hills was the most affluent and swanky residential community of that era. It's on a hill overlooking the city of Kingston. We arrived there, and the chief of staff introduced me to a few people. I then went outside to chat with Habbens. Habbens was a private, so we simply called him Habbens. The chief of staff, realizing that I was not enjoying the party, decided to leave. He lived at Up Park Camp.

We returned to Up Park Camp from Beverly Hills. The guard at the gate quickly lifted the barrier to let us in. The custom was that when driving an army vehicle, the driver was required to stop at the gate to be checked in and out. That process required that the guard at the gate enter the number of the vehicle—which was akin to a license plate—the driver of the vehicle, the time the vehicle departed, where the vehicle was going when it left and the time it returned. We left, and we were back inside Up Park Camp. The chief of staff was not subjected to such scrutiny.

Beverly Hills was about a mile from Up Park Camp. As we came through the gate, the chief of staff told me that he would be going shopping for his two girls on Christmas Eve, and he asked if I would go with him. Not wanting to say yes, I told him I was going to be the duty clerk at the Orderly Room. He told me that he would call the Orderly Room and ask the duty officer to relieve me. However, not wanting to go with him, I got in touch with a private male soldier named Private Evans and asked him if he would fill in for me. I told him I had an emergency, and he agreed.

Evans was an Orderly Room standby. He worked at the Alpha company clerk's office. If extra help was needed at the Orderly Room, he was the fallback. He lived in a barracks in the regiment. Having my replacement, I woke up very early that morning, caught a bus and headed for my parents' home in Hillside.

It was Christmas season. I do not recall how many days before Christmas I went to Hillside. However, on Christmas day 1977, my family received the saddest news, up to that point, of my family's existence. The oldest child for my parents, Todd, always came to Hillside at Christmas or on Christmas Eve. That year, he was on his way from Falmouth with his wife to our sister's, Marva, home on Christmas Eve. He had an accident on the way there. His car ran over a brink, and his wife was killed instantly. He, miraculously, escaped with minor injuries. He made it to Hillside on Christmas day to deliver the sad news. Fortunately, we were already finished with breakfast, so we were able to enjoy a part of the day before he got there. Once we got the news, that was it. Our whole Christmas season was ruined. Added to that sadness was the fact that they had twin daughters who were only two years old.

The girls were at my sister's home in Port Antonio, Portland, and my brother and his wife were on their way to spend Christmas Eve there and pick up the girls. It was my sister and her husband who, in turn, brought Todd and the girls to Hillside. I can still remember the girls crying on and off, calling, "Mommy, Mommy," and not understanding that they were never going to see her again. For his part, Todd took to the bed and that was where he remained for hours, possibly days.

I returned to Up Park Camp. It was customary for us to have physical training (PT) on Tuesdays. This usually took place across the JDF headquarters, in front of the officer commanding the Women's Unit office. Her name was Gloria Baccas. For this, we dressed in our white blouse, blue skirt, blue shorts, white socks and white sneakers. This was the same outfit that we were trained in at New Castle, but here we were not required to wear the beret. Everyone was required to be there, everyone except Int. They were in a separate world.

June Langley, Coppen, Gloria Baccas and another officer were there. I do not remember that officer's name. She was not at Int., but she came around us only when it was absolutely necessary. Sometimes she also gave herself a pass from PT. On the occasions when we paraded for inspections in our ceremonial dress and were "inspected" by the officers, she was always present. I think she liked that sort of self-importance. The women certainly thought so. They put it another way. They said she thought she was "nice." *Nice,* in our view, was someone who thought she was better or more important than others. It's a feminine expression. Men who had that type of self-importance were never described in a like manner.

Most of us looked forward to that time of PT. It was one of the few occasions when all the women got together during regular hours. We also looked forward to seeing Ms. Coppen. We were allowed to address the women officers by their surnames, provided it was preceded by "Ms." Ms. Coppen was fun to be around. She was down to earth. That was how we described her. She said things that made us open our mouths wide in disbelief and laughed, raucously. I think the other women officers were a little jealous that they did not possess that natural, without pretense, and easy way of interacting with us.

We generally did some stretches and trotted around Camp for about two miles. It was very informal, and we chatted while we were trotting. Ms. Coppen was usually found right in the midst of us, other ranks, chatting and carrying on just the way we did. True to form, the other officers were right in front, leading us. That was where officers belonged, and that was where they were usually found.

The Tuesday directly following my family's tragedy, I was walking from the women's barracks to muster with the other women for PT. As I approached the vicinity of the JDF headquarters, I heard a voice say, "Porter, come here."

I looked up and saw the chief of staff, and I looked at myself to be sure my outfit was in order. I then began to trot in his direction. By a wave of the hand, he told me to stop trotting and to walk to him. By then, Gloria Baccas, my officer commanding, her secretary, a woman soldier named Leal and some others were already standing in position. Before I even got to the chief of staff, Lieutenant Gloria Baccas shouted, "Private Porter, salute." She may have wanted the chief of staff to know that she was on top of things. After all, she did not know why he was calling me, but I did.

The Monday preceding that Tuesday, I had returned to work at the Orderly Room. There was an officer on duty named Second Lieutenant Danny Wayne. He was very fond of me. Twice, he invited me to the Harbour View drive-in to see a movie. I accepted, but a female soldier always accompanied me. I did not feel comfortable going alone, so I invited her. I sat in the front with Danny, and she sat in the back.

Second Lieutenant Wayne was the duty officer at the Orderly Room on Christmas Eve day in 1977 when the chief of staff called, desiring me to go shopping with him for his two girls. It was said the chief of staff was divorced. I did not know if his ex-wife was living in Jamaica or abroad. He appeared to have had custody of the girls. At some point that Monday, Second Lieutenant Wayne had come to turn in his Orderly Room report, which generally reported on anything of importance that happened in the regiment that night—did the patrols kill any criminal? Was any soldier shot?—those types of things would be reported on. In any event, he asked me what the chief of staff wanted when he called and asked for me at the Orderly Room? As I mentioned earlier, the chief of staff did tell me that he would call and ask the duty officer to relieve me. I was forced to explain to

Second Lieutenant Wayne the circumstances surrounding that call. And so, my conversation with Second Lieutenant Wayne gave me a heads-up.

The chief of staff replied to Ms. Baccas, "Gloria, it's okay." I approached the chief of staff, and he asked me what happened. He said that he called the Orderly Room, and the duty officer told him that I was not there. I quickly told him about the death of my brother's wife and that I was forced to go home for that reason. He was quite understanding and said that I should have informed him so that he could send me home—to Hillside—in a helicopter. I lied to the chief of staff because the tragedy was not why I left. It did happen that weekend, however, and provided me with the perfect excuse.

After this period, things in the army started getting a bit difficult for us, women, and for me, in particular. The male soldiers thought that the women soldiers were being given an unfair advantage.

We were allowed to wear our combat outfits to work, and the women were showing up at their units in shirt and trousers. We were dressed just like the men; although, some of the women's outfits were most form-fitting. Women were getting promoted in the units where men were working before the women arrived and had more seniority. The women, though, were being promoted on the strength of the Women's Unit, not on that of those differing units where those male soldiers belonged and to which the women were assigned.

It did not matter to the men that this was so. Ranks were equal, regardless of whether one was male or female, and it was not lost on those men that the women could now charge them. Another point of contention was that there was one barracks for women. The Women's Unit was young and needed to grow, and the intakes were coming in on a regular basis. In order to make room, the women were allowed to live off camp after only three months. This privilege was extended to a male soldier *only* when he got married. The army gave living allowance to soldiers who were given permission to live off Camp, so women were being paid more than men of the same rank.

We ate at the same mess hall as the men while we were living at Camp. They did not make things easy for us. They called us names and yelled out many unkind remarks. They started rebelling in other ways as well. They had begun to charge us. I recall how curious I was the first time I learned that a woman soldier was charged. Her name was Carol Coburn. She was tall, with beautiful, saintly eyes, and she was graceful. She worked at the air wing. I do not remember what she was accused of, but a corporal at the Air Wing charged her. We were all amazed and came to her defense, though, this was limited to berating the corporal in our barracks, although we did not know him.

When a female soldier was charged, she was required to appear before her officer commanding along with her accuser. In our case, it was Gloria Baccas. Both accuser and accused stood in her office. If there were witnesses, they waited outside until they were called. Similar to a court of law, the officer opened a book to the section that the soldier was charged under. She then read the charges to the accused, and the accuser was allowed to explain what happened. The accused then spoke. The regulations book had the guidelines for those proceedings. One was that an officer commanding could not award a sentence of more than fourteen days confinement to barracks. Anything more, had to be referred to the commanding officer of that battalion. That person was Colonel Nesby. Justice, army style, had nothing or very little to do with whether the accused was in the wrong; rather, more to do with who charged us and how our officer commanding perceived us, the accused. Almost, inevitably, we would be punished. The only time I heard of someone being charged and not getting punished was Leal, secretary to the officer comanding the Women's Unit. Leal generally took information from the barracks and told it to the OC, her boss. The information pertained to the women's personal matters and had nothing to do with the army. In so doing, she was earning herself points and privilege with the OC. Leal seemed to have realized the OC's insatiable appetite for this type of information, and soon, she behaved like the "untouchable." After all, it was Gloria Baccas, the OC, who decided if a woman soldier swam or sank.

That day when Carol went to "orders," an army trial is referred to as *orders*, I waited anxiously to learn what the outcome was. When I got to our barracks, I learned that she was going to the commanding officer (CO) for trial. We knew right away that this was going to be a long confinement to barracks. The army awarded these punitive awards in increments of seven. We were accustomed to getting seven, fourteen or twenty-one days' pay removed from our paychecks or the same incremental amount of days confined to barracks. When we were confined to barracks, we were not allowed outside of Up Park Camp, for any reason, during the period of confinement.

Carol had good moral values. She was a Christian for most of the time I knew her, and although she was the only Christian I knew in the Women's Unit, she was not shy or afraid of letting that truth be known. She lived her beliefs in front of us, and it was refreshing. Her code of conduct never seemed to change.

According to the reports, an air wing corporal liked her; he made it known to her, invited her out and she rebuffed him. After that, he started picking on her. It was that corporal that charged her. I do not know if that fact came out at the orders, but by army standards, that is not allowed. A woman can date a man of a senior rank or vice versa, if she so chose, but it should be kept a secret. A female soldier of the first intake had to resign from the army in order to marry her sergeant husband. In any event, Carol went before Col. Nesby and was awarded twenty-one days confinement to barracks. We were expecting it. Accordingly, we were not very surprised.

Things were changing, and they were changing fast. This, I believe, opened the flood gates of charges against us, women. Every Wednesday, there was a long line of women on Gloria Baccas's veranda, waiting to enter her office to answer charges. These charges were brought by men.

The word seemed to have got out that Gloria Baccas was extremely receptive, and the charges kept coming.

The second surprise came when Lance Corporal Berisford was charged. She was the same Berisford who was with us in New Castle. She worked as a medical orderly at the army's medical center. It was said that she was a nurse before she joined the army. This was the first time that a non-commissioned officer was charged in the Women's Unit, and we came to her defense.

The likeness we developed for her at New Castle had not changed. If we yelled out *Berisford* in the barracks, she did not remind us that it was *Lance Corporal Berisford*. I think as far as she was concerned, we could yell "Berisford" anywhere, provided some other stiff-upper-lip person of rank did not overhear and hold her to account, she was fine with that. When Berisford went before Gloria Baccas, she received seven days confinement to barracks. We all breathed a sigh of relief, although we attributed such leniency to the fact that Berisford worked at the Medical Center and even officers had to go there when they fell sick.

Sergeant Rudall, of the regiment Orderly Room, must have heard how well and how successful male soldiers were being at charging women soldiers, and he decided this was his opportunity to charge me. Colonel Rennock was away on a month's vacation. The adjutant was there, and the second in command was seeing to matters that Colonel Rennock ordinarily dealt with. It was Colonel Rennock's absence that Sergeant Rudall seized upon to charge me. As the Orderly Room sergeant, he knew the regulations book well. As a matter of fact, at the time of charging me, he had the book opened before him as if searching for something that would bring maximum punishment. He charged me for being insubordinate.

On the day of orders, we both left the Orderly Room and arrived at Gloria Baccas's office together. Sergeant Rudall's uniform was as well-laundered as ever. Leal, the OC's secretary, seemed very gratified that my time had finally arrived. Although Rudall was a sergeant, the fact that he was head of the regiment's Orderly Room, gave him a certain level of status way above other sergeants. He knew it and prided himself in it. I could tell just by the way he spoke to other sergeants and conducted himself. This was not lost on my OC either.

We were called in and she read the charge. She then asked Sergeant Rudall to speak. She listened to him in brief. He did not need to offer many details. Almost as soon as he began to speak, she stopped him. It appeared he was willing to give more information, but she interrupted and cut him off. When I was about to speak, as would be the norm, she cut me off and told me to either shut up or be quiet. Sergeant Rudall, being accustomed to these proceedings, seemed confused or perturbed. I do not know which it was. She immediately remanded me to the CO, Colonel Nesby.

After we got back to the Orderly Room, Sergeant Rudall was very nice to me. I never discussed the matter with him, but I have always thought that he realized that I was unfairly treated and may have regretted charging me. In his mind, I thought, he believed in discipline, even the army's version of it, but he also thought everyone should be given a fair chance to defend him or herself. It was too late. We were now going to Colonel Nesby, and the only reason to go there was to get a harsher sentence than the OC could give.

A week later, we arrived at Colonel Nesby's office, and we both stood there in front of him. Sergeant Rudall looked at me and smiled. I'm not sure what he intended to communicate to Colonel Nesby by that gesture.

He proceeded to present his case and although Colonel Nesby gave him all the time to speak, he simply said, "Private Porter won't listen to me when I speak to her."

Colonel Nesby appeared to have been listening for more, but there was nothing more to be said. He looked at me, and I had nothing to say. Colonel Nesby, now, seemed confused. He appeared to be wondering why my OC did not simply give me seven or fourteen days, as the case may be. Why did she send me to him for something so minor? He awarded me the customary twenty-one days confinement to barracks, the minimum that he was allowed to award me, and we left. Whenever I saw Colonel Nesby after that, he showed some gesture of kind recognition.

It was then I learned that Gloria Baccas did not like a bone in me. I served my twenty-one days confinement. It was not overly burdensome for the following reasons: At this juncture, I was living outside Up Park Camp and because I was working at the regiment, the Women's Unit had no control over my movements during the working hours. Sergeant Rudall, Lieutenant Sommers and Colonel Rennock, on his return, gave me permission to go outside of Camp during the days. They also, on occasions, authorized vehicles to take me to my apartment. I went there to check that everything was in order, and got fresh clothes, etc. Sergeant Rudall never charged me again, and after that charge our relationship got a lot better.

Crooks and I were avid supporters of the sports the soldiers of the regiment played, and rugby was one such game. A Captain Faber was in charge of the rugby team, and there was a big, tall chap named Charlie, who was a member of the team. He had a great personality, laughed easily and was funny—clean, funny humor. He was one of their top players. He came to the Orderly Room often. He was closer to Crooks than me. It could be said that Charlie was Crooks' good pal. There were times when they were talking outside the Orderly Room, and I would see Crooks out there cracking up with laughter and flailing her hands at him. I sat there and wondered what funny thing Charlie was telling Crooks now. Oftentimes, she told me once she came in.

The rugby team was having a party on a Saturday, and Charlie invited us. We went. It was held at someone's home, and it was a very nice place. I was introduced to Captain Faber. He took a liking to me almost immediately. I was not really interested in that type of attention because I knew he was a captain and that such relationship could bring a charge of familiarity. I was also attending movies with Lieutenant Wayne and did like him a lot.

Sometime after that party took place, I was called to Gloria Baccas's office and upbraided. She told me that she heard that Captain Faber liked me. I told her I met him at the party and could not help it if he liked me. I remember her rudeness as if it was yesterday. She said, "If a man likes a woman in the marketplace, he must know what he sees in her."

I avoided Captain Faber after that as best I could. At a later date, I saw him and told him of her rudeness. She could not charge me, however, because Captain Faber was senior in rank to her, and I told her that I had no control over how he felt about me.

After my first charge by Sergeant Rudall, I was charged a few more times by other male soldiers. As in the first instance, I was remanded to Colonel Nesby. On the first of these charges, when I appeared before Colonel Nesby, he told me that my OC, Gloria Baccas, told him that when he gave me the twenty-one days confinement, I did not serve it because Colonel Rennock was always allowing me to go outside of Camp. He was, therefore, forced to award me salary deductions as punishment.

While all of these things were happening, the army advertised for female drivers, and Crooks and I applied and were accepted. Colonel Rennock had put in a "good word" for us. Soon, we were off to a "driving cadre." That is what the training was called. There were two Land Rovers—referred to as "three-quarter tons." They were a bit larger than the ones we were accustomed to seeing. Staff Sergeant Graham was officially in charge of the training. He was a wonderful person, and one could not ask for a better driving supervisor. He was extremely patient and even when he had every reason to be upset, he ignored those reasons. I never heard him say an off-color word.

Two corporals were assigned as the driving instructors. There were males and females on the driving cadre. Initially, we learned to control the vehicle on the grounds of Up Park Camp. Once we learned to control the vehicle, we went outside on the regular streets. We drove all over Jamaica. It was the first time I had gone to most of the places we went. It was fun. We took turn driving, and we drove for an hour each time. The time went by, and after about six weeks we were ready to be tested in order to receive our driver's licenses. Testing was done by Staff Sergeant Graham. I recall that on the day of the test, he was making sure that we were relaxed. He walked me through what I needed to do in order to parallel park. That was the first part of the test, and when I did it, I was successful. We proceeded to the rest of the test, and soon, it was over. We were all successful.

I cannot remember if I asked to be assigned to the Transport Unit (TU), but I was now working there. I liked driving. I still do today. Duties at TU included, but were not limited to, picking up officers in staff cars at their homes and taking them to Camp. Commanding officers were assigned a personal car and a personal driver, just like the chief of staff. Other officers called to request a car to take them wherever they needed to go. *Wherever*, generally, meant army-related business.

On occasions, we picked up bread at bakeries if they needed them urgently. Those who were licensed to drive trucks generally transported soldiers to locations outside of Camp. The CO for TU was Major Taber. He was slim and loved fancy, fast cars. He had a few of them. At times, while in our barracks, we heard a particular car sound on the road outside, and everyone knew it was Major Taber. He was not a regimented sort of leader, though, he liked order. Wherever he was in charge, his soldiers spoke well of him.

There were two senior other ranks at TU—Staff Sergeant Graham and a warrant officer II, whom the soldiers called Sappa Lucci. I do not remember his proper name. Sappa Lucci was mainly in charge of the administrative tasks—correspondence and other such matters. Staff Sergeant Graham was directly in charge of the vehicles. Because TU was really about transport, Staff Sergeant Graham was much more popular. Everyone was always going to Staff Sergeant Graham, and he was always busy around the TU grounds.

By all indications, he loved his job and cared very much for the soldiers under his charge. There were three or four women soldiers at TU. However, he treated everyone the same. The male soldiers did not feel left out, and they were happy to aid us when we needed help. The soldiers liked Staff Sergeant Graham. They, obviously, did not care much for Sappa Lucci. Sometimes, at the end of the day when he was leaving for home, as he walked away from the admin office, the soldiers could be heard saying "Sappa, Sappa" in a heckling sort of way. He was very upset but could do nothing about it.

A few times, Sappa Lucci threatened to charge me. Staff Sergeant

Graham asked him, "Why?" He did not seem to have any good reason, except that he did not seem to like me and just wanted to "pull rank." *Pulling rank* was when a senior rank pushed around a junior rank just because he or she could. However, he was never allowed to charge me. I cannot recall ever doing anything at TU, at that point, that merited being charged, anyway. I do not remember having much interaction with Sappa. I dealt, almost exclusively, with Staff Sergeant Graham. For some reason, though, Sappa did not like me, and I believe Staff Sergeant Graham was acutely aware of this and may have confided in Major Taber regarding the same.

I had done nothing that merited charging by Sappa Lucci, up to that point, at TU, but he was looking for an opportunity, and I, unwittingly, gave him one. One day, I was assigned to go to Maxfield Avenue in Kingston to pick up some loaves of bread. I dutifully went and carried out the assignment.

On my return to Camp, I dropped off the bread at the storehouse and was making my way back to TU. I had just turned into the TU entrance and was about two chains from the TU admin office where Sappa Lucci worked out of. I noticed that the chief of staff's car was parked in the middle of the road with a door opened to its full extension. Habbens, the chief of staff's driver, was sitting in the car. I came to a full stop, got out of the vehicle and politely asked Habbens, "Would you please close the door so that I may pass?" He refused.

It was evening, and many soldiers had already left the unit. I needed to sign in the vehicle, which would officially conclude my assignment. I, again, asked Habbens, "Would you please close the door so that I may pass?" His reply to me was, "Go ahead and hit it off."

I was furious. There appeared to be no reason for the door to be opened in the middle of the road, except that he felt he could do whatever he chose by virtue of his position. There was also no reason, I thought, for his response to me. I decided to do exactly what he told me to do. I started up the Land Rover, put it in second gear, put my foot on the accelerator and drove. The door that he refused to close flew back and was crumpled.

The sound was heard in the TU office and in the admin office. Staff Sergeant Graham came out, put his hands on his head and said words to the effect, "Oh my gosh." He then asked, "What happened?" I told him that Habbens had the door wide open in the street. I asked him twice to close it so that I could pass. He refused and told me to hit it off. Staff Sergeant Graham was at a loss for words. He simply did not know what to say. Almost immediately, Sappa Lucci emerged from his office. He did not ask what had transpired. He shouted, "Charge her." I do not know where Major Taber was, but as soon as Sappa Lucci said that, Major Taber was on the scene. This is what he had to say, "Charge what? Charge who? Do you want to bring *expletive* disgrace on this unit? Take the vehicle to the workshop and have it fixed."

Habbens sat in the car, stunned. I do not recall him saying a single word. Major Taber left the scene, and I walked towards the TU office with Staff Sergeant Graham. As we walked away, Sappa could be heard saying, "The army mash up fi true." That would be Jamaican patois translated, *The army has really mashed up indeed.* I do not know if he said that to Habbens or to the wind or if Habbens even acquiesced. I was too upset to care at that moment. When I entered the TU office and the enormity of the moment registered, I burst out laughing. It was an almost surreal moment. I turned in the keys, signed the vehicle in and left.

The following day, I arrived at work and carried out my duties as if nothing took place the day before. Soldiers, in the regiment, could be heard saying to others, "Did you hear that a woman soldier hit off the chief of staff's car door?" A few days later, I saw Habbens driving a similar car. I did not know if that one was already fixed or if it was a temporary replacement, and I did not inquire.

The following day, as I was walking toward TU, Major Taber approached me and told me that he was being transferred to the Support Services battalion, as its second in command. That decision was made long before the incident. He said the information was going to be published that evening, and he also submitted my name to be transferred. I was going to be a clerk in the Support Services battalion Orderly Room. Major Taber volunteered that he was not going to leave me at the TU because he did not want *them* to kill me once he was gone. The *Standing Order* of that day had both our names, as he had said.

The *Standing Order* was a type of memo published by each Orderly Room. I knew Major Taber was right. I was not sure about *them*, but I knew Sappa Lucci would have had a field day with me. And, though, I was sad to leave Staff Sergeant Graham, I knew he would be fine without me, but I would not be without Major Taber.

It was on a Friday evening that the *Standing Order* was published, and I reported to the Support Services battalion Orderly Room that following Monday morning. Sergeant Rhead was in charge of the Orderly Room. It was located in a white building almost directly across the street from the women's barracks. It was a nice building with lots of French doors and windows. The building ran along a stretch of land on a straight path. The top end of the building was the Orderly Room; in the middle was Commander Haughey's office, and at the other end of the building was Major Taber's new office. I stopped in to say hi to Major Taber and to thank him for transferring me. I then returned to the Orderly Room.

Commander Haughey was commanding officer of the Support Services battalion. He was probably a colonel. I did not know. He was previously with the JDF coast guard. At the coast guard, they wore white uniforms with black lapels. Commander Haughey now wore regular khaki as other Support Services battalion officers did; however, he continued wearing his black lapels with his coast guard rank and continued using the title of commander. No one referred to or addressed him by rank; we simply said Commander Haughey.

I do not recall the events that led to my personal meeting with Commander Haughey. We met, however, and he said he wanted me to be his personal driver. I liked driving, and I was happy that he asked me. I drove him everywhere, including taking him home. One day, while we were on Mountain View Avenue in Kingston, I made a clumsy U-turn. It worked out okay, but I think for a bit he was concerned. When we got back to Camp, he joked to a few people, including Sergeant Rhead, that I nearly crashed him. He had a son called Neil, and Neil and I got along well. Sometimes, I picked him up at the house later in the day, after getting his dad and drove him to his father's office.

After the mandatory three-month requirement of living in the women's barracks, I requested and got permission to live outside of Up Park Camp. Crooks, another intake member and I rented a house in Meadowbrook Estates. It was a very upscale neighborhood. We rented a three-bedroom house. We each had a bedroom, but we shared the other facilities. We were able to afford the house because the army paid us living allowance.

Crooks knew a family called the Mandels. They made beautiful, mahogany furniture. There was a young man named Orville Mandel. Crooks told him about me, and she told me that he was a fine young man.

I agreed to see him.

One evening, he came to get me at the women's barracks. He was driving a Thunderbird. It was a beautiful car—off white canvas top and a light green body, with off-white leather interior. I was impressed as were the women soldiers who saw the car.

Indeed, Orville was a fine fellow. He worked in the family business making furniture. He and his brother shared an apartment in a high-rise building in the Constant Spring Road area in Kingston. He picked me up quite often at Camp. On weekends, we went partying at clubs in Kingston. I remember a favorite of ours was Rock club on Red Hills Road. We danced the night away. It was fun. He was soft-spoken, did not smoke and did not use swear words. My family members who met him were fond of him.

Eventually, I got my own apartment. Orville and I continued dating. In 1979, I became pregnant, and in May 1980, I gave birth to Yoshie Mandell, my daughter. About a year after Yoshie's birth, Orville migrated to the United States.

Army life continued. The JDF required women to commit to an initial three-year term. After this period was completed, we had the option of extending our service for however many years we chose, but a one-year extension was the minimum. By 1980, many of the women in the first intake who, by now had completed their three-year requirement, were leaving. Many left for the United States. My initial commitment to the JDF also ended in 1980, but I signed on for an additional two years, which took me to March 1982. As that time was approaching, I evaluated the situation and decided that I had had enough; the excitement was gone, and it had started losing its appeal. I was ready for another phase in my life. I decided that I, too, would leave for the United States of America.

# CHAPTER IV

# MY EARLY YEARS IN NEW YORK

I made the arrangements, including leaving my daughter, who was two years old, in the care of my brother, Sanjay, and his wife. On April 15, 1982, I left Norman Manley International Airport in Kingston and landed at JFK airport in New York. This was not my first visit to New York. I had earlier gone there on vacation and stayed with a good friend and former colleague, Anna. She joined the army as a member of the first intake, and we both worked at the TU. She encouraged me to migrate to New York. She told me I could stay with her, and I went to her apartment in Brooklyn, New York.

When I arrived at the apartment, another female was living there. I was not aware of this until the day of my arrival. Anna told me Holly arrived a week earlier and would be there for just another week.

After about a week of my being there, things started getting a bit tense. Holly began displaying certain hostilities toward me. I had done nothing to her and wondered what might be the reason for this behavior. It was a one-bedroom apartment; I was sleeping on the couch, in the living room, and she continued to share the bedroom with Anna, so I was not in any way getting in her way. This awkwardness continued for approximately two weeks. Anna said she felt terrible. She also said that she told me to come and stay with her, and Holly was treating me in that way, but, she continued, it was because Holly was jealous.

I was a bit amazed and inquired as to what she meant by saying *Holly was jealous*. She told me that Holly was a lesbian, was in love with her, and she was jealous because I was there. I pressed her for a better understanding of what or who is a lesbian. In a painstaking way, she began telling me what that meant. I had heard enough, and I could not believe that I had entered into such a world.

Of course, she told me that she, Anna, was not so inclined, but Holly was forcing this on her. I told her, "This is your apartment. How could you have someone here that you do not want to be here?"

Anna told me that she asked her to leave before I came, telling her that I was coming because she told me to come, and there was not enough room. Holly, she said, refused saying she did not have anywhere to go. Either, she had just broken up with her husband or was kicked out of her apartment. I do not recall.

I began to have second thoughts. I had not prepared for this. When I was on vacation with Anna, everything went well. It appeared at that time that going to live in New York would be a wonderful thing to do. Now, I needed an escape, but I did not know where to turn. I decided to get a job. Anna told me that I could get a home aide job, assisting old or sick people in their homes. She had done it for a while, she said, and it was not bad. I decided to try it.

One April morning, I went downstairs in an attempt to find an employment agency. I do not know how many degrees it was, but it was cold. I did not have a coat or any warm clothes on, and I did not return to the apartment to get some. When I left for the outside, I did not know how cold it would be. I looked through the window and there was sunshine. When there was sunshine in Jamaica, it was always a nice day. At that time, I was not aware that things were so vastly different in terms of temperature.

None of that mattered now, however. I was out, and I needed to find a job. I walked down Nostrand Avenue, and, eventually, I got a bus. When I got on the bus, a lady asked me why I was not wearing a pair of stockings, since it was so cold. This woman, realizing that I was not properly dressed for the cold weather, was concerned. I was touched by this act of kindness by a total stranger, and as I stood there holding on to the rail of the bus,

I felt like crying. There were other people looking at me, as well, maybe out of the same concern. I saw them, but I decided to be tough. It was my first experience being out in the cold and, initially, though, it was cold, the novelty of the idea was refreshing. I eventually ended up at Mulberry Street in Little Italy, Manhattan, at a home aide agency. This was the one Anna recommended. She also gave me the name of the agent she dealt with there. He was there when I arrived. He seemed to vaguely remember Anna, but he decided to employ me. I made my way back to Anna's place in Brooklyn. I tried not to seem too excited, though, I was.

She asked me how it went, and I told her I got a job. At that very moment, she told me I needed to give her a specific amount of money once I got paid. If I agreed with the sum, I could remain at her place. If I did not, I would have to leave immediately. I do not recall the exact amount of dollars she demanded, but it was an exorbitant portion of the already small amount I would be making. I decided I could not do it.

I called my daughter's father, Orville, who was residing in Borden to see if he could help me. He said he could not. God was on my side, however, and I made contact with a couple who also lived in Borden. The man was a long-time friend of my brother, Todd. I saw him a few times, as a child, in Hillside, but I did not know him personally. His wife was a registered nurse. I explained my situation to them by phone, and they decided to rent me a room in their home for forty dollars per week. I could afford that amount, and I accepted with gratitude. Had I not made contact with them, I do not know what would have happened to me in New York. I thanked God that he removed me from that situation with Anna and Holly and did not allow me to be out in the cold, literally, in a strange country with no one to turn to.

I moved into the Kleins' home. I paid my rent each week to them. A desperate young woman in a strange country can easily be taken advantage of and I was, repeatedly. I did not know my way around, and I had no one to turn to. As a result, I was forced to accept things as they were for a time. Eventually, I became more aware of how America worked, and I was able to find a room in a house not far away.

It was a two-apartment complex. Ms. Hobbes lived on the ground floor and Ms. Macy lived on the top floor. Ms. Hobbes had a two-bedroom apartment. She worked in Manhattan and came home only on weekends. She was renting the second bedroom furnished, for forty dollars per week.

This was where I moved to.

Ms. Hobbes was a very nice person. I was like an adopted daughter to her. She looked out for me. The first December I was living at her house—my first in America, she decided to host a Christmas party.

My brother, Sanjay's wife, with whom my daughter was living, decided that she too was migrating to America. She had a sister living in Borden—I was not aware of this information prior. She was coming to live with that sister. I made arrangements for my daughter, Yoshie, to travel with her to New York. They arrived a few days before Christmas. My daughter stayed with me. I invited my brother's wife, along with her sister and family to Ms. Hobbes's party. They came, and we had a good time. They, in turn, were having a Christmas dinner, and they invited us. Ms. Hobbes declined, but I went and took my daughter along.

There was a man, by the name of Tom, at the party who seemed very fond of my daughter. He played with her for much of the evening. I sat there and watched. We ate dinner, listened to music, talked and soon it was time to leave. My sister-in-law told me that Tom asked her if he could have my number. I went home and asked Ms. Hobbes if it would be okay to give the number out. She said yes. I did not have my own phone.

It was wonderful to have my daughter with me again after eight months. I was really enjoying her company. Ms. Macy lived in the apartment on top of Ms. Hobbes's, and she was a caregiver. I arranged to have her care for my daughter while I went to work. My daughter cried the first day I was leaving, but Ms. Macy assured me that she was going to be fine. I had the occasion to see and hear Ms. Macy interacting with the kids in her care, and I knew it was going to be fine indeed.

One day, Yoshie and I were home in Borden. Ms. Hobbes was away, and we were the only ones in the house. We fell asleep. Yoshie was two and a half years old. At some point, while I was asleep, someone poked me with a finger. I awoke to find Yoshie sitting beside me on the bed and sucking her finger, seemingly hungry. I, somehow, came to the conclusion that it was not my daughter who poked me. It may be because I thought the force of the poke could not have been that of a child that young.

In any event, I became startlingly awake and began using a colorful array of expletives. I believe, as a child growing up in Jamaica, I had heard, along the way, that if a ghost came in contact with you, you could use expletives, and this would chase and keep it away. This is what I was trying to achieve. I had my say and was now satisfied. I got up and prepared some food for Yoshie and me. The rest of the day was uneventful. It was about 8:00 p.m. that very night, and my daughter and I had just turned in. I closed the room door, and we were lying on the bed, wide awake. Suddenly, without warning, I heard the pots rattling against each other. The kitchen was next to my room, and the sound was loud and rather unnerving. I could see that my daughter was as scared as I was, and I did not want her to start crying, so I wrapped myself around her and told her it was okay.

We were cuddled together as we listened to this unexplained, insane clanking and rattling of the pots. I realized that my daughter was really scared, and I thought that I had waited long enough for the situation to change, but it did not. I got up, and as I did earlier in the day, I yelled out a colorful array of expletives. The more I carried on, the louder the rattling got. Eventually, I decided to pray. I started saying things like, "Oh God, please help us," and soon after that, the clanking and rattling stopped.

With some degree of fear, I decided to open the door and look out in the kitchen; there was no one there. I concluded, God saw that my daughter was hungry and sent an angel to wake me up so that I could feed her. Because I behaved so badly, instead of being thankful, he sent an angel to punish me. I do not recall if I told Ms. Hobbes or anyone else about this experience, and I do not know if my theory of the angel was correct.

After approximately two months, I returned my daughter to Jamaica. I was not yet in a position to have her live with me full time. Because Sanjay's wife was now living in the United States, I decided to ask my sister, Marva, to have my daughter live with her. She agreed.

Sometime later, Marva also decided to leave Jamaica to live in America. I again had to find a home for Yoshie. I now sent her to live with my parents in Hillside, my childhood home. My parents were getting older, and Yoshie was about seven or eight. I also wanted her to learn to play the piano. After discussing the matter with my sister, Peggy, who resided in Kingston and was a registered nurse, I decided to place Yoshie in her care. During those years, Yoshie traveled to the United States twice per year to be with me. She loved traveling on American Airlines and always had high praise for the air hostesses, in whose care she remained until they delivered her to me in New York or to her guardian in Jamaica.

Sometime after my daughter returned to Jamaica, either I contacted

Tom, the man I met at the Christmas dinner, or he contacted me. We started dating, and he visited me on a regular basis at the apartment on 332nd Street. He lived in Borden, as well. When I went to work, he sometimes stayed at the apartment and cooked dinner until I got home. I was a twenty-three-year-old young woman, and I was inclined to see a bit of life.

One Saturday night, I visited a night club on State Hall Road in Borden, and I met a young man there. He visited me at the apartment the following Tuesday. I was not expecting Tom. He assured me that he had some other engagement. Therefore, he said that I would not see him. While I was inside the apartment with the young man I met at the club, Tom used a key that he had secretly cut and kept to open the door to the apartment, and he came right in.

He did not knock. I could not believe what had happened, and I was mortified. The young man left, and I never saw him again. Tom never received my permission to cut a key for the apartment. Because I was renting a room in someone's home, I would *not* have given him a key. On the days I went to work and left him there, he used my key and gave it to me on my return. Tom was upset and stayed away for a week and then we started seeing each other again.

*Young ladies, when you see warning signs, please, never ignore them.*

Tom had four daughters before I met him. Two lived in Jamaica with their mothers, and two lived in the United States with their mothers. Tom was nine years older than I was. He had a decent job. He and I were paid on a fortnightly basis. When I did not receive pay, Tom gave me twenty dollars, and when I got paid, I gave him twenty dollars, and it came in handy. This helped us with our train fares during the blank week. Tom had recently entered the United States and was also trying to build a life. In addition to working, I was attending school at Borough of Manhattan Community College in Manhattan, New York. One day, I was a bit short on funds, and I asked Tom if he could assist me with twenty dollars to buy text books. Tom's reply to me was, "My kids need twenty dollars more than you do," and he never gave it to me. We continued dating, and I continued attending college.

Sometime later, Tom moved from Borden to live in Temple Hall. He shared an apartment there with his relatives. I visited on some weekends, and he continued visiting me in Borden. Tom also visited Maryland on a regular basis. Most weekends, he went there to spend the weekend with his friends. One of those weekends, I asked to go along, and he agreed. We arrived on a Friday afternoon. On that same Friday night, a woman and her daughter arrived. It did not take long for me to discover that Tom visited Maryland as regularly as he did because the woman was there each weekend, and he was having a relationship with her. No need to tell you how uncomfortable that experience was for me. We returned from that weekend, and we continued dating.

Tom and I dated, including sharing a home for six years, and then we decided to get married. While we made plans for the wedding, I heard the voice of God say, "Don't get married," or "Don't get married to him." I was very concerned. I believed it to be the voice of God, but I was not sure.

I told Tom that I did not think I wanted to go through with the marriage. I do not recall what his response was. I also told my older sister, Marva, about my concern, and she did not think that I should call it off. She actually told me that she thought it was the devil that said that to me.

Tom and I were living together. There was a personal benefit for Tom in getting married. Another weekend, we visited Tom's Maryland friends, and one of Tom's brothers was also visiting them at the same time. I overheard Tom telling his brother that the only reason he was doing the marriage was because of that personal benefit that he would get from doing so. When I heard that, I felt like *nothing*, but I still did not call off the wedding. I decided to go ahead, and we got married shortly thereafter.

In 1986, I was employed by a large New York law firm as a records analyst. I became aware of the firm when I ran into an acquaintance with whom I attended Willow Grove Secondary School. She was working with the firm and told me about it. I worked as an analyst for approximately four years. Soon, I received my Associate degree in Legal Secretarial Science from Borough of Manhattan Community College. After receiving that degree, I applied for a transfer to the Secretarial Services department to work as a legal secretary.

I reported to the Human Resources department to be tested for the transfer. The test was administered by the assistant human resources director in the absence of the human resources director who was on vacation and would return the following Monday. I did a typing test and a shorthand test, and I was successful at both. I was anxiously awaiting the return of Mariette, the human resources director, so that she could implement the transfer. Ralph, the assistant director, had told me that everything was fine, and once Mariette returned, he would give the test results to her.

The following day, while I was at work in the Records department, I got news that Ralph was stabbed several times and killed in Central Park that very night. I had never felt as sick as I did that day. I was totally unable to function. In addition to the fact that I did not know what would happen to the transfer at that point, I was very fond of Ralph, and he liked me as an employee of the company.

That Friday night, as I slept in my bed, I dreamed that Ralph came to my bedside and told me, "It is going to be okay. Tell Mariette that I placed the tests on top of the cabinet."

The following Monday, as I was on my way to Mariette, I was approached by my acquaintance—the woman who told me about the firm—in the hallway, and this is what she said, "You always were *Ralphie, Ralphie;* let's see you *Marie, Marie* now."

I proceeded to see Mariette at the Human Resources department. I did not feel comfortable telling her about the dream I had, so, instead, I told her that Ralph said the tests were on top of the cabinet. She told me that she had found them, and the arrangements were made for me to be transferred. As it was now official that the transfer was being made, the director of the Records department, where I was employed, started making things difficult for me. The human resources director, however, was very insistent, and after a few weeks, I left the Records department. A battle, that I was not aware of, had begun. I went to training to learn the company's way of formatting documents and correspondence. There were three of us in the class. All three of us were transferring to the Secretarial department from other areas of the firm. The course lasted for two weeks. At the end of the class, we were required to "float," which meant that we went from one lawyer to another to acquaint us with the different areas of practice, as well as to help us to be more familiar with the company's way of doing things.

On the day that I reported to the Secretarial Services department, I was summoned to the human resources director's office. The secretarial services director was also present. They both informed me that, though,

I had a perfect score on the "theory" aspect of the test, I had done poorly on the computer aspect. The computer aspect required us to transfer the theory into practical application. I asked them if they thought it made any sense that I would know what to do as I explained and demonstrated in theory, and then not apply it in the practical aspect. They looked at each other and said that it did not make sense. They asked me to sit in the Word Processing department for a couple of weeks so that I could have more hands-on practice. I agreed to do so, and it turned out to be a positive experience. I met some people there, and I learned many things that were not covered during the course.

Once I completed those two weeks in the Word Processing department, I was called again to the human resources director's office. She told me that a senior partner had asked for me to be assigned to him. He had a lot of paper to deal with. He had a secretary but needed another, primarily to handle the extra paperwork. I had dealt with the partner extensively as a records analyst, and he thought he would be satisfied with me.

I was assigned to him, and it went well for a while. He liked calling me Angelina. In time, though, I began having conflicts with his other secretary, and I left. After that, they did away with the number two spot for him. I began floating, almost exclusively, for partners. They liked my work, and many of them asked for me to assist them when their personal secretaries were out of office. I floated in one such position for a female partner for four weeks. She was the second female to become a partner in the history of the firm. She liked me, and she liked my work. When her secretary retired, a short time later, she asked me to become her personal secretary.

The Records department kept all files for the clients of the firm. Lawyers and their secretaries constantly called for information and files. Such requests were carried out by the analysts. On a few occasions, the director of the Records department reported to the director of the Secretarial department that I called over there and was rude to someone. That was a lie. While I was assigned to the Records department, that very director once called me into her office and told me, "It appears that the members of this department have more respect for you than they do for me." I was forced to tell her, "As best I know, respect is earned not asked for. I, therefore, have no control over that."

Another time, while she was having a feud with my German supervisor at the Records department, she again called me into her office and told me that I needed to tell her what the supervisor said about her. I told her I would not and could not do that. She told me that I should know who butter my bread. I did report that matter to the Human Resources department. Human Resources informed me that at least two of my co-workers reported to them that she was setting them up against me and that she was constantly picking on me. It was one of the reasons why Human Resources wanted to transfer me out of there very quickly. It appeared that she wanted to continue her assault on me by using such tactics.

My working relationship with the female partner, Ms. Roper, was like a match made in Heaven. She liked me and my work, and I loved and respected her. It appeared that some of the secretaries were ganging up against me. I do not know what the reason was, but they just could not abide me. I, nonetheless, thrived.

There were five partners' offices and five partners' secretaries in the suite where I sat. Three of those secretaries, with the exception of Kim, were troublemakers. They constantly went down to the supervisor and director of Secretarial Services to complain about me. They were, at times, quite hostile to me. Ms. Roper continued to compliment my work, and her clients were calling with rave reviews about me. One day, the general manager of Bank of America came to a conference at the firm. He asked to meet me. Ms. Roper came down, from the conference center, to the suite and told me that Mr. K was insisting on meeting me. I went, and I met him. There were a few more such requests. Another time, Ms. Roper told me that her cousin told her that she had the best secretary in the world. She trusted me and had much confidence in me. One of the benefits of working for a partner is that he or she, by virtue of being a part owner, has a say in matters of the firm, and she is able to protect you from your haters and adversaries. My adversaries talked about me; they lied about me, and she defended me. After all, I was constantly in her presence—she heard when I was on the phone; she saw me all day long. I stepped away briefly, at lunchtime, to get lunches for her and me at the company's cafeteria. She knew that my haters were being mischievous and that they were lying about me. She always gave me excellent reviews. My director's assistant once confided in me that Ms. Roper wrote on my reviews, in very large letters across the page, "GIVE ANGELA THE MAXIMUM PERCENTAGE RAISE ALLOWED." She also told me that Ms. Roper told my director to leave me alone and that if there was a problem, she would deal with it.

# CHAPTER V

# THE HELL I SUFFERED FROM THE OCCULT

In 1995, I purchased a home in Glen Cove, Long Island, New York. In that same year, some strange occurrences began manifesting in my life, and they were not medical issues. One day, while speaking on the phone at the office, without warning, I went from articulating and speaking clearly and distinctly to not being able to speak. When I attempted to speak, the sounds came out sounding like "tat, tat" and other weird sounds that I cannot describe in writing, and, though, I tried with every effort to speak, I could not speak clearly.

This went on for a while. At first, it occurred only when I was at the office. Soon, the same sounds, accompanied with a great degree of struggle to get my words out, started manifesting at home and then whenever and wherever I spoke.

On another occasion, I was at my desk in the office; I stood up and suddenly fell to the ground. I was not feeling weak or ill. I was quite frightened, and I quickly got up and sat on my chair, as if nothing had happened. All of these occurrences began happening after I started working for Ms. Roper. As these speech impediments continued to manifest themselves, Ms. Roper was most understanding and supportive. One day, I heard an Italian woman, whose desk was directly beside mine and who was secretary to one of the male partners in that suite, say, "If you did not buy a house on Long Island, that would not be happening to you." I pretended not to have heard and totally ignored the comment. Yet another day, I was at my desk and in walked the woman—the one I went to Willow Grove Secondary School with, ran into on the New York subway, told me about the firm and later became my, so- called, friend. I do not recall what her problem was, but she walked into the suite, with my boss present and behaved rather badly. She spoke loudly, was most menacing in her pursuit, and she continued this behavior for a while. Realizing that she had no intention of leaving anytime soon, I asked her to please step into the tax library, which was directly across the hall from the suite I was in. I was forced to leave my place of duty to try to pacify this individual.

One cold morning, while living in Glen Cove, Long Island, I went through my back door. That door was used as the entry and exit door. I was leaving for work. Just as I stepped out, I saw a multicolored bird resembling a fowl. The colors were extremely strange-looking and not typical to those I have ever seen on any fowl. This was directly in the back, in the neighbor's yard, with a fence separating the bird and me. The bird kept looking back at me as it walked in the same direction that I was going. I was on my way to my garage to get my car. I thought it most odd to see a fowl there, especially, since it did not look like a typical one. I proceeded to the garage, got into my car, and left for work. I arrived at work without incident.

That evening, I arrived home, went upstairs, as usual, and did some routine things I was accustomed to doing. A short while later, I went downstairs to the kitchen and began preparing dinner. As I stood in front of the stove, I felt a strange presence moving toward the kitchen from a hallway leading to the kitchen. It moved closer and closer, and soon, it stood directly beside me. I knew someone was standing there; I just could not see the person. He or she was invisible. I stood there for a brief moment, and, then, a harrowing feeling came over me. It was a feeling of great danger. I could no longer stand there. I opened the back door and dashed across the street to a neighbor's house. This was not the yard where I saw the strange bird.

These neighbors moved across the street about a year prior. I did not know them. They were a family: a man, his wife and four sons. Three of the boys seemed close in age, and one was a baby. We never had a conversation before. We waved to each other a couple of times. Now, however, I was in real trouble and did not know what to do. Just as I approached their door, Joe, the husband, came from somewhere to the side of the house. He asked me what was wrong, and I told him of my bizarre encounter. He ushered me inside and alerted Nancy, his wife.

As I was about to go inside their house, Tom had, by now, arrived home. He apparently saw me when I was making my way to the neighbors. He was now speaking to me from an open window in our upstairs bedroom. He asked what was wrong. I told him there was a fierce presence in the kitchen that caused me to flee. He said that I should come back home. I was being stupid.

Shortly after entering the neighbor's house, I began feeling really sick. It was a feeling that I cannot really put into words, except to say that it got progressively worse as the night went on. At one point, as I lied there on their living room sofa, I was feeling totally helpless and feeling, literally, as if the last bit of life was in me. Nancy asked me if I thought I was going to make it. I told her that I did not think so. She started singing worship songs and calling unto God on my behalf. After a while, I heard her say that she was going to call Ms. Lucy. She made the call, and a lady arrived wearing a white dress. I had a tiny bit of strength to ask, "What time is it?" I was told it was 2:00 a.m.

Ms. Lucy joined Nancy and Joe in singing and praying. They stood there, in the living room where I lied helpless, and bombarded Heaven with singing and prayers on my behalf. I fell asleep, and when I awoke sometime later, they were still there. I felt a little bit better, and as the morning progressed, I started feeling stronger and better.

Tom stopped by the neighbor's house, on his way to work, the following morning to check on me. Later that morning, at about ten o'clock, Ms. Lucy accompanied me to my house. I opened the back door, and she stepped inside. She immediately pulled back exclaiming, "My Lord, this place is awful; you cannot stay here." I took a few things, and I spent the day at Ms. Lucy's house.

Nancy recommended a church to me, and I attended the church that evening. I told the pastor of my dilemma and asked him if they would accompany me home. They did. They sang, prayed and blessed the house. I will always be thankful to that group of people because I never encountered that particular problem again. My problems, however, did not end there.

Another time, during this period of my life, I started experiencing an itching in my throat. Soon after, the itching changed to a croaking sound. When I spoke to people, there was a concerned look on their faces, though, they were polite enough not to say anything. Later, the croaking continued and progressed to the point where, when I swallowed, there was a slimy thing in my throat. Each time I swallowed, I felt this most uncomfortable slimy feeling in my throat. Soon, it became more pronounced as if whatever was there was growing in size.

There was a lady named Myra. She operated a beauty salon. I told her of the things I was experiencing, and she became very concerned. She suggested that I visit Haiti. I agreed, and she made the arrangements. Her sister, Anabel, traveled with me to Haiti, and we stayed at Myra's friend's house. I had heard a few things about Haiti and was not elated about going there, but I was desperate and did not know what to do. When we arrived at the airport in Haiti, I was pleasantly surprised. I knew Haiti to be an extremely poor country so I did not expect the airport to be so well structured. We were met at the airport and taken to her friend's home.

My next surprise was that her friend's home was very large and quite beautiful. She had a young boy living with her. He was not her son. His name was Savan. She regularly called, "Savan," and he answered, "*Oui*." It was there I learned that *oui* is French for *yes*.

A few days later, Anabel took me to see a man in Haiti. He seemed like any normal man. He lived in a small house and wore a pair of shorts. As I was unable to speak Creole or French, which is the language spoken in Haiti, Anabel did the talking. I do not know what she told the man. In a short time, though, we, along with the man, went into an open shed that was located close to his house. Soon, he lit a fire, said something and told me to cough.

To my horror, a huge lizard came out of my throat. I was horrified. In my disbelief, I screamed, "Kill it! Kill it!" The man assured me that he did kill it, and he said that it would not bother me again. Later, he said that there was something else he needed me to do. He gestured for me to go inside his house, and when I did, he pulled my blouse down and made a small incision with a razor blade. The horror continued as approximately four or five smaller lizards came out of the incision he made in my shoulder. He, too, was horrified as he explained, by way of Anabel, that the lizard had laid eggs in my body, and he needed to get them *all* out. He said that he had accomplished that.

That very moment, the slimy feeling left my throat, and I was able to swallow without any gross misgivings or difficulty. The man then told me that I am a child of God and should not be there—at his place. I was very touched and indeed amazed to hear a man of this repute giving me some godly advice. I was, nonetheless, very thankful for the advice and for his service.

He recommended that I go down to the Catholic Church in Haiti on a particular day, pay sixty dollars and have them do a mass for me. I complied. There were many people at the mass, and it was conducted in French or Creole. I really do not know the difference, in terms of the sound of the words. I did what he instructed me to do and felt that I received the benefits, although, I did not understand anything that was said or done. Mass finished, and I went back to our host's home. Our host, as well as Anabel, spoke English, but they communicated largely in Creole. That made me uncomfortable, but I tried to be the perfect guest, and I did not complain.

While we were in Haiti, we took a day's journey into the country to visit Myra's relatives. It was literally a day's journey, so we slept in the country. It was a bit like camping out, and I enjoyed it. The people were warm and accommodating.

The following day, we started on our way back to the city of Haiti. Our driver was Nathan, Myra's cousin. He was doing well along these, oftentimes, rough roads, but the journey was long. Soon, the vehicle broke down. We tried to fix it but to no avail. A truck came along, and we got a ride. The truck, however, was not going all the way to the city of Haiti. We were stranded yet again, and we knocked on the door of total strangers. It was very late at night. They opened the door, and our situation was explained to them. They invited us into their very small home and gave us what appeared to be their only bed. They left their home and went somewhere else to finish the night.

It was a long day, and Anabel and I fell asleep quickly on our hosts' bed. We awoke early the following morning, and the hosts made us a cup of tea and wished us well. We thanked them and caught a bus to the city. Nathan said he would arrange to go back and get the broken-down vehicle. After a week in Haiti, I was back in the United States, feeling a lot better and having a far different and better perspective of Haiti and its people.

When I returned to the United States, I called an older brother. I told him about the lizard that came out of my throat. I thought he would be amazed and sympathetic. I wanted to confide in someone, other than Tom, about this most horrible, unheard of, demonic thing that happened to me. He listened to me, and to my utter shock, he said to me, "Why did not you put it in a bottle?" It sounded cold, but I attributed his response to the fact that no one could have a meaningful response to something so far removed from what anyone could think or imagine.

The hell I encountered did not end there. Twice, as I traveled from Queens, New York, where I took the trains to and from Manhattan, I smelled a very strong smell of gasoline. It was in the middle of winter. I was stifling, almost unable to breathe. I looked around and realized that everyone seemed normal. I decided not to approach the driver to ask him to stop the bus. Instead, I opened the window. Fortunately, I was sitting closest to the window and no one complained. The smell dissipated at that moment, and I felt better. Another day, while traveling on that same bus route and also during winter, I was wearing a knee-high pair of leather boots. As the bus rode along, I suddenly felt a sharp object—somewhat like a needle but seemingly larger—pierced through my left foot, between my ankle and my knee. There was no sign of a bruise, but the pain was excruciating. I had no choice but to call on Jesus and wait it out. Soon the pain was gone.

One evening, I was on the bus. Suddenly, I began experiencing a horrible feeling in my body. I told a gentleman, who was sitting beside me, that I was feeling very sick. He asked me if I wanted to get off the bus and take a taxi. I was feeling so awful that I did not think I had the strength to stand and wait for a taxi. At least, I thought, "I am sitting on the bus, and who knows how long a taxi will take to get here?" I said, "No."

I bent over and prayed, "Lord, if only I could get home where I could get my Bible and be able to pray." That day, I did not drive and park. Soon after the bus that I was on pulled in, there was a bus going down Glen Cove. I went on the bus and in less than five minutes I was at my stop. The horrible feeling continued, and I was feeling weak. I prayed again, "Oh Lord, help me to make it up the hill and home to my bed."

I gathered all the strength I had and forced myself up the hill. When I got to the door, I opened it, entered the kitchen and put my things down. I went into the living room, held the rail firmly and pulled myself up the stairs to my bedroom. I threw myself down on the floor in front of my bed, reached for my Bible that was open on my bedside table and began to read and pray. A while later, that evening, I was feeling quite well again.

After these incidents, I began feeling afraid of leaving work and traveling home by myself. I felt extremely vulnerable. There was something, I thought, that was trying to destroy me. I told Tom about this and begged him to come to my train stop in Manhattan and wait for me there. He came, and nothing happened that day and nothing happened again on my way from work.

Notwithstanding, unfortunately, these weird occurrences did not end there. One day, I went into my garage in Glen Cove, and suddenly, it felt as if someone sailed an extremely large needle into the palm of my right hand. The pain was most excruciating, but there was no sign of a bruise. It was so painful that I felt I would faint right there, but I did not. The pain continued for a long, long time. Years later, I still felt that nagging pain return from time to time.

In my desperation and my need to be free from the unexplained things that were happening to me, I sought counsel from many people and found myself a couple more times, at least, in the places where the kind witch doctor in Haiti told me I should not go. One day, I told my primary health doctor of my experiences. He told me those were not the sort of things that doctors could handle. He further told me that I should seek help. I both respected and appreciated his candor, directness and honesty. It was actually this counsel from my doctor, in part, that sent me on my search to eradicate this problem that I did not understand, and I knew not its cause or origin.

I went to a place in Brooklyn, New York, on one such occasion. The man told me to have sex with him and that would heal me. I was desperate, I thought, but not *that* desperate. I promptly but politely explained to him that I am a Christian and could not do that. He made me a bath in a tub; I went and lie in it and then I left. Of course, I paid him for that.

I met another man along the way who told me that I was going to die, after which he told me to pay him one hundred and twenty five dollars. I told him I was ***not*** going to die and pretty much told him to get lost. I do not think that I paid him any money.

On yet another occasion, I went to another man in Brooklyn. He told me to sniff black pepper. It did not make me sneeze, and he determined that this was a big demonic thing that was affecting me. He got a fowl, broke its neck and did something with it. He then told me that my situation was grave because the spirit he dealt with cried, and then he told me I would die. I told him I was not ready to die because I had a daughter to take care of. Unlike the man I told to get lost, I took this man's words seriously. I was concerned, and as I drove home from Brooklyn to Glen Cove, on Belt Parkway, I prayed and talked to God. That day, after getting home and going to my bedroom, I heard the voice of God, clearly, say to me, "Don't worry, you're not going to die." This was my turning point. By now, I had spent approximately twenty thousand dollars, and, though, I had some relief, as in my experience in Haiti, I was still being plagued by this problem. God has told me that I am not going to die, I am going to trust God, totally, in this matter, I concluded.

I called Dean Wayne's ministry, and I spoke with someone who referred me to "pastoral care." She gave me a number for a person living in a town on Long Island, and I went to see her. There are many hills and quaint shops in this town, though, I cannot remember the name of it. Tom and I arrived at the house. A couple lived there. We chatted a bit. They showed us a lovely garden at the back of their home, and we began discussing my problem. While Tom and her husband went downstairs, she and I remained in her living room. She prayed and told me that "a powerful witchcraft spirit" was bothering me. After a while, a loud sound came out of me. After Tom and the gentleman came upstairs, Tom told me that the loud sound sounded like an animal. We thanked them for having us in their home as we left for ours. My quest for knowing and seeking Jesus had now begun in earnest.

During this phase of my life, I was called to the office of the human resources director; the secretarial director was also present. We had a conversation, and I recall the human resources director saying to me, "Are you going to let them kill you? No job is worth that." I replied, "If God wants me to die, I will die, but if he does not, they cannot kill me. I am not going to leave so that they can think that they can do these things whenever they want to have their way." And with that, I asked to be dismissed, and I left her office.

About a year after meeting with human resources, I was called to a meeting in the office of the head of the Tax department where I worked; my boss, Ms. Roper, was also present. He explained that they were aware of what was going on. He continued, "These people want to kill you, and we are not going to let them." As a result, he explained, they were terminating me from that position. While he spoke, Ms. Roper had her head on my shoulder and was very sad. They allowed me to leave early that day. When I left, I felt like a ton of something had lifted off me. That completed six years of working as Ms. Roper's personal secretary.

# CHAPTER
# VI

# MY INTENSE SEARCH FOR JESUS AND HOW HE BEGAN REVEALING HIMSELF TO ME

I started my intense search for Jesus by going to church. In five years, I had attended, on a regular basis, seven different churches of differing denominations. While I was attending church, I woke up very early each morning and scanned the channels for any that had something about Jesus. At the time I was searching, I received my television service by way of Cablevision; however, Cablevision did not carry Trinity Broadcasting Network (Christian TV). I regularly found Dean Wayne and a couple of Christian programs on secular stations between 4:30 a.m. and 6:30 a.m. I was starved for Biblical truth and a need to learn all I could about Jesus. As I had to go to work, I listened for those hours and then got up and started preparing for work. I was learning, and the more I learned, the more I wanted to learn. My thirst seemed insatiable, and I continued day after day.

After listening for a period of time, it began to seem to me that the people to whom I was listening were talking to me in a most direct and personal way. The more I listened, the more it appeared to be so. In 2003, a game show was holding a raffle to commemorate an anniversary. The show invited applications for the raffle. They were awarding fifteen Mercedes Benz cars. I prayed to receive one of those cars and sent in my application. I was now waiting for the notification that I was one of the winners. I was watching a local Long Island channel on the Sunday prior to the Friday when the winners were to be announced. There was a man on television, and he addressed the matter of the car very directly—so directly that there was no doubt in my mind that what he said was intended for me. He had never seen me. I did not know him. Therefore, I concluded that God must have told him what he was saying. I was amazed and extremely excited, and I jumped up in the bed, up and down, yelling, "Yes, yes, yes! I'm going to get the car!" At that point, I was now sure that I had won. The preacher on TV, however, did not say I had won. He said that I would get the car. I continued to await the notification.

The following Saturday, I went grocery shopping with Tom. We went to do an oil change for his car on Hempstead Turnpike in Franklin Square, Long Island. While they were doing the oil change, Tom said to me, "Let's take a walk to that car lot." I protested because, in my mind, I was waiting for my CLK Mercedes Benz notification to come in the mail. I had a car at that time, but I have always liked Mercedes Benzes, and having seen that raffle for fifteen, I thought this was my opportunity to get one for free. Tom was persistent, and I, annoyingly, gave in to his request.

When we arrived at the lot, we looked around. The only car I saw that I liked was a blue S430 Mercedes Benz. Tom asked me if I saw anything that I liked. Thinking that I did not have the money to buy such a car, and still annoyed, I shrugged my shoulders and said, "This is the only car I see that I like."

Immediately, after saying that to Tom, a guy alighted from the office with the key to the car and told me to get in. I again protested knowing that, as far as I was concerned, I could not afford that car. The sales guy persisted, and with my mouth pouting, I decided to get in. I sat in the car, and I liked it even more. It was, indeed, a car I would love to own. I told the sales guy that I liked it, and he began telling me how I could acquire it. He told me I could give him a down payment of two thousand five hundred dollars.

I was excited, and I ran to the bank, which happened to be close by, and I gave him the down payment. They dropped the price a great deal, and I arranged to return with the rest of the money on a particular date. I never received the notification I was expecting, but Jesus had worked, supernaturally, to give me a three-year-old, top-of-the-line Mercedes Benz car, which is a much better model than the CLKs that they were raffling and truly exceeded my expectations. I was now able to say that Jesus gave me my Mercedes Benz rather than giving the credit to an organization or a game show.

My interest in Jesus had increased. I realized that he, through the preachers and teachers of his word, was teaching me, guiding me, providing necessary information to me and blessing me immensely. One morning after praying and before leaving for work, as I knelt there, I heard a voice on the inside telling me that I needed to forgive. I was aware that I hated some colleagues on my job, whom I thought were doing many things to make my life miserable, and I asked forgiveness and named the people I thought were my enemies. While I knelt before the Lord, after finishing my enemies list, I heard the voice say, "Manda." *Manda* is a sister-in-law; while there may have been times when I did not approve of things she did, I did not think that I hated her. I, however, in obedience to the voice, which I believed to be the Holy Spirit who speaks directly to Christians on Jesus' behalf, quickly said, "Yes, Lord, Manda too. I forgive Manda."

After that prayer, on that day, I started noticing marked changes in my life. My enemies at work were still there, but the fear I once had, the misery I felt, the loathing I once held, were melting away, and I began feeling a great peace and felt, then, that I was in charge of the situation. I, at least, knew that the change was not being accomplished by me, but Jesus was, indeed, guiding me in these situations, and he was in control. I mentioned earlier that I attended seven churches during that part of my spiritual journey. Part of the reason was not so much my dissatisfaction with their way of doing things, but more that each time they approached me to become a member of their church, it was impressed upon me that it was time to leave that church, and I moved to another. On an occasion when I had left one, I was out of choices and did not know which one I should now attend. I prayed, "Lord, please let Dean Wayne say on his program, it's time to go back to church if you want me to go."

One morning, as I listened to Dean Wayne, I heard him say, "It's time to go back to church." I was again amazed and thrilled. I decided to go back but still did not know where to go. That morning, I went down to a bus stop on Glen Cove Road, almost directly across from Larchmont Avenue. At that stop, there was a woman named Maryann, whom I spoke with on occasions. She lived in the neighborhood. I greeted her, and, almost without any further comment, she said words to the effect, "You know, Angela, there is a church down there." She pointed to a Presbyterian church a short distance from us. I never had any conversations with her or anyone about looking for a church to attend. My only conversation, about this, was with Jesus, and I determined that this was where Jesus wanted me to go.

I went to the Presbyterian church for approximately four years. When I began attending the church, there was a male pastor, and there were many congregants. As attendance declined, they, the responsible parties at the church, decided that they could no longer afford to pay that male pastor the salary he was making and began searching for another.

The new pastor was a female. She once preached a sermon and said something about Jesus loving homosexuals. Even as a young Christian, I recalled in Leviticus that God, in the Bible, calls the act of homosexuality—man lying with man—an abomination, and I disagreed with her on that matter. I tried to get her attention after service to discuss the matter with her but did not get the opportunity to do so.

One day, she sent around a suggestion box, in one of the services with strips of paper for the congregants to say what was on their minds. I wrote that Paul, the apostle, said a woman should be silent in church and asked what she thought of that. Exactly two weeks later, she announced from the pulpit, that she would be leaving as soon as they found her replacement. She was leaving to take an administrative position within the Presbytery. It appeared to me then that she was stepping down as a result of my question to her, and I marveled to myself.

One Sunday, she had a meeting for those interested in becoming new members. I, along with five to seven others, attended. I believe that was the last Sunday I attended the Presbyterian church. The pastor did nothing wrong or offensive, but it seemed my time there too had come to an end.

I wanted to get baptized but did not know where to have this done. Someone told me about a Pastor Barker. He was the senior pastor at a Baptist church located in Floral Park Gardens on Long Island. I got his phone number and called him. He promised to call me back, and he did on a day I was sitting in my backyard in Glen Cove. We had a few discussions about the things of God.

As I was in this spiritual battle that I scarcely understood, I decided to discuss it with him. He told me without pretense or equivocation that he did *not* believe in demons or spirits. My response was, "How can that be when Jesus talks about them, on several occasions, in the New Testament?" I do not recall what his response was to that retort.

In any event, and thankfully so, he agreed to baptize me. I wanted someone to be there to support me so I asked Tom if he would go with me. He declined. My friend, June—now deceased—whom I met in the Jamaica Defence Force, attended with her kids, Karla, Cami and Joe. She lived in Crown Heights, Queens, New York, at the time. I had told her of my intention to get baptized, the need I felt to have someone there, and that Tom said he would not go.

On the day of baptism, as I lined up with the others, I looked around and there they were. I do not recall her telling me that she would be there. It was a good feeling seeing them, and I was most appreciative of the fact that they came. After baptism, I received "the hand of fellowship." This is a time when other members of the church shake your hand and welcome you as a new member. I also got some documents, which would acquaint me with church procedures. That was the last time, however, I went to that church.

On a Saturday morning, shortly after being baptized, I was lying in bed with Tom. It was customary for me to be awake and just lie in bed on Saturdays, after a hectic week of rushing to and from work, just to recoup. I began shaking violently. It felt like electric bolts were going through my body, but it did not hurt. Rather, it felt good. I was jerking, uncontrollably.

A short time later, as the jerking persisted, Tom asked, "What's that, what's wrong with you?" I replied, "It's okay."

I had seen others in churches demonstrating similar shakings, and I recognized that what was happening was the work of Jesus by his Holy Spirit. I lied there and allowed the Holy Spirit to have his way. After a while, the movements stopped, and I heard the small voice inside of me speaking to me. I continued lying there, and the voice continued to speak. When I realized that Jesus was speaking and was continuing to speak, I jumped up, grabbed what I was able to find close by and began to write. The message was about me in the future, Jamaica, Europe, America, Asia and Africa. I wrote the messages in a book, which I kept for years but left in a red doctor's bag along with other valuables at downtown, Kingston, Jamaica in December 2009.

The following Saturday, after the Holy Spirit shook me, I was again lying in bed, and the Holy Spirit began speaking. This time, I heard him say something regarding a tsunami in the region of Asia. I wrinkled my face in a quizzical look because I did not know the word *tsunami*. As I wrinkled my face, I saw a mound of water rising in the air. I did not know what it meant, but I became aware when I heard, a few days later, that a tsunami had occurred over in the region of Asia.

One day, I was sitting at a desk at the New York law firm where I worked. I was substituting for someone who was away from the office that day. As I sat there, I heard the voice on the inside say, "Joe is going to die in a skiing accident." I did not know a *Joe* so I did not pay any attention to what I was told. Later that evening, I heard, by way of the media, that *Joe* of a prominent New York political family had died in a skiing accident in New York. I straightened up as it came to my remembrance what the Holy Spirit had told me that day.

I began to ponder what that meant for me. What did Jesus want me to know? Another day, after the *Joe* accident, I was again sitting at a desk, in that very law firm, when I heard the voice say, "RK—I have chosen not to put the name here—and his wife are going to die in a plane crash." This was on a Friday at approximately 1:00 to 2:00 p.m. Recalling the "Joe" incident, I decided I needed to tell someone. I dialed Lindy, my director at that time, but her phone went unanswered. I reasoned that she must be out to lunch. At that very moment, the thought came to me that with all the things going on with me, if I told her, she might conclude that I am crazy. I did not try calling her again. The following morning, or that Sunday morning, I heard that RK and his wife had died in a plane crash. This was the second time, in a very short time, that the Holy Spirit had alerted me to the deaths of these individuals belonging to the same family. Even today, I'm still wondering, *Why?*

Another day, I was standing in the firm's elevator along with the managing partner of the firm and others. As he stood there, the voice of the Holy Spirit said to me, "He's going to die of cancer." As the elevator traveled up, I looked at him and thought, "He's young, and he looks healthy." We continued up; we stopped at floor after floor, and soon, I dismissed the thought. Sometime in 2007, I sat at home in Florida, and the managing partner came to mind. I went to the Internet and did a search for his name. To my utter shock, I read there that he died of cancer.

On a regular day while traveling to work, I boarded the "C" train in Queens, New York, that was going to Manhattan. The train rode along, and I sat and hummed a song. At some point while humming, a great peace came over me, and, in that moment, I saw an electrified body come out of my body. It actually separated from my body, and there were two entities. The electrified body was transparent and had the appearance of being lit. Shortly after, I found myself in a room. The room was lit with a natural yellow glow, resembling butter. There were no light bulbs. It was a long rectangular shaped room, and I was the only one there. I did not know why I was there, and I stood and waited for a while. A little later, a man stepped out into the room. He was wearing a floor-length, off-white robe. He was white and of slim build. He approached me and put a similar robe to the one he was wearing on me, and without saying anything to me, he stepped away, appearing to disappear through a door, which led from the room in which I stood. A little later, I began to struggle, telling myself, "I'm dead, I'm dead." Almost immediately, I saw my electrified body merge into my fleshly body, and I woke up—or came alive. There was an even greater peace in me after that experience, and I continued humming as the train continued on its journey.

In 2004, the Lord spoke to me and told me that I was going to be leaving the New York law firm in mid-2005. I wondered to myself, *To do what?* I also thought that things were finally going well at work, *so why now?* I kept the thought in my mind, and I continued going to work and performing my duties.

The Secretarial department had hired a new manager by the name of Anya. When she arrived at the firm, we got along well. Without any warning, it appeared that she started acting negatively towards me. She called me to her office often and made work-related threats.

One day, I was called to a meeting by her. I think I had complained to Human Resources that she was harassing me without reason. When I arrived at her office, the human resources assistant director, Sophie, was there, and Sophie was pregnant. As my manager, Anya, presented her case, which in Sophie's view was non-existent, Sophie got very upset and told me, in Anya's presence, to be careful because, "They are trying to do you in."

I was very touched by the gesture. In the past, Ms. Roper defended me, but here was Human Resources, with no skin in the game, dressing down my manager, in my presence, as to her gross unfairness. Shortly after, Sophie left the firm. It may have been on account of her pregnancy. I do not really know.

Sometime around February 2005, I felt that pull and inclination to leave the law firm. I asked the Lord, "Where should I go?" He told me to go to somewhere warm. As I went around working for the various partners, Joanne had told me about a friend she had living in Naples, Florida, and how nice and beautiful it was there. I told Tom of my desire to leave New York and that I would like to move to Naples. We made a few week-end trips to find a place, and, soon, I found one that I liked. I gave notice of my intention to leave the firm to Human Resources and to my manager. Anya, my manager, told me to come say goodbye before I left. I promised that I would.

On June 8, 2005, I terminated my employment with the New York law firm. Before leaving, though, I kept my promise to Anya to say goodbye. I called and informed her that I was about to leave and asked if that was a convenient time to see her. She said yes. I went to her office, and we had a little chat. Coming to the end of our conversation, she asked me how it felt to be leaving. I said, "I feel like I came from the street to deliver a package, and now I'm leaving again."

She said, "Angela, you must be going to a wonderful life." I looked at her, smiled and said, "Goodbye." With that, I was finally gone from Seward & Strong LLP.

# CHAPTER
# VII

# MY JOURNEY FROM NEW YORK AND LIFE IN NAPLES

Mid-July 2005, I sold my house in Glen Cove, Long Island. Before placing the house on the market, I prayed about it. The Lord told me that I should use Remax as the listing company and that I should ask for a male agent. He further told me that an African would purchase the house and that he could afford it.

I got up on a Saturday morning, found the number for a Remax in the area and called. When I called, a lady answered the phone. I explained my situation to her, and she replied, "Okay, I will ask her to come over." I immediately told her, "It cannot be her. It has to be him." She replied, "Okay, I will ask him to come over."

A man arrived at the house at 4:30 p.m., the time arranged. His name was Jermaine. The house was placed on the market. The following Friday, I had an appointment for a showing. Three men arrived at the house—the potential buyer, his agent and his cousin. At the completion of the tour, as we walked towards the garage, which was detached from the house, the potential buyer asked me where I was from. I told him Jamaica. He told me he was from Nigeria. We exchanged a few more words, and they left. A few minutes later, I received a call from his agent asking for the information of my agent. I provided the information.

After waiting for much of that day, I had not heard from my agent. I decided to call his office. He was not there at the time, but he called me the following morning. I told him we had an offer and asked if he had received that information. He said no; he also said that he had someone else who wanted to see the house. I told him that we had an offer, and I was not interested in any further showings. However, I told him that I would accommodate that person since she was already scheduled, but no other. The afternoon that the lady was to show up, she called to say that she was unable to find a babysitter and could not make it.

My real estate agent thought that we should continue showing the house until the contract was signed and we had the verification letter from the buyer's bank. I told him, "No more showings." We had an offer; that was it.

You see, what he was saying was logical from his point of view, but Jesus had told me that the buyer would be African and that he could afford it. The gentleman was Nigerian, and he was a radiologist. As far as I was concerned, he was the buyer.

Some days later, as I pulled out of Florida on a transatlantic cruise that would take me to four European countries by way of Bermuda, I called home for a status report. I was told that the inspectors were there carrying out their inspection. I had prayed that morning, before leaving home, that all would go well with that, too, and, now, before hanging up my cell phone, I declared that everything was going to be fine. It was, and we closed on the home on or about July 11, 2005.

A few days later, Tom and I were on our way to Naples, Florida. We had purchased a house there that was under construction and was near completion. It was due to be completed shortly, and we were going to be living in a rented apartment for a couple of months. I was also going to be starting a new job on July 18 at a law firm in Naples.

Tom and I were traveling by car. About the time we were passing through Georgia, Tom's cell phone rang. It was his sister. She was calling to ask which bank we had got our mortgage from. I was curious about her question and wanted to know why she was asking such a question. We had decided to pay for the house in Naples with the proceeds from the sale of the house in Glen Cove, and we had approached Citibank for a mortgage of ninety thousand dollars. Citibank carried our mortgage for the Glen Cove house, that was just sold, and had approved this one, as well.

Shortly after Tom spoke with his sister, my phone rang. I answered, and it was Citibank calling to inform me that the ninety-thousand dollars mortgage was denied. I protested by asking them, "On what grounds? How can you deny a mortgage you already approved?" I also told them that I was in possession of the approval letter they sent me. They would not budge. They had no meaningful response, and I was getting nowhere with them. I carried on about my many years of banking with them and eventually gave up in frustration and told them, "Thank you for the information and goodbye." For much of the journey, I was fuming. I had no understanding of what transpired because they provided no explanation. I was, nonetheless, not deterred. I knew Jesus was with me, and I firmly believed he had an answer to what just happened.

We arrived in Florida and moved into the temporary apartment. Tom had received a transfer to a hotel on Biscayne Drive in Miami. I was going to be working on North Miami Trail in Naples. The drive would be too much for Tom to travel back and forth daily so he rented a room from one of his daughters who lived in the Miami area. He stayed there Sunday evenings to Friday mornings.

I did not know anyone in Naples, other than my real estate agent, but I decided I had to quickly get the mortgage sorted out. One day, while I was at lunch, I ventured out and saw a bank. I went in and inquired about a mortgage. They told me that the lady was out to lunch and would be back shortly. I waited nervously because I did not want to return from lunch late, since I had just started a new job. Soon, I was told she was back, and I was shown to her office.

We spoke about the mortgage, and I found her to be warm, professional, caring, understanding and relatable. Her name was Debbie. She said that she would call me with the answer, shortly, if I could not wait. I kept checking the time while she ran the numbers, and soon, she told me she had an approval. It was a wonderful feeling. I went back to work feeling jubilant, knowing that the mortgage was fine.

I had sent my car, from Glen Cove to Florida, by a moving service, which transported vehicles across America. It had not arrived there by the time I did. Since I was not sure how long it would take, I had sent it in care of, Julie, my real estate agent in Naples. Consequently, I had to take cabs to and from work. As I got better acquainted with the folk at work, we spoke a bit about me. As the newcomer, they seemed interested in learning about me. I told them about my car situation. A female attorney pledged to take me home and pick me up in the mornings until my car arrived.

About a week later, while at work, I received a call from Julie telling me that they delivered the car at two o'clock that morning. She said that the truck was too big to get into her lane, and her husband had to go out, at that time, and meet them for delivery of the car. I jokingly told her that it was her bright idea to have it sent to her, one for which I was most thankful. Julie asked me if it was okay for her to drive the car to the company's parking lot, where I worked, and leave the key under the mat. I told her that was fine. She was aware that I had only just started the job and did not want me to get in any trouble.

I met Julie, by way of the Internet, when I was looking for an agent to assist me in finding a home in Naples. She turned out to be a wonderful person. She was the first person I knew to have driven a hybrid vehicle. One day, as we were traveling in her car to Golden Gate Estates, I told her that I felt the real estate market was at its plateau and would shortly come down. I was speaking prophetically, though, I had not known it at the time. I do not remember what her response was. She had her own company, which she ran from home, and she told me that she was doing very well.

On the day I interviewed for the job, in Naples, Julie and I had an appointment scheduled for after the interview. The interview lasted longer than I had expected. My phone was on, and, to my utter embarrassment, Julie called right in the middle of the interview. I had to apologize and explain that it was my real estate agent who was trying to find me a home and had scheduled an appointment for that very afternoon. Fortunately, the interview was going well; they liked me very much, and they did not see it as a problem.

A few days after starting the job, my two bosses, along with the others with whom I worked, took me to lunch. Others drove their cars, but since mine had not arrived, I rode with my senior boss. He drove a beige Mercedes Benz 350. It was new, and I could tell that he liked it very much. I complimented him by saying, "Nice car!" I did not mention that I, too, owned a Mercedes Benz—the S430 I told you earlier that Jesus gave me.

On the day Julie delivered the car, I went to lunch at my customary time. My senior boss had requested that I go to lunch when he did, and I did just that. Both of my bosses were friends, and they went to lunch together, most of the time. I went downstairs and entered my car. I was not aware that they were coming directly behind me. Just as I sat down, I heard Raymond, my junior boss, say, "I heard her talk about a car. That's not a car; that's a *caar*." I was not sure how to act on the basis of that comment. I started the car, said hello to them and drove out of the parking lot to find some lunch.

One afternoon, I was sitting at the apartment in Naples. I believe it was a Friday. As I listened to the television, I heard that a hurricane was headed for New Orleans. I sat there and began saying words to the effect, "Yes, Lord, destroy it—the mardi gras and all the things they do there that are wrong." I was in support of the hurricane coming and beating up on this place. That was that, and I had completely forgotten about the hurricane or anything else I had said.

The following Tuesday, I decided to drive home from work on my lunch break. As I was traveling down the street, where my temporary residence was located, I heard on the car radio that New Orleans was under water and also that the devastation that had occurred was continuing. It immediately came back to me what I had said a few days earlier as I sat in the apartment on the couch. I was shocked, so shocked that, as the realization hit me, I was forced to grab the steering, hold it firmly, as I thought about it and wondered what it all meant in the larger scheme of things, where I was concerned and what God might be doing in my life.

The house I purchased in Naples was now complete, and I closed on it in mid-September 2005. A few days after moving in, I heard of hurricane Wilma. It was headed for the Naples area, and we were told to prepare for a direct hit. I was alone at home, and I did not know what to do. I prayed, "Lord, please do not let the hurricane come here." Immediately after praying, I saw, as by a vision, a white material coming down and covering my property.

On the expected day of the hurricane, we were given the day off from work. Sometime about midday, it started raining, and there was a little breeze. I had never experienced a hurricane before so I was very excited. I had seen the white material come down from above, over my property, so I knew it was going to be okay. I went out on the lanai, at the back of the house and watched as the palms waved their fronds in the wind. I thought, *Is this it?* I danced and allowed the little girl in me to enjoy a novel experience.

Later, I heard, on television, that many trees were down in Naples. Not even a limb came down on my property. I decided to get in my car and venture out to see what damage they were talking about. I did not get very far. It was pretty bad. There was no water at the office, and we did not go to work the day after Wilma struck. When I did return to work, my boss, Joram, told me that he was in his house, and the hurricane sounded like a train wreck. I told him it must have missed me because I had no such experience. A little rain, a little wind—that was all I got. I lived about three miles from my boss.

I left the Naples firm after four months. Prior to my joining the firm, a woman named Dana worked for my two bosses. They promoted her, they said, and I was taking her position. She, however, saw it as a demotion. One day, I heard her, none too subtly, tell the mailman that they put her all the way in the back, while I was now sitting up front, but, she added, they will see.

The arrangement was for her to teach me what I needed to learn in the position, but she was not enthused about it. She seemed, rather, to undermine most of what I did, resulting in my making notations on hard copies as well as on the computer. Once, she tried to make mischief by lying on me; I immediately pulled the notations I had made. She was very surprised, and everyone realized, at that moment, what she was really about. My senior boss, Joram, at that point, decided that Raymond, my junior boss, should teach me. Raymond told me that it was Joram's fault why Dana was behaving that way because Joram was making such a big deal of me.

One day, Joram left for West Palm Beach to see clients. The administrator was away, at another office, that day. I went down to the file room and, while I was there, Dana came and accused me of something. I told her she was wrong. There was a bit of back and forth between us. When the administrator returned, Dana and the woman, who worked in the file room, went and complained. The following day, the administrator and Joram asked me to a meeting in the conference room.

I listened as they waxed eloquent with praise for my work. The administrator then told me that "I was not the right fit." I was not offended. I was happy to be leaving, but I thought it was a stupid comment. Here was an administrator, in a very large American law firm, telling the only dark complexion person in the Naples branch of the firm that she was not the right fit. I thought, *How candid, how honest.* There is a tremendous lack of honesty in society today, which often leads to a breakdown in integrity. Therefore, though the comment was stupid, from the standpoint of America being such a litigious society, after four months of working closely with Felicia and Joram, I believe they came to respect me in a way that assured them that, while such remark could have negative consequences, saying it to me was fine. I simply told them, "Thank you for having considered me for the position. It was a pleasure working with all of you, especially with you, Joram."

Again, I felt, at that moment, as if a heavy load was lifted off me, just as it felt when I left the position working for that partner in New York. It was a great relief. I had had enough of Dana and her antics. One does not go to work to fight battles. He or she goes there to try to add value to that company by being good at what he or she does.

Before I left that day, I sent a few e-mails to Felicia, the administrator, in which I told her that they did the right thing. I also told her that I believe it was God's timing, not theirs. She wrote in one of her e-mails to me that she, too, believed God had a plan for my life, and the happenings of the day were part of "his master plan." I thought, *Wow!—spoken like a true prophet.* That afternoon, as I walked out of Stone & Rock, LLP, I felt better than I had felt in the last two months.

Though, I was in Naples for just over a year, I began feeling a pull to leave. I sought Jesus on the matter. He told me to enjoy what I liked of Naples because I would be leaving there. I liked it in Naples, but I thought, *Who am I to contend with God's advice?*

I spent my post Stone & Rock, LLP days gardening, etc. There were many snakes where I lived in Naples. One day, as I backed out of my garage, I saw little heads looking up on the west side of the house. I counted nine snakes, in the same location, lying in the grass with their heads up. This was somewhat abnormal but not surprising. They often frolicked on the pavement, in front of the house, as if they owned it, and when I threw objects at them, they behaved as if nothing happened. On many occasions, they could be seen crawling around the house and looking for a way to get in.

Between September and October 2006, I placed the house in Naples with an agent for sale. She was recommended by Debbie, the lady who approved the mortgage for me in Naples. When the agent came to my house, she told me that there were many homes that were similar to mine on the market and that the market was slow. As a result, she said that she would send me a letter every two weeks updating me on the progress she was making. I told her that would *not* be necessary because the house *would* be sold in two weeks. I got the feeling that she might have laughed in my face had I not come highly recommended by Debbie. She repeated the "letter" disclosure once more, and I chose to ignore the second mention.

She returned some days later with her team to take pictures for a layout brochure. It is said that in Texas they do things big; well, in Naples they do things nice. She compiled a number of binders with the pictures she had taken. They were beautiful. A week later, as I was about to leave the house for some shopping, I heard the voice of God say, "You're going to be getting an offer, and whatever it is, accept it."

I had not heard from the agent, at this point, but I kept my phone at the ready to grab it once it rang. The following morning, at about eleven o'clock, she called to tell me that someone wanted to see the house at four in the afternoon. I told her that I would go somewhere at that time. The morning after the showing, she called with an offer of ten thousand dollars below the asking price. I called Tom for his agreement and then accepted the offer. The contract was signed a few days later.

We began looking for a home in West Palm Beach. We viewed a house and then stepped outside to discuss it. Immediately, I heard God say, "Don't get it." Just then I said, "I do not like it." Tom, at that point, said he liked it. We made an offer and soon we signed the contract. On October 30, 2006, I left Naples for West Palm Beach.

# CHAPTER VIII

# MY MOVE TO WEST PALM BEACH

On my way to West Palm Beach, I stopped in Miramar, Florida, and spent the night with my brother and his wife. The following morning, I was on my way to my new home. That night, Tom came home from his daughter's home in Miami. He found a job, a couple of weeks later, in West Palm Beach. I slept in my new home for the first night. The following morning, I woke up and went outside. To my great surprise, there were approximately one hundred ants' nests that came up overnight on the one acre of land. It baffled me as to where all those ants' nests came from and where they got all that dirt to build those nests in that short time, but I did not allow the thought to consume me.

I spent the next days and weeks decorating the house. After a few weeks of living in the home, I decided to make some changes. I got custom drapes, tore out the flooring and put in twenty-four-inch marble tiles, a custom entertainment center, an enclosed pool, some landscaping and other minor changes. The purchase price of the house was five hundred and sixty thousand dollars. The upgrades cost an additional one hundred and fifty thousand dollars.

My mother had not visited me for some time in America. The last time she visited, I was living in Glen Cove, New York. I decided to invite her for a visit. She agreed, and on May 5, 2007, accompanied by my sister, Peggy, she traveled to Florida. Tom and I met them at the Fort Lauderdale airport. We got home and she settled in the side of the house designed for mother and mother-in-law. Mother and I spent our days driving around West Palm Beach. She had a good first week. On the beginning of the second week, Mother was visited by her only living sibling—her sister. Her sister then decided to spend a week with her about four weeks into my mother's visit.

Now, my mother, her sister and I were driving around West Palm Beach. My mother was shopping for her friends, children and grandchildren in anticipation of her return to Jamaica in two weeks. My aunt returned to Hollywood, Florida, on Father's Day. We drove her home and spent the day with my brother in Miramar. At the end of the day, we left for West Palm Beach.

The following week, my mother and I continued shopping. Monday through Thursday was uneventful. Friday night, Mother went to bed as usual. I generally spent some time with her each night, curled up in her bed while we chatted about old times as well as other things. That Friday night was no different. However, Mother woke up that Saturday morning, and I saw her frantically trying to open the sliding glass door leading to the pool, which was still under construction. I asked my mother if she needed to get out there. She opted, instead, to go to a swing that was located in a breezeway at the left front side of the house. She sat in the swing and began swinging away. I was making breakfast, but I kept going out there to see how she was doing. She appeared to be having the time of her life. Some parts of her hair were sticking up as the breeze blew, and it was a most beautiful picture of my mother.

That Saturday evening, Tom left home to meet one of his brothers somewhere in West Palm Beach. He returned a couple of hours later. Just as Tom entered the family room, my mother who was watching television in the family room where Tom always watched television, got up and went to her room to lie down. I accompanied her to her room. Some minutes later, she said that she was not feeling well. I remained with her in her room. At that point, she told me that on Friday night she got out of bed to go to the bathroom, which was a couple of steps from her bed, and someone pushed her, causing her to stumble into the shower and hit her head. I did not know what to think, and I still do not know what to think.

I knew my mother was telling the truth, but the mystery that lingers is, *Who pushed her?* It was then I realized that my mother may have been disoriented when she was frantically trying to open the door on Saturday morning. The problem is that Tom and I were the only ones in the house with my mother. Was my mother then pushed by a demon?

My mother continued to feel worse as the minutes ticked away. I called my sister, a registered nurse in Jamaica, who traveled to Florida with my mother, to see if she might be able to shed some light on our mother's illness. She told me she did not know. I then called my aunt's daughter who is a registered nurse in Hollywood, Florida, to see if she could tell me anything. She suggested getting my mother's "vitals" taken.

I decided to take my mother to the hospital. Mother was reluctant to go, but I encouraged her by telling her that we needed to take her blood pressure, etc. Sometime around midnight, that Saturday, Tom drove us in his pickup to the Palm West Hospital, West Palm Beach. Mother and I sat in the back seat. Upon arriving at the hospital, they conducted some tests, and my mother was admitted. My aunt and her daughter came to see my mother at the hospital that Sunday.

My mother had sickle cell, which she lived with, managed and led a regular life with for a number of years. The tests revealed that her spleen was enlarged, and the doctor recommended chemotherapy. After consulting with my mother, to see if she was agreeable to the chemo treatment, the doctor was given the go-ahead.

Mother responded extremely well to the first dose. Tuesday night, June 26, 2007, I was with my mother in the hospital as I had been since she was hospitalized. I was joined that Tuesday evening by my brother, Sanjay, his younger son and Tom. We all sat there and conversed while Mother joined in the conversation, even joking at times. I was there until very late that Tuesday night. Sanjay, his son and Tom left at about 9:00 p.m. I told Mother that I would leave when she fell asleep. I ended up leaving at about 2:00 a.m. As I drove out of the parking lot, I began speaking in tongues and praising God. I did so during the drive all the way home.

When I arrived home that night, Tom told me that my brother's son was sleeping in my mother's bed. I asked Tom why he was not sleeping in the guest room or with his father. Tom told me that he said the two beds in that room were too hard, and he did not want to sleep with his father. I was extremely upset that he was sleeping in my mother's bed, but since it was very late, I allowed it to be.

The following day, Wednesday, June 27, 2007, I woke up but could not get out of bed. There was a heaviness on me. I felt weighed down, not in spirit but in my body. I, eventually, got up and made breakfast. We ate, and I packaged some food for Mother, just as I had done the past three days. Sanjay, his son and I arrived at the hospital. My mother was sitting up in the middle of the bed, totally unsupported. I told her I had her breakfast, and she was very happy. A nurse told me that she had eaten a good breakfast earlier that morning. I told the nurse, "She likes her Jamaican breakfast."

Just as I fed some of the food to my mother, one of two nurses in the room attempted to put something in her IV tube. I asked the nurse to allow me to feed my mother before doing so. She replied, "Okay."

My mother was now enjoying her food. I gave her another spoonful, and she was chewing it. Just then, the other nurse bent over and forcefully put something in my mother's IV tube. Immediately after she did that, my mother stopped chewing and leaned over. I then heard my mother say, "Angie, water, water, Angie." I quickly pulled out a bottle of water from my pocketbook and tried to give it to her. She was unresponsive. Those were the last words my mother spoke, and they are indelibly seared in my psyche. I called out, and many people came running into the room. The nurse who forcibly put the medicine in my mother's IV was among them. They scrambled to resuscitate my mother and said they did. They then quickly moved her to ICU.

I called my sister, Marva, who left work, at that moment, in Philadelphia and caught a flight to Florida. I called Tom; he left work and came to the hospital; I called my aunt, and she came along with her nurse daughter. Just then my brother, Todd, called and asked me what was happening there. I told him, and he asked me to keep him posted. I made some other calls, as well.

I left the hospital to pick up Marva at the Fort Lauderdale airport. When she arrived, Mother was on life support. She had been on it since they moved her to ICU that day, and I had been numb for much of it. I could not believe that my mother, who was enjoying the breakfast I brought her only moments ago, now lied there on life support because a nurse—in whose care she was placed—decided to force medicine in my mother's IV, while she was eating and who, obviously, should have known better.

Later that day, I looked at my mother while she lied there on life support, and she had a radiant glow on her pinkish looking face. My mother had a beauty radiating from her that could only be described as from God. Later that night, my sister, Marva, began to feel very ill; we decided to leave for home so she could get something to eat. We left Mother's room in ICU, knowing they were getting ready to remove the life support from her. We asked them to allow it to go out on its own. At about midnight, my house phone rang. Palms West Hospital had called to say the heart monitor had gone silent. My mother, who visited Florida for a six-week vacation, would have to return to Jamaica in a casket for burial. The hospital listed *five* causes of death on my mother's death certificate. The hospital also sent me, by mail, a handwritten letter to express their sadness and regret at my mother's passing. She was laid to rest in Hillside, the only home she's really ever known, on July 7, 2007. June 27, 2007 was the saddest day in my life.

# CHAPTER IX

# HITTING ROCK BOTTOM

After the funeral, I returned home to West Palm Beach, Florida. It was customary for my nephews Joshua and Brian, his younger brother, to visit for the summer. Joshua had done it for the past eight summers. They enjoyed and looked forward to these vacations. I did not want to disappoint them, and I also felt it would be somewhat therapeutic for me, in getting my mind off my mother's death, and I decided that they should come. They arrived with their mother. She accompanied them on the flight, and she spent two weeks with us. The boys stayed for six weeks.

Prior to my mother's passing, there were plans for one of Tom's daughter's to visit us. It would have been the week following my mother's funeral. She was going to arrive with her husband and two-month old baby. As a result of the recent developments, I asked Tom if he could ask them to stay with her uncle in Fort Lauderdale to allow me some time to recoup. Tom, not seeming to understand the magnitude of all I had gone through the past few days, lambasted me—and asked me, "How is it that your family can come and mine cannot?" I pointed out to him that my sister and nephews were close family. We had just lost our mother and grandmother, respectively, and were all mourning our loss. Of such, if I failed to be a good and gracious host, they could relate and understand. Tom said his daughter and her family would come, and they came. Barely two weeks after I lost my mother, who came to that very house for a vacation and died suddenly, I was hosting Tom's daughter, her two-month old daughter, her husband, my sister and my two nephews.

I mentioned earlier that my mother was staying in the suite designed for mother and mother-in-law. When Tom's daughter decided to visit, Tom decided that he wanted her to stay in that suite, even, though, my mother was there, and her visit would overlap my mother's stay. It may be useful to note that apart from that suite, there were two other guest rooms, a full bath and a half bath available in the guest wing of the house. After my mother died, Tom's daughter stayed in that suite. Indeed, Tom got his desire. Tom's daughter and her family spent their time between us and her uncle in Fort Lauderdale, where they spent the majority of their time.

Almost immediately after returning from my mother's funeral in Jamaica, I started feeling ill. I have always experienced good health and did not know what the cause of this feeling was. I could not explain the feeling other than to say my arms felt ill; my body felt ill. It was a strange feeling. I visited the doctor during the time my sister was visiting. While I was at the doctor's office, my sister asked me to allow her to speak to my doctor so that she could explain to him. I told her that I was not going to allow her to speak to him. I was trying to sort out these strange feelings that *I* was experiencing and could not explain, yet she somehow thought that she was able to articulate to *my* doctor what she thought I was feeling.

As the weeks went on, I continued to feel the very strange feeling all over my body. In the middle of August, the feeling persisted. I looked in the telephone business directory for the number of a church in West Palm Beach. There were many churches listed. I saw the number for *Acts 2*. I had seen that sign as I drove around West Palm Beach. I decided to call them. I explained my situation to the assistant pastor who answered the phone and asked if they would come to my house and pray with me. He said a group would come over.

On a Wednesday evening, approximately six people arrived at my home on Little London Street. There were five women and one man. The man's name was Parker. His wife, who worked as a nurse, was also present. We had a prayer meeting, which lasted for about two hours. We sang and held hands in a circle and prayed. We went to each room in the house and sang and prayed. Before leaving, they encouraged me to attend church. I attended that Sunday following their visit; I continued attending on Sundays and Wednesday evenings, and that became the pattern for some months. Almost immediately, I began feeling a change. I kept feeling better and better until the feeling was completely gone.

I continued going to *Acts 2* for a while. I do not remember my reason for leaving, but I did stop attending there and found another church called Redemptive Life. While I attended *Acts 2*, I noticed that everything significant—the worship, the preaching—everything was done by the pastor and his immediate family. The greeters were not family members, but the pastor, his wife, his son, his daughters dominated everything.

It was a good size church, and I often wondered why was it that other members of the church were not asked to be a part of his small family worship group that led the worship on Sundays and Wednesdays. Certainly, there must be others in the church who could sing and would welcome the opportunity to be part of the choir. While I attended, I never heard the invitation extended for anyone to join the choir. I did not like that so it might be that my decision to leave may have been influenced by that.

I was now attending Redemptive Life Church in West Palm Beach. I was startled, on my first few visits, when I saw the number of offerings they collected in a single service. There were, at least, five different offerings in a single service. The first time I heard of the "Levite" offering was at Redemptive Life Church. Once, they also collected a "first lady" offering.

I had seen the pastor on TBN's *Praise The Lord* program and was impressed by his performance and learned that he was in West Palm Beach, and so when I needed another church to attend, I sought him out. I went to the Internet, plugged in his name and found the name and location of his church. When I got there, I noticed it was a good size church but not large by today's mega churches' standard. The pastor's messages were inspirational, and I enjoyed them most of the time. Soon, I invited Tom along. I purchased a Bible for him while we lived in Naples, and I was encouraging him to seek a relationship with Jesus. He attended a few times and was no longer interested. The last Sunday he attended, about five minutes into the pastor's message, Tom got up and went outside. He never returned until the service was over. I do not know if something in the sermon offended or affected him, but that was the last Sunday and the final time he attended.

In February 2006, while I still lived in Naples, my sister, Peggy, told me about an investment opportunity in a company named CashPlus in Jamaica. Her husband had been investing in it for a while and it was working out good for him. I had some money, at that time, that I had no immediate need for, and I decided to try it.

I flew to Jamaica and met with the chief executive officer, a male. I posed a few questions to him; one of which was, "How can you afford to pay the interests you do?" He showed me a number of products that were on display in a front office of the building, which was located in New Kingston, Jamaica. He also told me of the huge success the phone card was having in Jamaica and said that they were the proprietors of those, as well as some other hugely successful companies in other countries. His explanation seemed logical, even plausible, and I left feeling rather impressed and pleased that Jamaica, finally, had a venture I could invest in. I returned to Naples feeling determined to invest in CashPlus.

I called and spoke with Cahill, the chief executive officer. I had spoken with him on my personal visit to the company and told him of my decision. He put me on to a woman named Marjah. I started by investing five thousand dollars. After two months, realizing it was working the way he said it would, my confidence was heightened. I upped my amount, significantly. Throughout 2006, it performed as expected, and I was thrilled. I told my sister, Marva, about it, and she decided to get in, as well, and she did. Soon, my brother, Sanjay, also got in. Sanjay said that knowing how careful I was about investments, if I thought it was fine, he would try it.

Just about that time, CashPlus informed me that they were increasing the percentages on new monies that were sent in. I asked CashPlus to return to me the one hundred and ten thousand dollars that were already invested. In turn, I would send another one hundred and twenty thousand dollars. I spoke with Cahill and explained this to him. He told me to speak with Marjah. Marjah instructed me to fill out the requisite forms. I did and faxed them to her. She told me she was working on returning the original investment to me. I went ahead and sent off the additional one hundred and twenty thousand dollars of new investment, before getting back the original one hundred and ten thousand dollars that they had promised to return to me.

One Friday evening, in October 2007, I received a call from my sister, Peggy, who simply and in a matter-of-fact way stated that she heard on the radio in Jamaica that CashPlus was having some problems. The following Monday, I spoke with Cahill by phone, and he assured me that they had everything under control. I would later learn the truth that CashPlus was a pyramid scheme, even before Bernie Madoff's came to light. I learned that PricewaterhouseCoopers was hired to perform the final audit. Investors were told that we would receive a fraction of our money back. It has been twelve years, and I am still waiting to receive that portion of my two hundred and thirty thousand dollars that CashPlus took down with it.

I had recently purchased the house in West Palm Beach for five hundred and sixty thousand dollars, and I had paid down over two hundred and fifty thousand dollars toward the purchase. The money I had in CashPlus was all the savings I had left. Still, I refused to be despondent. I had done foolishly, I now discovered, but God does not forsake us, even when we do foolishly, and I had faith in God. When I received the news of CashPlus's looming demise, with my life's savings tied up in it, I declared what God says in Romans 8:28— "And we know that all things work together for good to them that love God, to them who are the called according to his purpose." I trusted God and his word; therefore, I was not alarmed. I told Tom that and drew a most sarcastic remark from him telling me that, "It is because you do not have the mental capacity to realize what is happening or just happened to you."

I knew we had a mortgage of approximately three hundred thousand dollars on the house, along with some other responsibilities. Regardless, my trust was securely in God and whatever happened, I thought, *God is in control.* At the time this happened, I had about twenty thousand dollars in the bank. I used that money until it was exhausted. I paid credit cards. The mortgage was approximately $2,800 per month. I paid $2,300 and Tom paid $500. All the other bills were split fifty-fifty between Tom and me. I continued paying my $2,300 of the mortgage payment and my fifty percent of the other bills until all my money was gone, and I had nothing left.

Sometime earlier, a niece of mine had called to inform me that she had received a fifty thousand dollar settlement on a car accident that she was involved in. At the time she told me, I encouraged her to send some money to her dad and place the rest of it in a bank certificate of deposit.

However, after hitting rock bottom, I called her and asked her to lend me some money. She promised that she would get it from the bank and send it to me that Monday. I never heard from her again. At the time, she was residing in Nebraska.

About two years later, in January 2010, I was riding on a bus in Tampa, Florida. I saw someone that looked familiar. Not expecting to see her in Tampa and the fact that she looked somewhat different, I looked at her and said, "You look like my niece." She said, "I saw you and thought you resembled my aunt." We chatted on the bus ride until she got to her destination and got off the bus. We never mentioned the loan or anything relating to it.

After the CashPlus debacle, I tried to get a job but was not successful. Things were getting worse, financially. It was customary for Tom and I to split the food bill, as well. Tom was working; I was not. Tom continued giving his usual portion of food money, and I had to make do with that. By the grace of God, I managed. I plugged out appliances that were not in use, at particular times, turned off lights, and used them only when necessary. It cut down dramatically on the light bill, and Tom did not have to pay much more than his fifty percent for that either. The first month, after I had completely exhausted my last twenty thousand dollars, I was having a conversation with my sister, Marva. Later that day, she called and offered to pay that month's mortgage. I told her that was awfully kind of her, and that I hope that I would, one day, be able to repay the amount. She said that I should not worry about it. I borrowed an additional one thousand two hundred dollars from her, at the same time, to make good on a deal that a bank called to offer me on my outstanding credit card debt to them.

My brother, Carlton, who resides in Jamaica, sent me one hundred dollars each month. That aided me in getting basic things that I needed, and I was very thankful to him. One day, I asked Tom for ten dollars. He wanted me to tell him what I needed it for. I never thought that I would be brought down to that level, but I was and God was there with me. After missing two months of mortgage payment, we received foreclosure notice on the house. It would take five years, however, for the bank to foreclose on it. God was faithful to ensure that I had a roof over my head.

Sometime in March 2007, I went to Mercedes Benz in West Palm Beach and purchased a new CLS 500. With the trade-in of my S430, for which they paid me fifteen thousand dollars, I paid an additional fifty three thousand dollars. After a month of driving the car, it developed a terrible sound. I brought the car to the dealer, and they test drove it and confirmed the sound. They, nonetheless, depreciated the car by twenty five thousand dollars.

In order for me to get a car of the same model and year, I was asked to give them another twenty five thousand dollars. The only other option that they proposed was for them to give me a check with the twenty five thousand dollars, depreciated amount, subtracted. I was forced to take the check and resort to leasing a car of the type that I originally owned. Now, after losing all my money, I called Mercedes Benz and informed them that I would turn in the car. They told me that I should keep it until they picked it up. I insisted on turning it in and drove it to the company on Okeechobee Boulevard. I had the feeling that had I not turned it in, they would have allowed me to keep it for a much longer time, even though I had not paid them for a few months. Looking back, I realized that God was giving me favor with them, too. I became totally broke between April and May 2008. On August 9, 2008, a Saturday, before attending Tom's niece's barbecue, he told me to go to the bank with him so that he could remove my name from his bank account. He said that the reason he did it was that I owed the IRS some money, and he did not want them to take it out of his account. We went to the bank in Royal Palm Beach, Florida, and filled out the necessary paperwork. It took about half an hour, and it was done that Saturday.

# CHAPTER X

# HOW GOD LED ME FROM DANGER TO SAFETY

I had been feeling that the Lord was impressing upon me to leave Tom and the home in West Palm Beach behind since mid-2008. It was something I wrestled with. On one occasion, I called a few people of God and asked if they thought it might be God impressing this on me. One day, the feeling came on me so strongly, and I actually stood in my living room and contended with God, asking him how could he ask me to do this? In early 2009, between March and April, the feeling was so fierce that I could no longer remain in the house at West Palm Beach. I had to leave. I felt afraid. I felt an ominous feeling—a darkness that suggested that if I did not leave, I would not be safe.

In March 2009, I made the decision to leave. I called my mother's sister in Hollywood, Florida, and told her that I needed to leave home and needed a place to stay. She said it was fine for me to come to her house. I should go ahead and come, and she would discuss the matter with her daughter—who was at work at that time—with whom she shared the home. I packed some things, went to Nath and Cynthia, my sister's in-laws and asked them for some pocket money and a ride down to my aunt's residence. Nath gave me twenty dollars. I was broke, and that was all the money I had. Cynthia and I got into her car, and Nath drove us to Hollywood, Florida.

We arrived at approximately 3:00 p.m. All three of us went to the door, carrying my things, and my aunt came to open it. She greeted Nath and Cynthia. I then bade them goodbye and went inside. My aunt took the bags and suitcase I had brought and told me that she was putting them away for the moment. She appeared to have put them in a storage area. She then went to a refrigerator in that same area, got some food in a plastic container, and heated it for me. I ate the food. A short time later, my aunt's youngest daughter stopped by. They were conducting what appeared, to me, to be a sort of coded conversation. I wondered to myself why my aunt and cousin would be talking like that. Only weeks before, when my mother was in West Palm Beach, they were all at my house.

Prior to leaving West Palm Beach that day, just after speaking with my aunt, I called another of my aunt's daughters in Jamaica. I do not know why I called her, but I felt the need to and so I did. I told her that I was going by her mom and would be staying with her for some time, that I had just finished speaking with her mom, and she said that it was fine to come. My aunt's daughter was really taken aback. She replied, "Are you sure *Mom* said you can come?" I replied, "Yes, I just got off the phone with her." My cousin again asked, "*Mom*? Are you sure Mom told you to come?"

I did not know the reason for my cousin's skepticism. Now, listening to the coded conversation between my aunt and her daughter, and remembering what my cousin in Jamaica had said earlier, I decided to leave. I took a folder I had, along with a small shoulder handbag, and I told them that I was going for a walk. I left everything else I brought at my aunt's. Shortly after stepping out my aunt's front door, I started feeling a terrible sick feeling in my stomach. I walked a while until I saw a McDonald's. I went inside, got a cup of tea and sat there until they were ready to close. I began walking in the general neighborhood, not going anywhere specific but just being out there. I did not call my aunt to report my whereabouts. After everything that transpired that day, I did not think I should trust my aunt, and I did not want to be bothered.

It was quite late, and I was still out there walking around and sitting on the occasional park bench I saw. At one point earlier in the evening, when I was feeling quite ill and before going into McDonald's, I had seen an ambulance and approached it. They asked me if I was okay, and I asked them if they would take me to the hospital. They said, "Yes," but I declined.

Now, at approximately midnight, I was approached by two policemen. They asked my name, and I told them. They told me that my aunt had called to say that I left her house that evening, and she had not heard from me since. The policemen said that my aunt further told them that I showed up at her house with nothing—no clothes, etc., and that I showed up without her knowing that I was coming to her house. I told them that I had a conversation with her earlier in the day, and she told me to come, and I brought two very large bags and a suitcase, which she took from me when I entered her house.

Having received that information from the police, I was most gratified that I had left her house when I did that evening. I knew my aunt was not crazy, and I decided that whatever she was up to, I could not trust her. The officers asked me if I wanted to go to a hotel for the night. I told them that I had only twenty dollars. They said that it would cost more than twenty dollars. They also said that there was a way for me to get somewhere safe to stay for the night, but I would have to agree to be there for three days and that I would be subjected to an examination. They said it was called the "Baker's Act," and it was run by a hospital. I told them I would think about it.

They gave me about an hour to do so. I told them I did not want to go. They said they could not allow me to remain on the street. They called an ambulance; when it arrived, the attendants in it reminded me that they were the ones I had spoken to earlier in the evening. I was scared. I did not know what to expect, and I was learning very fast that I no longer knew whom to trust.

The ambulance arrived at the hospital, and I was taken to an area. There was a male orderly booking in patients that night. He was in a room, with an opening, from which he communicated and dispensed medicine. He appeared to have a Jamaican accent. As the night wore on, from time to time, I went to the window to ask him questions as to what to expect. He gave me a few answers and kept telling me to wait. After being there for approximately two hours, I noticed two young men, wearing white or latex gloves, standing close by and looking at me in a rather menacing way.

I became both concerned and even more scared. I asked them who they were and what their function was. I do not recall their response.

I was the only patient in that area at the time. Soon, I was given a hospital gown, which I put on. Sometime later, a door opened that appeared to have led from a basement or a lower floor, and another four or five men, wearing gloves, came into the area where I was. Without any explanation, they forcibly grabbed me, forced me to sit on a metal chair, pulled my underwear down and stuck a needle in my buttocks. Immediately, after receiving that needle, I became groggy and disoriented. They put a mattress on the floor in an adjoining room and led me to the room. I was the only person in that room.

I remember feeling that I was going to die. I felt that if I ever fell asleep, I would never wake up again. I walked around on the mattress praying to Jesus to not let me die. I fought the sleep for as long as I could. I became exhausted trying to fight off the sleep. I kept praying while I kept going around and around the mattress in the room. After a time, I heard Jesus say words to the effect, "Blessed are the little children who die in the Lord." Almost immediately after hearing that, I fell down on the mattress and fell asleep. I do not know what they injected me with or why they injected me; I was healthy and did not complain of any problems. The stomach problem I had earlier was long gone, and I did not tell anyone about it.

I do not know how many days I was asleep. I was awakened by a man late one day. I knew it was late because he asked me if I had eaten all day, and I told him no. He said he was going to take me to a room. I followed him. I was still disoriented and did not know what was going on. On my way to the room, he stopped by a doctor. I vaguely remember sitting down before someone who told me that he spoke with my husband and, based on conversations with him, he came to a diagnosis. I had no clue what he was talking about. I was still disoriented.

After leaving the doctor's presence, I was led to a room. I must have fallen asleep immediately after I got there. When I woke up, a young woman, with whom I shared the room, wanted to know what was wrong with me. I asked her, "Why? She said that I had been sleeping for two days. I asked what day it was, and I believe she told me Thursday. I saw a doctor later that day. I do not know if he was the one that saw me initially; however, he said that I would be released to the care of my husband on

Friday.

Tom showed up on Friday to take me home. He had picked up my things from my aunt's house. I told him the police said that she told them I did not bring anything there with me. Tom asked me if I could recognize anything. I did not know the reason for his question, but, amazingly, whatever they did to me in that hospital was still having its effect on me at that point. Everything seemed strange.

This was the beginning of a bizarre series of events. A few weeks later, I happened to walk out to the family room of my West Palm Beach home. It was night. The moment I got out there, Tom also appeared, but he was going to one of the guest rooms nearby. Just then, I felt a zing-like burst of electricity and a sound where I was standing. I felt as if I was going to fall, but I did not. I noticed, at that very moment, that Tom looked at his watch as he made his way to the guest room. Just then, I felt a strange sensation, and I began feeling ill. I called 911.

I was grateful when a woman answered the phone. I explained to her what had happened and told her that I was feeling sick. She told me that an officer was on the way to my home, and she offered to remain on the phone with me until he got there. A short time later, two officers arrived in two police cars. They spoke with Tom, privately, and then spoke with me. They decided that it was not safe for me to remain there that night. They spoke with Tom and I outside the house, and they did not want me to go back inside to change out of my pajamas. They took me to St. Mary's Hospital in West Palm Beach, and I was placed under the Baker's Act. I was, indeed, grateful to have left home that night. I do not know what might have happened, had they allowed me to remain. I spent a week at the hospital and was again released to Tom's care.

It had now become a regular habit for Tom to tell me that he was going to call the cops to "Baker Act" me. I had also noticed a couple of strange events involving the movement of some long sharp kitchen knives at home. Those events made me feel very unsafe. I decided I needed to find a safe place, away from home. One afternoon, I told Tom that I was going out to Royal Palm Beach. I intended to find a place to which I could escape. I stopped by Acts 2 church, spoke with a gentleman there and then left.

I decided that I would attend service at Redemptive Life church, and I did. When I got there, I spoke with a woman I had met during the months when I was a regular visitor there. I was not a member, but I attended church there each Sunday and Wednesday and considered it my church home. I told her how unsafe I felt and that I needed a place to stay for the night. I told her that I did not feel safe going back home. She suggested that I speak with the pastor's wife.

The service started a short time later. The members were encouraged to *sow* seeds during the service. I needed a miracle; in my estimation, my situation was grave. I did not have any money, but while I sat there, I heard the co-pastor say that we could *sow* jewelry if we did not have any money. *She must have read my thoughts,* I reasoned. I immediately took off my Wertheimer, gold plated, diamond studded watch and sowed it. It was an expensive watch. The service continued; the pastor preached and then it concluded. I was glad when it ended because I needed the opportunity to speak with the co-pastor. I asked to speak with her and was told I needed to speak with her through a "surrogate." I do not know the surrogate's name, but while I spoke with her, she was extremely hostile.

I had no idea what I had done to arouse that level of hostility in her. In any event, I related my sad tale, telling her that I felt it was unsafe to return home that night and needed a place to stay. *Could they help me?* She had absolutely no sympathy for me. She became irate and told me that they did not even know me, etc. Reluctantly, after the co-pastor overheard her carrying on, she inquired as to what was the matter. The woman explained to her, and I, drawing near enough so that she could hear me, added that I was having some issues at home. I felt very afraid to go home and needed somewhere to stay for the night. I was wondering if I could stay with her or was there a church sister she could recommend for me to spend the night with?

Now, it was the co-pastor's turn to be disgusted. She looked at me as if I was someone who did not matter, someone who had no value in her eyes, and in a scornful manner, she said, "I couldn't take you into *my* home, and how could I ask a church sister to take you into her home when I do not even know you." I felt like I was punched in the gut while having stale urine thrown in my face. I thought, "The pastor's wife, co- pastor of the church, a woman of God—this is the way she responded to someone in need who comes into her church begging for help?"

I had second thoughts of "sowing" my Wertheimer watch that I had, only a few minutes ago, placed in *her* hands, personally. She told me, when I handed it to her, "God is going to bless you for sowing it." Now, she's telling me, with scorn and ridicule, that she did not even know me. I consoled myself with the thought that it would go to the work of God. I had not really given it to her, I reasoned, I gave it to God. I stepped away, with a sinking feeling in my stomach, thinking that if this is the *Church*, that I had witnessed up-front and personal, I did not like what I just saw, just heard and just experienced.

Men and women may reject us, but Jesus never will, and he is only a whisper away. Shortly after leaving the co-pastor's presence, two young ladies approached me. They may have overheard the conversation, I really do not know. They said that they knew of a place, not too far away, and they would take me there. I got into a car with them, and they drove to a building. Upon arriving there, they went inside, spoke with someone and assured me that I was going to be fine. After their assurance, I went inside and started feeling quite comfortable.

I was given something to eat. Sometime later, I was shown to a room that I shared with another woman. It was comfortable as was the bathroom. It was my first experience being in a shelter. I had heard of shelters but had no concept of what they were and what they offered. The following morning, I woke up and was served a good breakfast. I was then interviewed by a woman in an office in another area of the building. After speaking with me, she said the place I stayed last night was a very temporary shelter, usually for a single night. She said there was a more long-term shelter where women are protected—the place is secret and women's identities are kept secret. I would be taken to a police station where I would give them a code name. She provided me with that code name, which she said she would also give to the police. She told me to go home and get my things.

I took a bus from the office to a plaza in Royal Palm Beach, where I generally had my nails done. I asked for a ride from one of the workers there. She willingly obliged, and we went into her car and drove away. When we arrived at my home, I approached the front door, attempted to open the door and found that my key could not open it. I tried another door and the same thing happened. I was shocked and wondered what that meant. I apologized to the woman who drove me, telling her that I was sorry that I took her from her job and wasted her time. She was extremely gracious and said it was no problem. We left, and I asked her to make a brief stop at Cynthia and Nath, who a couple of months ago had given me twenty dollars and drove me to my aunt's home in Hollywood. I gave them a brief update and left. The woman who gave me the ride drove back to her place of business. I thanked her. They wished me well, and I left.

With only the clothes on my back, I boarded a bus. When I reached the police station, it was dark. I was hoping to get there earlier, but I was instructed to get there at 8:00 p.m., the time they would be expecting me. I arrived and gave my code name to an officer and the "all clear" was given. I was very afraid as I entered the back seat of the police car. He drove me to the location of the secret shelter. When we arrived there, he escorted me into the building, and he spoke with one of two ladies in an office. They, too, were expecting me.

The policeman left, and the two women began interviewing me. They asked me questions, and I answered. As I answered, they entered the answers into a database. They asked me about my fear of being home. I explained to them, in details, about the long kitchen knives and the strange and unusual movements that I had noticed, the past days, along with a few other details. I also told them that I went home to get some clothes and found that the keys I had could not open the doors. When the interview ended, I was given a brief orientation of the place— the physical layout, the rules, etc. After that, I was shown to a room.

There were four bunk beds, a few ladies and some kids. I was shown a box in which I was told I might be able to find a few pieces of clothes to tide me over. Next, I was taken downstairs to the kitchen by one of my roommates. She told me that I would need to find a job since we would have to buy our own food. There was, however, a cupboard where there were a few "public" things that anyone could use. I had no money and no personal stack of food so I quickly looked into the public cupboard. I recall thinking that there was nothing in there that I ate. I hard boiled a couple of eggs, ate them and went to bed.

The following morning, I went downstairs to the kitchen to see what was in the public cupboard that I could make for breakfast. It was about seven o'clock. It had every appearance that a female resident had let two men into the building. I distinctly remembered being told by one of the women, who interviewed me, that men were *not* allowed in the building. Immediately, it was as if the voice of God said to me, "Run." Instinctively,

I ran up the stairs and locked myself in a bathroom. I did not know what was going on, but where I was, it did not look good for me.

The men came up the stairs and were somewhere in the passageway. I heard them tell a resident, "Tell her you want to use the bathroom." The resident repeated what he told her, and I replied, "Use another one." They were out there for a long time. Though, I was told this place was secret, I was now forced to call my sister, in Jamaica, on my cell phone, to tell her that I was at this secret shelter. I said, "Two men are trying to get to me. I do not know who they are. I am locked in a bathroom, just in case anything happens to me."

At times, they could be heard saying, "Angela, come out." I remained there, holed up for hours, and I was praying. I prayed and I prayed and I prayed. My prayers were answered. I heard the voice of God say, "It's okay to make a dash for it now." I was terrified. I questioned myself for a moment, "Is it really God?" I decided the only way to find out was to use my faith. I quickly made my way down the stairs, opened the door, scaled the iron gate, which was locked and which helped to secure the place, and I was quickly out in the street. I ran and ran and ran until I came upon a large tree about a half mile down the road. I looked back and saw no one coming after me, and I sat behind the tree and rested. A while later, I began to walk. I was now in a built-up area of town.

I was less afraid, but I was very cautious. I asked a man I saw what town it was, and he told me. As I walked along the sidewalk, I thought to myself that it was a beautiful, affluent-looking place.

I do not recall how the circumstances surrounding this episode began, but a short time after I arose from sitting behind the tree and began walking, a gentleman bought me a Sub Sandwich, and he told me where I could get some water to drink. I walked across the street and asked the restaurant operator for a drink of water. He asked me if I wanted a drink instead. I gratefully replied, "Yes," and he filled up a cup with lemonade. He said I could return if I needed some more. I thanked him, went back across the street and finished my sandwich and the drink.

As I sat there, a few youngsters passed by and joked with me in a fun loving way. I joked with them in return and smiled. I went back across the street and took the restaurant operator up on his offer of another glass of drink. He remarked, "Looks like you're very thirsty."

I said, "I won't get into it, but yes I am." He offered me another if I wanted one. I thanked him and said, "I think that will do it." I came back across the street and sat down. Indeed, God feeds the sparrows, and he fed me that day too. It would not be his last act of feeding me when I had no money and no food.

I sat there and pondered what I was going to do. I called my sister, Peggy, to inquire about some money my brother, Carlton, had asked her to "Western Union" to me. I was told it was sent. I caught a bus to West Palm Beach. The driver was a woman I had traveled with a couple of times in the last few days. On those occasions, we had a few conversations. I think she was Jamaican or said her husband was Jamaican. I knew she knew that I was down and out. She may have seen a look of despondency in my eyes, and, certainly, my hair was in need of proper grooming. The way she talked and looked at me, I could tell. When I stepped up on the bus, she smiled and said, "Hi," and she looked at me sympathetically. I rode the bus for over an hour and then came off, prematurely, at the wrong place. I was then forced to walk a long way. The buses, I believe, ran on the hour. I was desperately trying to get to a location where I could pick up the money. I finally made it to a Publix supermarket and went to the Western Union there. The woman, who worked in that area, checked and told me that no money had come in for me. I called my sister again to inquire what was going on. I believe she told me she sent it. I waited until 7:00 p.m., the time the woman told me they would close and still nothing came.

My brother had sent me over one hundred dollars, and I had planned to get a motel room for the night in West Palm Beach, where I would weigh my options. I was not able to do so now. I was out of options and out of money so, as much as I hated to and was still very afraid, I decided to go home.

I walked along Okeechobee Boulevard until I reached the Berean Baptist Church. I had attended services there with Nath and Cynthia. It is where they worship. I went inside and asked someone if I may be allowed to use their phone. My cell phone was out of charge at this point. A kind gentleman led me to an office, and I called Tom at home. He answered the phone, and I said that I was coming home. Would he please come to get me at the Berean church?

Tom replied by saying that I told the people at the *secret* shelter that I was afraid because of strange activities with the kitchen knives; they contacted the police, and the police contacted him. I thought to myself, "Some *secret* place that was." He went on to say that the police told him that if I contacted him to come home, he should contact them before having any contact with me.

Remembering how eager Tom had been to tell me that he would call the cops to Baker Act me, at the slightest anything, I became both concerned and alarmed. I left the office and went across the yard to a hall where they were holding a meeting. I wanted to talk to someone to ask them to be present with me if and when the police showed up. They dismissed me by telling me that they were having a meeting. They were singing and clapping their hands so I determined that it was a worship service. I pleaded with them, but they told me that I was disturbing their meeting, and they closed the door. My concern was that I somehow feared that there may have been a crooked, rogue cop in the force, working with Tom to destroy me. After those two men, whom I spoke of earlier, showed up at the *secret* shelter, my concern turned to alarm, and so I felt I needed help.

Just as they closed the door, a police car drove up. It was driven and occupied by a white male officer in uniform. When I saw the car, in my fear, I ducked into a garden by the side of the building. I was wearing a pair of pants, a sleeveless blouse, and I had a tiny shoulder purse over my left arm. He pulled up beside me, alighted from the car with his gun pointed at me and said, "Don't move; if you move, I will *expletive* kill you."

About a minute or two later, entering from Okeechobee Boulevard in the Berean church entrance, was a Toyota Corolla. With gun still pointed at me, he said, "Is that your husband?" I said, "I think so."

Tom pulled up to where we were and came out of his car. They looked at each other and then the officer told me to lean on the back of the police car. I complied. The officer, roughly, pulled my small shoulder purse from my shoulder and handed it to Tom. He also plucked my pair of gold earrings from my ears and gave them to Tom. Next, with his gun still pointed at me, he told Tom to search me. Tom came over, put his hands in my pants pockets and searched me.

When Tom was finished, the officer continued to speak harshly to me. Tom told me to do what he says and everything would be fine. I was complying from the start, and I continued complying, needing no exhortation. As far as I was concerned, I was not guilty of any crime. A woman in the United States of America, feeling unsafe or afraid in her home, has a right to leave and find a place of safety. That was what I tried to do. I was not rude, in any way, to the officer, and he did not accuse me of anything. He held me at gunpoint and roughed me up while speaking to me harshly. I never knew that a police officer in the United States of America could tell a civilian, in this case Tom, to search anyone.

When Tom was finished with his search, the officer placed both my hands behind me and handcuffed me. As he was about to push me in the back seat of his car, I glanced at Tom with a look of bewilderment, as in, *What's going on?* Tom gave me a nasty look that said, in my view, *Serve you right.* The officer, literally, pushed me in his police car and closed the door. I do not know what he said to Tom, but he said something to him. He drove off with me in the back of his car with my hands handcuffed behind me. I had not known that this type of treatment could be meted out to an innocent female in the United States of America, and here, too, again, as with the co-pastor at Redemptive Life church, I had called upon a group of church people at Berean Baptist Church in West Palm Beach, Florida, for help, and they refused to come to my aid, at a critical moment in my life, when not much was required of them.

They say that they are representing Jesus. At those moments, though, I saw or experienced *nothing* of Christ in them. I know some things about God, more specifically about Jesus, and I was not going to allow their ungodly behavior to deter me.

The police drove away, and I started to pray. He drove to a shopping plaza, where there were a white man and a white woman, both dressed in dark clothing. They were not dressed in police uniform. I had no way of knowing if they were police officers. He pulled up to them, dragged me out of the back of the car, pulled the cuffs off, pulled my hands in front of me and handcuffed me again. The man and the woman, without any explanation, stepped up to me and started running their hands all over my body in a menacing way. When they were finished, the officer in uniform who drove me there, pulled the handcuffs, pulled my hands behind me again and handcuffed them there. And, as he did at Berean Baptist Church, he again, literally, pushed me in the back of the car and closed the door. He then drove away.

I had gone to St. Mary's Hospital twice before. I had also lived and driven around West Palm Beach for a while. I had no concept of where I was. There was nothing familiar. I asked him, "Where are you taking me?" He replied, "To the hospital."

I did not believe him. After the way he mistreated me, the strange manner in which he acted, the seemingly long drive along roads where I did not see any street lights or buildings, I thought he was going to kill me. I asked him, "Do you know God?"

He replied, "Yes."

I said, "Why are you doing this?" I do not recall what his response to that question was.

I started singing. I thought if I am going to die, let me die praising God. After that, I began praying in tongues—the heavenly language. He continued to drive, and I continued praying in tongues. After what seemed an eternity to me, he pulled up outside a building that was a hospital. I said, "Oh, you did not kill me," and he said, "I told you I was taking you to the hospital."

He pulled up his computer on the dashboard area of his car and in big capital letters he typed, while I looked from the back seat, "PATIENT WAS BAKER ACTED BEFORE. HER HUSBAND SAID SHE IS A BURDEN TO HIM. HE SAID HER FAMILY MEMBERS DO NOT CARE ABOUT HER, AND HE ALONE HAS THE PROBLEM." The date on his computer, as I recall, was July 28, 2009.

I was shocked to see that note and wondered why he needed to give such a note to the hospital. Was this a *go-ahead* to the hospital to dispose of me, I wondered. We went inside; he took the handcuffs off, handed the note to the person booking in patients, told me good night and left. I was told to wait in a room.

Except for a little boy of about nine years old, I was the only patient there. There was a lady sitting in an office. When I saw the boy, I suddenly remembered that in a vision, God had showed me that little boy with a cut down his back who needed an organ. God showed me that they were going to try to take the organ from me to put into that boy, but they would not be able to do it because the machines were going to break down.

The boy came into the waiting room about five minutes after I arrived there. He was eating food from a foam food container, and he had a hospital gown on. The back of the gown was open, and I saw a cut that was stitched running down the full length of his back. With that realization, I began to sing praise songs and started speaking in tongues, and I did not stop. I walked up and down the room while continuing to praise God out loud. I saw a man dressed in light green hospital scrub uniform going in and out of a room across from where the boy and I were. There were large machines in there. After a while, he came out and muttered something about the machine or machines stopped working. When I heard that, I said, "Thank you Lord." It now seemed so apparent that what God showed me was playing out right in front of me.

Soon, there was an announcement that they would not be able to continue because the machines were down. When I heard that, I asked myself, *Can this really be happening?* This is exactly the scenario that God showed me.

I continued praising God and speaking in tongues aloud. The lady, sitting at a desk, in the office suggested that I sit down in a "very comfortable chair." I told her I did not want to sit down. However, I started feeling a bit like sitting down, and I did. Later, I recall being in a hospital gown and being helped into a wheelchair. I believe they injected me because I was unable to recognize much at this point. I do not recall the name of the hospital.

I recall being driven through a gate in an ambulance at about 5:00 the following morning. I believe that was when I was taken to St. Mary's Hospital. The doctor who saw me when I was at St. Mary's, at an earlier time, was the one who saw me again. When I was there earlier, he commented that I had a lovely personality. And now he said, "Oh, you're back!" I told him I'm afraid to be home and needed a safe place to be. After a week, he released me, and I was again back home. When I arrived home, Tom said that two of my family members said that they would be willing to come and testify so that they would keep me in the hospital—in a mental ward, supposedly permanently.

When I told him he was lying and pressed him for names, he gave the name of my daughter. I never asked her anything about it. Tom also said he knew I was not going to remain home. I told him he was right. After that note I read on the police officer's computer, what transpired with the police officer that evening and at the hospital, I was more determined than ever to get out of there.

I needed somewhere to go. I had a conversation with my sister, Caryn, in Jamaica. She later spoke with my sister, Marva, in Philadelphia who said I could come by her. My daughter, who worked with an airline as a supervisor, at that time, purchased a ticket for me. I packed three large boxes with things I would need. I shipped two boxes by post to my sister's place in Philly. One would be shipped later, I thought. Carlton, my brother in Jamaica, sent me money on a monthly basis. It was some of this money I used for shipping. I traveled with two suitcases. I was met at the airport by my sister, Marva.

While in Philadelphia, I tried desperately to find a job but was not successful. I went on an interview, a good way from Philly town where my sister lives. My daughter drove me to the interview. The job was offering twenty-seven thousand dollars. I told them, if offered, I would take it. They were concerned about the distance. They said that I would have to get up at 3:00 a.m. to make it there on time. I said that I would do what was necessary. In the end, I did not get the job.

My niece placed an advertisement on craigslist for me. In response, I received an e-mail from a male looking for a "personal assistant." I replied quickly thinking it to be a legitimate offer, but after a few e-mails, I quickly recognized that was not the type of personal assistant I wanted to be. The questions he asked had nothing to do with the type of personal assistance I was trained to give. I realized that in dealing with the world of cyberspace, you have to be careful, and when you are desperate, be doubly careful. I ceased responding to his e-mails.

My sister had gone out of her way to accommodate me. She had a three-bedroom house. Two of her sons were still at home, and I was sharing her bed with her. Her boys, with whom I had a great relationship over the years, now seemed far removed and distant. I had started feeling extremely uncomfortable. I needed to get out, just to be out for some fresh air and to gather my thoughts. I told my sister that I was going by my niece. I called my niece, Damaris, after leaving my sister's house, and asked her if I could stop by. She gave me an excuse, which basically meant no.

I ended up taking the bus to a hotel. I sat in their Lobby and enjoyed their festivities. I took a cab home at a very late hour. I had to wake my sister from her sleep to let me in. After she let me in, she mentioned something about calling Tom and telling him. I wondered, what did she not understand about what I told her—that I was afraid of Tom, afraid to be home with him and was now trying to leave. *Why would she say that?* I wondered. I made the mistake of saying, "I'm going home." No sooner had I said that, she latched on to it, and she said, "Yes, go home."

I immediately begged, or rather pleaded with her that I was not serious; "I'm just upset, confused, not understanding what's going on," I said. She said, "You said it, and you cannot take it back. I have tried, and now you must go." I was turned out of my sister's house. After that decision was made, I noticed my nephew, the younger one, became happier and more talkative. I was with my sister for two weeks.

I contacted my daughter, and she made arrangements for me to fly back to West Palm Beach. My sister offered to drive me to the airport, but I declined. She gave me fare for a cab, and I was off. I had barely stepped foot into the house at West Palm Beach when Tom again said, "I know you'll be gone in a few days, right?"

I said, "I cannot stay here." Now, I felt more tormented and afraid than ever. I was now feeling that if I did not leave, I would have a nervous breakdown.

I called my brother in Miramar. He had regularly spent weekends with me in Naples and West Palm Beach. We had a good relationship. I told him I needed a place to stay for a few days because I felt like I was going to have a nervous breakdown if I did not get out of there. I then asked directly, "Can I come by you for a couple days?"

He said, "No." He then told me not to go to Jamaica. I told him Jamaica seemed the only option I have left. I was not upset that he said no, but I was disappointed. I continued to plan.

Earlier, I heard the voice of God telling me *not* to go to Jamaica. As a result, Jamaica was a last resort. I did not know what to do. I just knew I could not remain in that house at West Palm Beach. I asked Cynthia and Nath if I could stay with them for a while. They declined, saying that they did not want to get between Tom and me.

I called my sister, Peggy, and told her I had no choice but to come to Jamaica. She suggested that I ask our brother, Carlton, if I could stay with him. I called, and Carlton immediately said, "Yes." I took my two suitcases, untouched from my return from Philadelphia, and Tom gave me a ride to the Fort Lauderdale Airport.

When I arrived in Kingston, Carlton was there at the airport to meet me. He welcomed me with a warm smile and open arms. I arrived in Jamaica in the first week of September 2009. I was having a good time at Carlton's place. We went out together; he allowed me to drive his car to church, supermarket and other places. I used his daughter's computer.

I cooked and tidied the house. Carlton and I chatted about all sort of things. One day, while my sister, Peggy, was visiting, Carlton said, "How is it they said Angie is crazy, is not it the same Angie we've always known? I do not see any change."

Peggy concurred saying, "Yes, that's what I'm thinking. It's the same Angie. I do not see any change." It was the first time I was learning that it was being said by some in the family that I was crazy.

After being with Carlton for six weeks, relaxing and having a good time—I even got Carlton and Kate, his daughter, to attend church with me—Peggy came by one day and told me that Todd, the eldest sibling, called her and said, "How is it you told Angie to come to Jamaica and left her with Carlton who is not well?"

Peggy was steaming with fury, and she said, "How dare Todd suggest that there is something wrong with you when you're the same person, and Carlton is really enjoying your company." For some unexplained reason, I now felt like taking a break from Carlton. I told him he was terrific, and he really was. He had shown me no negative attitude in my time there. "However," I said to him, "I will keep you as my base and spend some time with the others."

He said, "Why?"

I said, "I just feel like it."

That Friday, I called my sister, Caryn, and asked if I could spend a little time with her. She asked, "How long?"

I said, Two weeks, no longer than a month." She said that she would think about it.

The next time I called to see if it was okay, she said she had consulted with a woman at her church—who told her it was not a good idea. Her daughters, she said, also did not think it was a good idea. I asked, "Can I just come for the weekend?" The answer was still no. I was shocked. In my years, visiting Jamaica, my sister and her daughters always wanted me to spend some days with them. I generally spent a day or two with them, spending the majority of my time, with Mother, in Hillside. Just a year or two earlier, December 2007, when my sister and one daughter visited Miramar, Florida, they spent nearly a week with me. I drove to pick them up; we went shopping and had a good time. I then drove them back just before they were to return to Jamaica. I also bought her daughter her first laptop computer on that visit. I wondered why they were acting like that.

I called Peggy and told her that I needed to leave Carlton that Friday. She came and got me, and I was now staying with her and her family. Shortly after getting there, my sister's attitude changed. I did the laundry, cleaned the house, ironed the boys' school clothes, cooked dinner, etc. I do not know if any of that was appreciated. At times, I would ask my sister simple questions of a non-personal nature. If she did answer, the answer was laced with sarcasm.

I spent a lot of time in the room where I stayed while being there with them. One day, my sister volunteered that she would invite me to church, but her church members were going to ask a lot of questions such as, "Why are you in Jamaica?" I replied, "So tell them." She said that she couldn't be bothered. I told her it was not a big deal for me. I was fine being home. They attended church on Saturdays. I attended on Sundays.

On a day that my sister, Peggy, was at work, her husband said to me, "In the past, you did not want to stay with us, but now you're here." My sister has never invited me to spend time with them. Whenever I returned to Jamaica, on vacation, my time was spent primarily with my aged mother, cooking and cleaning and just enjoying some quality time with her. Additionally, I recall spending time at their home at least twice before. I did not say this to him, but thought, "How dare you? Are you aware my name is on your deed because I gave money to my sister in the purchase of this house? Are you aware that when you got married, I bought all the champagne along with so much more? Are you aware that every summer when your boys visited the United States, I bought their tickets with my funds, shopped for them with my funds and sent them home, laden down, with clothes, toys and so much more?"

I never told those things to anyone. That's not who I am. I am simply noting my outrage here to say that when you are down, some people will try to kick you further, if you allow them.

One night, I went to church in the area. A fellow church sister gave me a ride home. She and her husband dropped me off at the gate and left. I went to the living room door and knocked. My sister's husband sat in the living room at the computer, and he did not budge to let me in. I stood there, for a while knocking, as if begging to be let in. My sister, who was at the back of the house, came out to open the door for me, eventually. I was almost brought to tears thinking, as I stood there at the door, how far I had fallen and how people reveal their true selves when they think you have nothing more, in terms of material things, to offer. While still at my sister's house, alone one day, I stood in the living room and thought about my situation. These words suddenly came from deep inside me, "They are treating me this way because they think I am finished, but I am not finished; I will rise again." Shortly after that, my sister told me that she was going to call my other siblings and ask them to help her pay for a place for me. She said that she felt I needed my independence.

A Sunday in November 2009, my sister called to say that she had found a nice place, but the woman, whose house I would be sharing, needed to interview me. The woman was supposedly a teacher. She rented a house and was subletting a room in it. I would share her kitchen and bathroom. It was close to Carlton's home. The monthly rent was eleven thousand Jamaican Dollars, and I would pay an extra two thousand Jamaican Dollars for use of her refrigerator, stove and washing machine. We agreed to take it.

Before I moved from my sister's home, I was lying on the bed in the room where I stayed. I clearly heard the voice of God say, "Don't move." I said, "Lord, they want me out. I have no choice but to go. It is their house."

Another day, I was again lying on the bed in the room; I was listening to a Christian radio station called Love FM, by way of the radio on my cell phone. The male announcer said, "You do not have to go; do not move." I knew it was a message from God to me, and I thought long and hard about this message, but my sister kept moving in that direction with her plans, and after everything I was experiencing there, I felt I had no choice, and, with a level of trepidation, I went along on the day that my sister came and told me that she was ready to move me to this place. God told me not to go to Jamaica, and I felt that I had no option as to where to go and so I left for Jamaica. Now after everything, God was again saying, "Don't move."

When I got to the new place, I made sure everything was locked, that there was not an extra key to my room and that I had keys to every door. There was a large, red and heavy iron door at the back of the house, which led to the backyard. There were two bolts on the inside. I asked the woman for the key to that door, and she assured me that there was no key to it. She said, "We simply bolt it on the inside, and that is fine. It is safe." I believed her.

Each night, I made sure the locks were locked and the door was bolted. I locked my room door with the key and bolted it as well. One Sunday, after coming home from church, I placed my pair of designer sunglasses on the dresser in my room and went into the kitchen to prep some chicken for dinner. When I returned to the room, the pair of sunglasses was gone. I knew the woman, with whom I shared the home or her friend who was visiting that afternoon, had to have taken it. I decided to be more careful.

On two occasions, I went out and came back just as it was getting dark; as I stepped into the room, I heard the voice of God say, "Leave now." I said, "Leave now?"

I proceeded to put down my bag and was getting ready to unwind. I always kept my phone radio on Love FM, and I was always listening to it by way of earphones. Just as I put my bag down, I heard the man on the radio say, "Yes, leave now." I immediately picked up my bag, locked the room and left. I never returned for the night.

On another day, I went out and came back just at the onset of dark. I was in my room for approximately five minutes. Suddenly, I heard the voice of the Lord say, "Ask her for the key to the back door."

I said to the Lord, "I asked her before, and she said there was no key for the back door."

The Lord repeated, "Ask her for the key to the back door."

I stood there contemplating, with my phone radio playing in my ears. I then heard a man on Love FM say, "Ask her for the key, and when you get it, leave by way of the back. Don't use the front gate."

I went and unbolted the large, red and heavy door, at the back of the house, and, to my utter shock, the door was locked. In shock, and with a level of indignation, I said to her, "Where is the key to the back door?"

She said, "There is no key to the back door. I told you there is no key to the back door."

I yelled back, "The door is locked. Give me the key."

She produced the key. I opened the door, went through and climbed over the back wall. As I was going over the wall, I heard her say, "She must be psychic."

I said to myself, "It's not psychic; it's God." I left and caught a cab just as I got over the wall. I did not know where I was going, but I trusted God.

When the cab arrived at a brightly-lit area, on what appeared to be a busy street, I asked the driver to leave me there. I did not know the area, but it was quite busy, and I thought it was okay. I debated with myself as to where to go. I boarded a minibus headed for Kingston. Along the way, I stopped the bus and came off at a wrong stop. The area was dark. I walked down a street and then realized I did not know where I was. It was a bit eerie, but I continued to trust God.

I came back to the main street and waited by the side of the road. I then realized that I needed to be on the other side of the dual carriageway. I crossed over and to my surprise, a rather unpleasant one, I had to walk nearly a mile, on that other side, to reach the bus stop going to the Portmore area. Eventually, a bus came; I stopped it and got on. I traveled on the bus until it reached another busy area. I realized that something was up, and, though, I did not know what was going on, I needed to be careful.

I walked in a certain direction, and I happened upon a café with an inside as well as an outside area. Quite a few females were seated on the outside of the café, and I felt it was fine to sit on the inside, where there were only a few people. A television was on in the café, and I began watching.

I was in the café for about an hour, and I decided that I should find a place to sleep. As I was about to leave, I saw two white jeep-like vehicles across the street, opposite the café. At least one appeared to be a police vehicle. Lest I be accosted and asked any questions by them, I decided to wait a bit longer at the café. After approximately forty-five minutes, they were still in position across the street. I decided I had to find a place to sleep so, though, I was scared, I began walking. I walked past where they were, while discreetly gazing in their direction to ensure they were not coming in my direction. As I got farther and farther away, I noticed they were still there. I walked until they were no longer in sight.

After walking for about two miles, I told myself that I had to find a place to sleep. I saw a street and turned into it. I passed by a couple of homes and then I saw a building, which appeared to be unoccupied. It was not a house. It could have been a basic school or some such building. I decided to turn into that gate.

It was dark but not terribly dark. There were reflections of street lights or moonlight. I sat behind the building on a overnight bag I had with me, and I decided to spend the night there. Just as I sat down, the idea came to me that someone may enter the property and would see me quite easily. I looked and saw a large concrete canal, apparently built to take water down its path. It was deep, wide and unattainable. I walked down just a bit and saw an embankment. There were a few shrubs that would offer me a cover if someone came by, I thought.

I slipped under the shrubs, lying down with my head on my overnight bag. I was there for about two minutes, lying and looking at the moon. I started singing, almost in muted tones, *Guide me, O thou great Jehovah pilgrim through this barren land.* At about thirty seconds into the song, I heard giant-like footsteps coming toward the building. I froze in fear and told myself I must not even shift my position, lest there be leaves or anything that might make a sound and give away my position. I was even afraid to breathe. I remained quiet and still. I turned my head to see where the giant steps were coming from. To my utter surprise, I saw the form of a man. He was huge, with the broadest shoulders I have ever seen on anyone. He walked in and stopped at the side of the building. I then heard water running, as if coming from a hose. It continued for a while. A bit later, insect-like things started biting me on my toes and hands. The pain, from the bites, was excruciating. Even with this pain, I remained still. I told myself, either I was going to endure the harsh pain or be discovered. I began to quote many scripture verses. After a while, the water stopped, and I heard a vehicle, sounding like a motor cycle but with a toy-like sound, going around and around the building.

The stings continued, and I continued repeating scripture verses. At certain times, when I said particular Bible verses, the stings got more painful. I do not know why, but at one point I remember saying, "I want everything you have for me, Lord." After I said that, I was stung even more painfully.

I lied there as still as dead, as I endured the vicious and punishing bites from those things. The scooter, or whatever it was, continued going around and around the building. I must have passed out from the nonstop, excruciatingly painful bites and stings, after between twenty and sixty minutes. I was out for a while—some hours, maybe, and, then, I was awakened by a loud male voice which said, "Wake up, you may go now." The voice boomed into my consciousness in a way that jolted me up and into action. When I woke up, it was still dark. I climbed up the embankment wondering why one of my eyes was half closed.

When I got out, the man was gone. I saw tracks of a single wheel vehicle that went around the building. I went out the gate and turned right, down the street, and began walking. After walking for a while, I saw a taxi with some people in it, and I joined them. The taxi took me to a gas station, and the driver told me that I would get a taxi there to take me home. Shortly after, that other taxi came, and I asked him to take me to my address. When we arrived at my address, there was a blue car parked, with someone sitting inside, as if waiting. I sat in the cab while I waited for that car to leave. I felt, in my spirit, that the blue car may have been waiting on me for evil, though, I did not recognize the car or its occupant. The cab driver did not ask me why I was just sitting there in his car. He patiently sat there and allowed me all the time I needed. After a time, the blue car drove away. I waited for some minutes, and I exited the cab.

I went inside the house and was surprised to see that the woman, with whom I shared the house, had not gone to her teaching job. She was in the kitchen. I greeted her, went into my room and packed a red canvas and leather doctor's bag with my important documents, jewelry and a few treasured pieces that I really did not want to part with. I then said to her, words to the effect, "I'm leaving. This has nothing to do with you, but I think the time has come to leave."

I left my two suitcases with all my clothes, along with the bed, mattress, dresser, two comforter sets, a small television set given to me by Carlton, a couple of pots, a chair, groceries in the kitchen cabinet and a dozen ivory soaps. I did not tell my brother, Carlton, or my sister, Peggy, that I was leaving. I just headed off.

The bag I had, with all my important things, was heavy. It was weighing me down. I struggled from one transport to another with it. Eventually, I got downtown, Kingston. There, you get minibuses going to Jamaica's fourteen parishes. At that time, I was not sure where I was going. As I struggled with the bag, I again noticed a couple of policemen in white jeeps. I wondered if they were watching me. I looked at them and continued struggling with the bag. I heard a voice say, "Put the bag down." It was not the voice of a mortal. I thought it must be God, but I wondered why God would be telling me to put down the bag when he knew it contained all my valuables. I hesitated, while observing the policemen from the corner of my eyes. I struggled on.

I had my earphones in my ears, with my phone radio on Love FM, as I was accustomed to doing. The male host on the radio said, "Put down the bag. You're struggling with the bag; put down the bag." I immediately turned left into a store, asked for a shopping bag, placed my folder in it, and I left the bag, with all my valuables, there, on the pavement in front of the store. It was December 2009.

I boarded a bus headed for Morant Bay, St. Thomas. I spent the day in a quiet place in Morant Bay. In the evening, I boarded a bus going back to Kingston. I changed bus on Windward Road in Kingston, and I went on a City bus that was going to Half Way Tree in Kingston. There were many teenagers, in their school uniforms, on the bus. As I stood there and listened to their conversations, which one could not help hearing, I thought of how much times have changed. They were loud and raucous. Their conversations seemed to have nothing centered on school or anything they learned that day.

The bus swung, almost violently, from a less busy street on to an extremely busy one. I looked up as I held on more firmly to the rail in front of me. As I did so, I saw a large billboard in the distance, with an Air Jamaica aircraft, advertising flights from Montego Bay. At that moment, the thought came to me that I must go to Montego Bay and catch a flight back to the United States.

I arrived at Half Way Tree on the bus. I came off and walked around for a while. I went into a pharmacy and bought a bottle of worm medicine. I had started losing weight, and Jesus told me I had a tapeworm. I then went into a clothing store and purchased a blouse and a couple of panties. At this point, I was left with the only clothes I was wearing. I visited some other stores, basically seeing what the stores in Jamaica offered by way of shopping. I thought to myself, *Jamaicans do not necessarily need to shop abroad*. The quality and cost of goods appear to be comparable to the United States'. It began to get later. As it drew closer to late evening, I again started thinking about a place to sleep. Later that night, I found an affordable motel and spent the night there. Very early the next morning, I woke up, got dressed and headed out. I walked to Half Way Tree Road. It was about a thirty-minute walk from the motel. I waited there for a long time. I, eventually, saw a taxi and stopped it. I cajoled the driver to take me Downtown for three hundred Jamaican Dollars. I instructed him to take me to the minibuses going to Montego Bay, and he did.

As I boarded a bus, I was careful to be sure that no one was following me. I sat on the bus until there were enough passengers. The bus pulled out, from its parked location, for its journey to Montego Bay. I was relieved, and I said to myself, "Good; thank God; goodbye, Kingston."

The minibus breezed along. I had no idea what I would encounter in Montego Bay, but life appeared to be an adventure, and I was continuing on it. The bus stopped at a rest stop. We exited the bus, used the lavatories and purchased snacks. As we loaded up to leave, a young woman, sitting on my row of seats, yelled out that her ring fell and she could not find it. Everyone looked under his or her seat, and, soon, we were on our way again. We traveled some miles away from the rest stop, and there, on the right side of the road, was a sign with a strange word on it. I recognized it immediately, the moment I saw it, as the exact sign and the exact word I saw in a dream a few nights before. I do not remember what the word was. It was not a common word— certainly not one I knew to be in the English language. After seeing it, I felt some level of confidence that I was on the right path.

Later, the driver called out, "Montego Bay." I asked, "Where in Montego Bay are we?" He said, "Where do you want to go?" I had no clue where in Montego Bay I wanted to go.

I asked, "Where is the airport?" He pointed in a direction and said, "Over there."

I later realized "over there" was not very close. Eventually, I got to the airport. I had a return ticket to Florida but needed to pay the *change fee*, which I did not have. I decided to call Tom and ask for a ticket back, which was about the same price as the change fee. He got into an argument with me and told me that expletive starting with "F" followed by you.

My daughter was working with an airline, at that time. Her fiancé was also working with an airline. I called and asked her for a ticket to Fort Lauderdale. I do not remember exactly what transpired at this point, but I was under the impression that she would send me a ticket. I waited at the airport all afternoon and never received a call from her. I kept checking with the airline to see if a ticket had come through for me; they kept telling me "nothing." I was almost out of money and did not know what to do. I decided that I would sleep at the airport until the following day. As night fell and I continued waiting at the airport, security told me I could not stay there. I was nauseated by the whole thing.

I had approximately two thousand Jamaican Dollars. I knew no one in Montego Bay and did not know what to do. I went outside, and I saw a man by the name of Paul. I asked him if he drove. He told me yes. He operated a taxi. I told him I was not feeling well and needed to go to the hospital. He obliged and took me there. He stayed with me until a doctor saw me, which was quite late. I was really hoping to remain at the hospital until morning. However, the doctor examined me and found nothing wrong with me.

Paul asked me, "Where to?" I told him I needed a place to sleep, but I had almost no money. He said that he knew some people with a motel who charged two thousand Jamaican Dollars per night for a room. He took me there, and I checked in for the night. I still had no clue where in Montego Bay I was. I woke up quite early the following morning. I walked to a location where I was told I could get a public taxi to town. I waited for a very long time and, eventually, I got one. Because I did not know where I was and where I wanted to go, I got out of the car prematurely and had to walk a very long way before finding a place where I was able to get some breakfast.

I had left my phone charger in the bag that I had put down in Kingston. Now, I was forced to buy one out of my almost nonexistent funds. I was determined to get back to America. My phone was the only lifeline I had to anyone. I made a few calls, but I was not successful in making any headway. Paul had given me his number and told me to call him if I needed a ride. I called him and asked if he would give me a ride to the airport. This was going to be my second day at the airport, attempting to leave Jamaica. When I arrived at the airport, I asked Paul how much I owed him. I do not recall his response, but I promised to send him ten thousand Jamaican Dollars, and he seemed excited at the prospect.

I went to the airline desk, yet again, and checked if my daughter had sent me a ticket. There was none. Though, I did not plan on letting my sister, Peggy, in on my departure at this juncture, I was now forced to call and inform her that I was leaving, and I asked her for one hundred and twenty four dollars. Before agreeing, however, I had to promise her that Tom would pay her back.

I was now able to purchase a ticket to Fort Lauderdale, Florida. My sister, Peggy, promised to take the two suitcases, that I left at the rented house, to the airport in Kingston and meet me there. I asked the authorities at the Montego Bay airport if I would be allowed to go outside and retrieve my suitcases when the aircraft stopped in Kingston, and they assured me that it would be no problem. I told my sister that I would see her there.

Upon arriving at the airport in Kingston, I called my sister to be sure that she was there. I proceeded to get the *okay* to go fetch my suitcases, but I was told it was not allowed. I called my sister again and told her what they said. I asked her to keep the suitcases for me. I reboarded the aircraft in Kingston and had an uneventful flight to Fort Lauderdale. I went through Immigration and Customs there with one suit of clothes on my back, a small black shoulder purse and a paper bag, which contained my blue folder. I had called Tom and asked him to pick me up at the airport, and he was there.

We exchanged a brief greeting, and we headed for West Palm Beach. Some minutes into our journey, my phone rang. It was my sister, Peggy, asking to speak with Tom. I told him that she was on the phone wanting to speak with him, but he brushed it aside. I told her that he was driving, and I asked her what was the matter. She told me to tell him that she would get flowers. I had no idea what that meant, and I do not think I told him what she said. I determined that whatever that meant, I was in God's hands while I was in Jamaica, and I would continue to be in God's hands. We rode on mostly in silence.

When we arrived at the house in West Palm Beach, Eric, Tom's nephew, of about sixty-five to seventy years old, was there with his teenage son. In a conversation I had with Tom while still in Jamaica, he told me that they were there. I greeted them and proceeded to the private quarters. I felt strange and isolated, and I made the decision to remain in the mother-in-law suite.

When I tried to go into the kitchen to fix some food, it was as if I needed to get permission from Eric to do so. It had every appearance that he had taken over. Once, I was making a meal—this was about two days after getting back—he came into the kitchen to scrutinize what I was making. He went as far as to open the pot. I got quite upset and told him, "Don't ever do that again."

One day, I went into the washroom and decided I would do some laundry that was there, which I recall was mainly Tom's. I started the washing machine. A few minutes later, Tom came into the washroom looking rather somber-faced. I said to him, "Am I in the way?" He replied in a gruff tone, "Yes, you're in the way." I thought to myself, "This is my house, too, yet I cannot go into my kitchen without some man come breathing down my neck, scrutinizing my every move, and I cannot even be in the washroom without being told I'm in the way."

Another day, I was over in the suite where I was now staying. Tom was at work. I smelled a strange, awful odor coming from the direction of the kitchen. It certainly was not food. I came out and asked Eric what that awful odor was. I do not remember what he said, but it appeared to me that there was a conscious effort, on their part, to chase me from my house, or make my life there a living hell. I decided I could not trust them.

This was an area where the houses were not close together, and they were, for the most part, large. If something were to happen to me, no amount of screaming or yelling for help would attract anyone's attention. I was in a house with three men, two of whom I barely knew, who cared nothing about me.

I decided to take every precaution to protect myself. I took refuge in that suite. I brought in whatever food I found, which was minimal, some water and vegetables. I locked and barricaded the door to the suite. I told Tom I was going to be fasting for a number of days and did not want to be disturbed.

Before I barricaded myself in, I noticed that Eric's son came over to the suite almost daily to use the computer. It appeared to me that his purpose for being there was more than just being on the computer. It now appeared that I was not even allowed to have that small space in a large house. I determined that whatever they were up to, I was going to keep them out and also to truly seek God. God had told me to go on a fast. It was to be seven days at first. He then extended it for another seven.

I arrived in West Palm Beach, from Jamaica, somewhere around December 11, 2009. After realizing that I was not welcomed there, and feeling both afraid and uncomfortable, I told Tom that I heard the Holy Land in Orlando was looking for workers. I decided to go to Orlando to look for work. I went to a number of places there but had no success. Eventually and regrettably, I had to return—yes, to West Palm Beach. On my return, after a week, nothing had changed. As a matter of fact, I was now more afraid to be there. A few days later, I decided I had to get away again. I just could not remain there, in that house. I had left my two suitcases in Jamaica and needed some personal items. Under the guise of going shopping, I asked Tom for one hundred and sixty dollars. After much back and forth, he gave it to me. I left on a Greyhound bus for Orlando, again. I knew that there was something in Orlando that God wanted me to have. I was not sure what it was or how I would achieve it, but here I was again, twice in two weeks going back to Orlando. I spent a week there and encountered some amazing things—things that transcended where I was and what I was going through, really amazing.

After a week in Orlando, on this my second visit, with no clear direction as to where to go and not being able to find a job, I decided to call Tom and ask for a bus ticket home. The price of the ticket was approximately forty dollars. He railed about my being in Orlando. I told him that I believed God wanted me to go there for some reason, which I have not yet determined. He told me to let God pay my fare back. I told him, "I will."

On that Sunday, I attended a church service in Orlando. I explained my situation to the pastor there, and they gave me the money to buy a ticket. I arrived in West Palm Beach on December 25, 2009 (Christmas Day). When I arrived at the house, Tom, Eric and Eric's son were about to leave for Fort Lauderdale. I spent that afternoon alone at the house. Feeling uneasy and afraid, I took a blanket and decided to sleep in an empty lot behind the house. While I was sleeping, I had a dream of a neighbor standing over me who was there to kill me. I awakened and heard God say to me, "Get up and go inside the house." I did.

It was very late; it may have been about 2:00 a.m. I went to the door and put the key in and realized it was bolted. I knocked on the door and Eric came and opened it for me. I was very grateful, at that moment, that Eric was there. The following morning, Tom said to me, "How did you get in?" I said Eric let me in. Tom was very upset with Eric.

On January 1, 2010, I started fasting, as God had directed me. I ate a light salad each day and drank water. After about a week, I was out of vegetables and grapes. I was now forced into an absolute or total fast.

Each day, Tom came outside the door to the suite where I was and said he was leaving for work. I generally responded in a like manner, "Okay." A few days into the New Year, 2010, he said Eric and his son were leaving. One day, after they were supposedly gone and while Tom was at work, I ventured out and went over to the guest wing. I discovered that one closet was piled high with their personal belongings. I wondered why they had not taken their things, since Tom had said they had found a place in the Fort Lauderdale, Florida, area. I closed the closet, went back to my quarters and never said a thing.

From this moment, my life became more of a living hell. The light that used to be on, outside, in front of the house was now turned off by Tom, and the whole place was very dark. It caused me to be more concerned and afraid, but God was with me. God has a way of getting instructions to his people when he needs to. I daily and constantly watched Christian television, and God sent me messages by way of it. He sent his men and women to tell me to be sure that each night I go and check that the dead bolt was on, so that no one from outside could get in with a key, and I did.

One night, I went to check the door, long after Tom had gone to bed, and found that the bolt was not on, and I put it on. Since I barricaded myself in, it meant I had to move away the furniture that I stacked in front of the door, in the suite, in order to get out to the main area of the house, but when God instructs, I follow, and I faithfully checked each night, when I was sure Tom was gone to bed.

On another occasion, a man of God warned me about a gas cylinder being used to try to destroy me. God was very specific in telling me that it would be done on a Saturday and that a hose would be used. On this particular Saturday night, I was in the bedroom in the suite. I began to feel a bit dazed. I was lying on the carpet and now I sat up. I smelled gas. I decided to open a tiny window in the kitchenette in the suite. Because I was afraid, I thought no one could get through that window easily, while if I opened the bedroom window that was large and low, my safety could be easily compromised.

The house was fully alarmed. If you opened a door or window when the alarm was "armed," the alarm would go off, but if the alarm is not armed and you open a window or door, there would just be a beep. When I cracked the window, Tom, immediately, yelled from the other side of the house, "What are you opening the window for?" I replied, "I just need some air."

Knowing what God had said about the gas and that it would be on a Saturday, I was very careful not to mention anything about smelling gas. Tom said I was to close the window because I was making him cold. I again told him I needed some air. I also told him there is no way he could be cold because he was in a totally different area of the house. I continued, "Furthermore, there is only a small crack to let some air in." He said, "In the morning you will see."

I remained perched on a countertop with my nose at the open area of the window. About a minute or two after Tom said his piece, he went outside the house and came right back in. I believed that he took the cylinder outside and placed it in the garage. I no longer smelled any gas. I also concluded that he had not put the alarm on that night because he wanted to go in and out undetected and possibly to leave the windows in his suite open. I realized that Jesus had saved my life again.

At about eight o'clock that Sunday morning, Tom got up, and in keeping with his threat of, "In the morning you'll see," he drove out. At that point, I was watching Christian television. A preacher was preaching at his church in Texas. Suddenly, what appeared to be a replica of my foyer came on the screen. The preacher was in a posture of a cop with a gun, and he said that I should not go out there because if I did, I was going to be shot and killed.

About half an hour after Tom drove out, he returned. Soon after, about ten to fifteen minutes, a strange male voice was heard in the foyer calling for me to come outside. I asked him what he wanted, and he said he was a cop; Tom told him I had not come out for days and that he was concerned. I told him that I had seen Tom on Friday, and Tom knew I was fine. He said he wanted to see my face. I told him he could listen to how strong my voice was and know that I was fine. He remained outside telling, and coaxing, me to come out. I refused. He said he would remain there until I came out.

I started praying aloud in my intellect and in the Spirit. I took Psalm 119 and began reading it aloud so that he could hear. I also began repeating a number of Bible verses, very loudly, so that he could hear. After about forty-five minutes of my refusal to come out, and my praying and declaring God's words over my present situation, the cop, or whomever he was, decided to leave.

The following Tuesday—after that Sunday—as I continued my fast, barricaded in my suite, I heard a knock on my door. When I asked who was there, I was told cops. I looked through the window and saw a fire truck and two cop cars at my gate. The cops said that Tom told them he called me and did not get a response. They wanted me to come out, and I, again, refused. I told them if they wanted me to come out, they would have to break the door down. They did. Two men from the fire department forced the door open and came in. They saw that I was fine.

They were impressed with the way I barricaded the door. One told me I did a fine job. They took my temperature and blood pressure, which were both fine, and they left. Just before they left, I heard one cop say, "By Tuesday morning you'll be dead." There were other occurrences that took place during this time. I will not, however, get into those.

One day, my brother, Todd, called to have a conversation with me. In addition to other things, he told me that Tom said I had given away all my clothes. I told him that was not the case and proceeded to explain what had happened at the airport. I told him to tell Tom not to worry. I still had lots of clothes, and what I needed, God would provide. I ended my conversation with my brother, and, soon, the phone rang again. Tom answered, and I quietly picked up another phone. I heard Todd saying to Tom, "How is it you said that Angie is crazy? I just spoke with her and she was fine. She sounded normal and rational as usual." Tom replied, "Yes, sometimes she makes a little sense, but most time she doesn't."

I realized, at that moment, that Tom was telling people that I was crazy to the point of not even being able to hold a proper conversation. I now had a key piece of information, which allowed me to see the sinister nature of some of the things that were happening. I began to pay closer attention.

Whenever Tom drove out, I went to the window and looked. On a few occasions, I noticed that he slowed down at a neighbor's gate and the neighbor immediately drove out after him. It was that neighbor I saw in the dream that night while I slept in the open field behind my house and whom I dreamed would kill me, when God woke me up and told me to go inside.

One day, I looked through the window and saw the neighbor with a number of very large white plastic bags. I stood there for a few minutes observing him. That night, as if led by the Spirit of God, while Tom was asleep, I went into the kitchen. God spoke and said, "Open that door." When I looked in the cupboard, I saw one of the very large, white plastic bags that the neighbor had, in addition to a large, thick black bag. There were a couple of other highly suspicious items. After seeing these things, I heard the voice of God say to me, "What other proof do you need to see that your life is in danger?" God then instructed me to move them from where they were to the garbage compactor in the kitchen. I did as he instructed me, and I quietly returned to my quarters. The following day,

Friday, I was again watching Christian television.

A woman named Bernice, wearing a bright blue suit, sat and spoke into the camera. She said, "God sent me to tell you that your life is in danger; you must leave, now." I knew she was speaking to me. God has a way of letting me know when he's speaking to me by way of others.

I put a coat on. I took my folder and placed it in a shopping bag, and I took a handbag and left. I walked around for about two hours but did not know where to go. Eventually, I returned to the house. Later that day, the house phone rang and I answered. It was a call from a real estate agent informing me that a man would come to see the house on Saturday at one o'clock, which would be the following day. The house was up for sale. I immediately started tidying up the suite that I was in. Tom also called later that day and asked if I wanted him to take something for me to eat. I told him I would like to have some vegetables to make a salad and some grapes.

Tom was later than usual getting home, and I kept looking out the window to see him arrive. I had not eaten in days and was very hungry. Eventually, I saw Tom and that neighbor drove up at the same time. He and Tom were never friends, as far as I knew. They appeared to have become quite close lately. Tom came in and knocked at my door. I opened the door, and he handed the things to me. I thanked him, and I closed the door. I proceeded to wash the things in the kitchen in my quarters, and I began eating them. Shortly after, before I was finished eating, a horrible feeling came over me; I put the dish down and the horrible feeling continued. I started to pray. I felt as if I was going to fall, but I did not. The feeling felt like the presence of evil. I picked up the phone and called two Christian television stations and asked them to pray for me. I told them I had just eaten something and felt like I was dying. They both prayed with me.

By now, Tom had disconnected the service for the computer. He had also disconnected the long-distance service for the house phone, and he also terminated my cell phone service. There was no way of getting to anyone outside the local area. Thankfully, the Christian stations were toll free numbers. Shortly after I prayed with the individuals at the Christian stations, I began feeling better, and soon, I gained some strength.

When I began feeling better, God told me to go out to the family room. I did as I was told, and there on a small side table were a Philips and a flathead screwdriver. It occurred to me that they were placed there in anticipation of something happening, in order to pry my locked door open. God instructed me to remove the screwdrivers and put them in another place, and, again, I did. I went back to my quarters and locked myself in. God had again saved me. Later, as I listened to Christian television, I heard Marilyn talking about the poison gourd. I also recounted what Bernice had said on Christian television, earlier that very day, that God sent her to warn me that my life was in danger, and I should "leave now."

I woke up that Saturday morning in anticipation of the man coming to see the house at 1:00 p.m. that day. I straightened up the place and got dressed. I had my radio on Moody Radio, a Christian station. As I listened, there appeared to have been a panel discussion going on. They spoke about a situation, similar to mine, where the man was to come and see the house. I listened and pondered the situation. There was something said to the effect that the man could shoot me before I realized who he was.

As I thought about it, I reasoned that the man may be looking for open access to harm me by posing as a potential buyer. I decided that I should not be there when he came. I thought of leaving but considered that Tom would call the cops if he knew that I was leaving. I wondered how I would leave. I went to the window to look at another neighbor's house and wondered if I could escape through there. Just then, I heard the lady, who was part of that panel, say, "Yes, go there." I concluded that was God saying, "That's a good path." I heard God say, "You will be out there for three days."

I decided that I would take my passport alone, but immediately the voice of God said, "Take a pocketbook." I took a pocketbook containing my passport and a purse with ten cents—one dime—and waited. It was about 12:30 p.m. when I heard the clear intoning of the voice of God say, "Go." I knew Tom would not challenge me at that point.

The arrival of the man, who was to view the house, was imminent, and God had said to go, I reasoned. I told Tom I was going for a walk. He said, "Okay." I calmly walked out into the street and turned into the neighbor's yard that I looked at that morning when the lady said, "Yes, go there." A man and his two sons were outside. I told them I was cutting through their yard to go through the forest-like area. I asked the man to tell Tom that I was gone and would *not* return.

I made certain to stay away from the streets. I walked in the bushes, ending up at times on some back roads and then back in the bushes. I walked for many miles. My feet started hurting and were getting swollen. I found myself, as the night began coming down, in a town beyond Royal Palm Beach.

I felt I could go no more that night and was not even sure where I was. Soon, I saw a Palmetto plant, in a secluded area, and decided to spend the night there. I placed my head on my pocketbook and fell asleep. It was not the first time I was sleeping outside since trying to get away from home, and it would not be the last. I had the assurance that, with all that was happening, God was with me, and that gave me the courage I needed.

When I woke up that Sunday morning, I did not know what to do or where to go. I started walking. I walked and walked. I made sure to stay away from the main roads, just in case Tom had sent the cops after me. Before long, I found myself standing under a tree on the road going in the direction of my house while I waited for the rain to end. I had to retreat quickly, and I began walking down streets, in a remote area, with very few homes.

A short while later, a woman stopped beside me, in a beaten up car, and asked if I wanted a ride. I told her yes and got in. We exchanged a few words, and she dropped me off in front of the Royal Palm Beach police station. I was petrified because I had the feeling that the cops who harassed me, in the past, were from there.

I quickly got out of the area and started walking on streets in a more residential part of Royal Palm Beach. At first, I saw a man, in his yard, with some bottled water. I was very thirsty and asked for two. He quickly and graciously gave them to me. As a matter of fact, earlier, long before I saw the man with the water, I heard the Lord say, "There's going to be a man in his yard with water, ask him." I thanked the man and walked on.

A little later, as I walked up another street, I heard God say, "Knock on that door and ask for a sandwich." I bravely approached the door and knocked. An Indian lady answered the door, and I asked for a sandwich. She seemed only too happy to oblige. She invited me in and offered me a seat in her living room. She made me a meat sandwich and a hot cup of cocoa. I ate, and we chatted for a while. Her husband was there, as well, and he joined in the conversation. After a while, I felt I did not want to wear out my welcome, and I thanked them and left. They appeared sorry that I was leaving. They also seemed sorry for me. They asked me if I was going to be okay, and I replied, "Yes."

I walked on and soon there was a downpour of rain. I turned into another home and asked for an umbrella. They gave it to me along with a comb and a few things for my hair. I spent a couple of hours with this family—a woman, her husband and a small girl. They seemed to be enjoying my company, but I felt a sort of unease with them. I was telling them about the way the police were treating me, and I thought, later on, that I had told these total strangers too much.

The rain continued to come down quite heavily, and they were very happy about that. They seemed to think I was trapped in their home and could not leave because of the rain. They implored me to wait until the rain stopped, but I refused their offer, and I left in the pouring rain. My hairdresser worked at a salon in Green Acres. Green Acres is a few miles from Royal Palm Beach. She also worked on Sundays. With nowhere to go, and having no money, I decided to visit my hairdresser. I wanted to ask her for whatever money she could assist me with. I was very tired and felt beaten down, but I kept walking. I thought I would never reach my intended destination. It appeared so much farther, now that I was walking, than the many times I drove over there. With great determination and a rock-solid trust in God, that he would give me the strength to get there, I kept walking—one slow step after another. To my utter dismay, when I finally reached, the shop was closed.

Someone, who ran a business next door to theirs, gave me the phone number for my hairdresser's aunt, who was the actual proprietor of the salon. I called her. She told me that she was ill. She recently had surgery and was recuperating. She lived in a ritzy gated community in West Palm Beach, and by her and her niece's account, she threw lavish well-attended balls. They also told me that her house was quite spacious. I wished her a speedy recovery, and she provided me with her niece's phone number.

I asked for another call, to my hairdresser, from the kind store owner next door. Soon, she drove up in a silver S430 Mercedes Benz. She asked me what was going on, and I told her that conditions at home were horrible. I told her that I did not have a phone to call anyone. I also told her that I was seeking some money to purchase a ticket to Orlando. She asked me how much the fare would be, and I told her about thirty-six dollars. She said that she could give me twenty dollars. I told her that would help. I asked if I could spend the night with her, and she said yes.

She drove us to her house. She showed me to a room, with a small bed, where I would sleep. I thanked her. There was an ominous feeling, though. I just did not feel comfortable. I thought that she no longer appeared to be the person who had done my hair so many times and with whom I had kidded, laughed and had so many conversations. She was Jamaican, and she was relatable. I kept my wits about me and did not allow my discomfort to show.

She said she was going to the supermarket to pick up orange juice and a few other things. She also said that she was going to pick up a couple of friends, and she did. We all went to the supermarket. She dropped them off and then returned home. She too lived in a gated community. I was not aware of this. The house she was now living in was not the one we discussed when we all talked about our homes. I was aware that she was trying to get a nicer one, and this one was nice. There was a young man, at the house, whom she introduced as her brother.

Shortly after returning from the supermarket, and just as it got dark, she left the house and said she would soon be back. She drove down a road that ran beside her house in the gated community. Because I did not feel comfortable, I did not want to get too comfortable. I came outside and looked to see if I saw where she went.

I asked her brother where she went. He said that she went down the street. A little while later, I saw a police car coming toward her house, and I heard her brother say, "Run." I took off running, and the car came after me. Her brother shouted to me to cut across some other houses which, I did. Soon, I was out of the gated community and back on the main road. I dashed in some bushes, as soon as I was on the main road, and I remained there until I was sure it was safe.

I do not know what she told the police. I never saw or spoke to her again. I am thankful that her brother was there that night. This was night two since I walked away from my house. With nowhere to go, I simply went across the street, from where I hid from the cop, found a place, placed my handbag under my head and lied down. Eventually, I fell asleep. I awoke at various points in the night and heard sounds as if someone was walking on dry sticks and leaves, just beyond me, but I was not afraid.

As night turned to day, I awoke, took up my handbag and made my way to the main street. I started walking toward West Palm Beach and away from Green Acres. It took a while, but I, eventually, made it to Okeechobee Boulevard and walked until I saw a McDonalds. I went inside and purchased breakfast from the twenty dollars that my former hairdresser, who now turned on me, gave me.

This was day three since leaving my house, and I did not know what to do. As I was about to finish my breakfast, three ladies came to my table. I explained my situation to them and told them that I did not know what to do. They told me to pray. I bowed my head and prayed. When I was finished praying and opened my eyes, they were gone. I heard the voice of the Lord say, "Sell the bracelet that is on your hand." I looked on my hand, and there was a bracelet. I had two of those bracelets that were exactly alike—white gold and diamond and yellow gold and diamond. I had left them in the Doctor's bag that I had put down at Downtown Kingston. I realized that the three ladies were angels, and they had placed the bracelet on my hand while I prayed.

I walked until I saw a number of pawn shops on Okeechobee Boulevard. I entered two and asked how much they were willing to give me for the bracelet. The second one said one hundred and sixty dollars, and I accepted that offer. I signed a declaration saying that it was *my* bracelet, took the money and left. I returned to Okeechobee Boulevard, and I waited for a bus that would take me to the Greyhound bus terminal. I arrived at the terminal. I looked around to be sure that I was not being followed, and I proceeded to the ticket counter to purchase a ticket to Orlando.

The bus departed West Palm Beach at approximately 1:00 p.m. and arrived in Orlando at dusk. I came off the bus, and I had no clue where to turn. I then heard the still small voice of God, on the inside, directing me, "Turn left, turn right, etc." I followed as I was directed. I walked for a very long time.

At one point, there was a helicopter hovering above as I continued walking. I wondered if those were cops looking for me. I continued walking anyway. Later, I stood before a building with a sign that read "Goodwill." I realized that God had shown me to a place where I could shop for clothes at a minimal cost. I noted the place and started going on that street in the opposite direction.

I walked for a while and then waved down a taxi. I told him I needed to go to an inexpensive hotel. I told him about one I had seen on an earlier visit to Orlando, and he took me there. It was forty-seven dollars for the night, and I paid. I was given the entry card to the room, and I went to the second floor. It was not a large place. The second floor was the topmost. Once inside, I washed my socks and other personal items and put them to dry.

I was awakened at some point in the night. To my utter surprise, there was the male proprietor trying to use a card key to get into my room. I jumped up, went to the door and asked him, "Just what are you doing?" He said, "Sorry, sorry," and he left. I thanked God that the door was bolted and that he awoke me, at that very moment, to see the supposed intruder.

The next day, I decided to move on to a place where I stayed before and where I felt safe. Still left with some money from the sale of the bracelet, I purchased a bus ticket and made my way down to the Goodwill I discovered on Monday. I purchased a few pairs of jeans—Lauren, Calvin Klein—and by the way, they were new. I also purchased a dress, a few blouses, slippers, etc. I now had some clothes. On my way back from shopping, I stopped at a hairdressing salon, and I asked the proprietor for a "free" shampoo and set. She surprised me by agreeing, and I thanked God for the favor. I went into her bathroom and changed into one of my new outfits that I purchased only a couple of hours before. I began to feel and look alive again.

On Christmas Day 2009, just before I left Orlando for West Palm Beach, God had mentioned the name "Pastor Tims." I had seen him on Christian television and knew that his church was in Orlando. Now, I decided to look him up. I asked around and was told where he could be found. On Thursday morning, I set out on a long bus ride to visit Pastor Tim's church in Apopka. I asked the bus driver to put me off when I got to a particular location, and he did.

When the bus stopped, there was nothing in sight except for a gas station a little way off. I walked over there, and there was one car. The driver was buying gas. I asked him if he knew Zachary Tim's church. He told me yes and offered to give me a ride there. He said it was not close, and he was right. I was glad, very glad that he was there, and I did not have to walk all that way. It was also an isolated area.

On my arrival, I asked for and was shown to the office. I introduced myself and explained why I was there. I was shown to a very nice area and was told to wait there. The reception I received was warm—the type I had always been expecting from people or organizations who name the name of Christ. It was a very nicely situated place—decoratively and otherwise.

As I sat there enjoying the ambiance, I was interrupted by a young woman who greeted me and led me to a conference room. I thought, "Now, here is a man of God who knows how to run a godly organization." The atmosphere was extremely cordial and professional. Everyone appeared to know what he or she was about and acted accordingly while remembering that they were representing Christ and being sure to reflect that in their actions and their approach.

In the conference room, I explained to a man and woman a few of the experiences I had in the past few days. I was not quite sure what to make of their silence. The woman kept looking at the man and vice versa. I was being honest and truthful, I thought, *So what if they thought it was bizarre?*

When we were finished in the conference room, they gave me a blue towel, soap and some other toiletries. I was shown to a bathroom beside the gym, and I took a shower. When I was finished showering, I was directed to a room where they had lots of good clothes. I was encouraged to take whatever I wanted. Having purchased my Lauren and Calvin Klein jeans at Goodwill two days earlier, I decided to take a few suits that I could wear to church. A few jovial women joined in to assist me in picking out the suits while offering their advice about what they thought was nice. There was a mood of camaraderie, which I enjoyed.

Later in the day, at about noon, I was invited to the lunch room. There were entrees to choose from, along with other pastry-like edibles. After lunch, they invited me to hang around for church worship, which started at 7:00 p.m. I spent much of that time in the gym watching the youngsters shoot hoops and engage in other activities. I also found a very chic overnight bag to put the clothes I had picked out in, and I began to feel that things were looking up.

I joined with some of the ladies that evening, and we went into the sanctuary for service. We sang praise songs, and I was surprised to see how well-attended the Thursday night service was. Soon, Pastor Tims and two other men entered. This was the first time I was seeing him in person. He was quite slim and did not seem to take himself too seriously. When it was time to preach the night's message, he went to the pulpit, and his message spoke directly, in part, to me. For example, I mentioned earlier that God had mentioned Pastor Tims on December 25, 2009 while I was in Orlando and before I returned to West Palm Beach. Though, I did not recall saying this to anyone, he said, in his message, words to the effect, "Yes, God told you to come here, but he doesn't want you to stay here, maybe someone else." I took that as a word from God.

Now, I was both relieved and concerned. *If not here, where?* I was relieved that God had spoken directly to guide me by telling me not there, but was now concerned that I had no money, no contact, and I did not know what my next move would be.

When the service was over, I made my way to a few women and told them I had no money and no place to stay. Someone told me, "Wait here." I did. Moments later, a woman came up to me and greeted me. She told me that she and her family had recently moved to the area from North Carolina. She said that she heard of my situation, and she and a few other women agreed to pay for a motel room for me for two nights. She would then arrange for a women's home for me to stay. She told me to come with her, and I followed her to a black Mercedes Benz car. Her husband was sitting in the car with their two children—a boy and a girl.

They said they lived in the area, knew of a decent motel, and they would take me there. Before we arrived at the motel, they went to Kentucky Fried Chicken and purchased some food for me for two days. We arrived at the motel, and they paid the proprietor for two nights' stay.

The following day, she called to inform me that she was able to get me into the women's home. She said that the name of the woman in charge of the home was Ann, and she had, personally, spoken with her. Shortly after the conversation, I heard God say, "Don't go to the home, and be careful."

I went to the motel proprietor and asked for a change of room. After a bit of a tiff, he accommodated my request. I was moved from the third floor to the first. I asked him not to give any information about me to anyone, including the people who accompanied me here last night. I used the time in the motel to wash my hair, and I did some other personal grooming.

On Friday, my final night at the motel, I heard God say, "Go to Tampa." I was quite baffled. I could not understand why Tampa. I had no connections there, and I knew no one there. As a matter of fact, I went to Tampa twice before, some years earlier. I did not like the place and vowed I would never live there. That was then.

I decided to ask God for confirmation. While watching Christian television that Friday night, God sent the word by two men confirming that he wanted me to go to Tampa, indeed. I was instructed by God to leave at 8:00 a.m. I woke up and prepared myself for the journey. I went across to the office and checked out. The man in the office told me that some folk came checking for me, and he told them he did not know where I was. I was thankful that he did. I did not want to seem ungrateful to the people who were so helpful in paying for my two nights' stay there, but they were indeed strangers, and I needed to be careful, as God had said.

I left and walked through the gate. I had no clue where I was and did not know where to turn from where I was. I asked, "Lord, where should I turn?" I heard, "Left," and so I turned left. I had no clue what I was seeking "left." After a while, the idea came to me that I needed some breakfast. I saw a man and asked him where I could get some breakfast. He told me the Waffle House was in front of me down the road. I walked on until I came to the Waffle House. I believe I had $2 or $4 left at that point.

A sweet young woman, who was a waitress, came and asked me for my order. I was torn as to what to order. I felt like having eggs, but I could not afford it. As if she knew my dilemma, she left and came back to tell me that they were having a special whereby I could get six waffles for, I believe, $1.99 or $3.99. What I remember is that whatever the price was, that was all the money I had, and I quickly reasoned that since I did not know where I was going to be the rest of the day, I could eat two of the waffles and take four with me. I told her I would take the special for six. I then thanked God for meeting my need, by working it out so that I had enough for the rest of the day. I asked her for a container to put in the remaining four waffles. Now that I had eaten, I decided to leave for Tampa.

I had no money left. I was broke, not even a dime was left. I started in the direction from which I earlier came. I walked a long way before seeing someone whom I was able to ask where I could catch the Greyhound bus. He told me it was far, but he pointed in the general direction. I continued walking until I came to a shopping plaza. I believed that since God had sent me to Tampa, he would make a way for me to get there.

I decided to use my faith by asking or begging for my fare. I approached a store and asked a female Asian proprietor for ten dollars. She told me to come back later. When I returned later, she told me she did not have any money. Shortly after, I saw a man calling to me, and I answered. I told him I needed a fare to go somewhere. I was broke. He told me that he was expecting someone to bring him some money. He said he was there waiting for the person. He asked me to wait until the person got there, at which time he would give me some money. I asked him if the person he was waiting for could be trusted. He said it was someone he knew very well.

I waited and waited, but the more I waited it appeared he was more interested in having me around to talk to. I needed money for my fare, but I also needed to get going. I was desperate, but my trust was not in the man; it was in God. I left that location, and I began walking again. It was, indeed, a very long way. Just when I thought I could not make it, I stopped a taxi and asked, "How far away is the Greyhound bus station?" He told me I was close, and, eventually, I arrived there.

Since the time I had left my house in West Palm Beach, God told me not to call anyone in my family before seven days. It was now exactly seven days. Still in need of my fare to Tampa, I called Marva, my sister. I said, "I am trying to get to a city, and I need twenty-six dollars to pay for the ticket."

She said, "Where are you?"

I said, "I am not going to tell you."

She said, "What city are you going to?" I did not answer that question either.

She said, "If you are not going to tell me, I cannot help you."

I said, "Okay, I'm in Orlando, but I will not tell you what city I'm going to."

She said, "If you want a ticket to go back home to West Palm Beach, I will buy it, but I am not buying you a ticket to go anywhere."

I am really not sure why she was so invested in my being in West Palm Beach. In any event, I pretty much told her that was not going to happen and moved on. Next, I called Tom. I said, "I am in Orlando. I'm fine. I asked the neighbor to tell you that I was gone and would not return. I hope he told you." He replied, "Yes, but I told the police you are missing."

I said, "How could you tell the police I am missing when the neighbor told you I was gone and would not return?" I continued, "I am an adult and have a right to make my own decisions." He became quite mad, and I hung up the phone.

I then called Marva's son, Rush. I told him I was asking him to buy me a ticket for twenty-six dollars on Greyhound. I provided him the phone number to Greyhound as well as the phone from which I was calling. I told him I was using a stranger's phone, and I did not have much time. He promised me that he would purchase the ticket and that he would also call me back. Having waited approximately ten minutes and not having heard from him, I decided to call him again. The call went to voice mail. The lady whose phone I had borrowed was now anxious to get going. I assured her my nephew promised, and I knew he would come through for me. I asked her if she could allow me another five to ten minutes. She agreed, and we both waited patiently for that time to elapse. It did, and I called again.

Again, the phone went to voice mail. At first, I thought he may have been on the phone, with Greyhound, purchasing the ticket for me, but now I came to the sad realization that he had lied to me and had placed his phone on voice mail so that I would not be able to reach him. I thanked the woman for being so kind and returned her phone. I thought how amazing that a complete stranger would be so kind, while my family seemed so cold and far removed.

I saw a man sitting off in the distance. He appeared to be looking in my direction. I walked over to him and said, "Hi, my name is Angela. Can you please buy me a ticket to Tampa?" He said, "Are you sure that when you get to Tampa things are going to work out for you?" Knowing that God was sending me there, I said, "Yes."

He immediately got up and went to the counter, with me following behind, and he bought me a ticket to Tampa. After that, he apologized by saying he was sorry that he did not have some spending money to give to me. I assured him it was fine. He had already done so much. I thanked him profusely. He told me that he was watching me while I spoke on the phone, realized I needed help and was hoping I would come and ask him. His name was James. I took his phone number and promised him that when it turned out well, I would give him a call to let him know.

Shortly after I received the ticket and returned to the general area, I looked outside, and immediately in front of the building, there was a car with four Orlando police officers alighting from it. They were dressed in green pants with a beige shirt. They were behaving in a rather frantic way, as if the President of the United States was just shot in that location. I knew right then that Tom had alerted the West Palm Beach police, who in turn alerted them to the fact that I was at the Orlando Greyhound bus station, and they were there to "Baker Act" me or possibly force me to return to West Palm Beach. I assumed that they were looking, expecting me to be somewhat disheveled looking, having being told that I left home with one suit of clothes on my back and no money.

Here I stood, looking at them with my hair nicely done, decked out in my brand new pair of Lauren Jeans and a knitted pink cotton sweater, a pair of heels complete with my quite expensive-looking traveling bag. I stood there for a while and stared directly at them. They came into the building and were looking around. They looked at me, but I thought to myself that I did not fit the profile of what they were told. I calmly walked into the ladies' room, took out my Bible and began reading verses from Psalm 119. I also prayed and asked Jesus to make them leave. I heard God say to me, "Go outside in approximately five minutes, and they will be gone."

I counted to sixty slowly, five times, and decided that was approximately five minutes. I went back to the waiting area and found that, indeed, they were gone. I breathed a sigh of relief and thanked God, yet again. A few minutes later, they announced boarding for Tampa. I stepped up on the bus, found a seat close to the rear and sat back. As the bus pulled out of the station, and I now realized that I was on a bus to Tampa, a sense of relief and freedom came over me, as I thought I would now be free of Tom, the cops, the harassment and the fear. I did not know what awaited me in Tampa, but God told me to go there, and I was on my way. He has never failed me; he was not going to now.

# CHAPTER XI

# A NEW PHASE—THE START OF A NEW LIFE

The bus drove through many cities. Finally, I saw signs with Lakeland. I had been there once before and recalled that it was in the general Tampa area. I asked someone how long it would take to arrive in Tampa, and I was told one and a half hours. I sat back and took in the sceneries as the bus drove on. At approximately 5:30 p.m. on January 23, 2010, I stepped off the Greyhound bus, and I stepped on the ground in Tampa, Florida. I did not know what my next move was going to be. God had mentioned Joy Dempsey's church. Immediately after coming off the bus, I saw a taxi parked in front of the Greyhound building. I approached the driver, and I asked him if he would take me to Joy Dempsey's church. He said the cost would be twenty dollars. I told him I did not have any money.

He said no one would be there at that time on a Saturday. I told him thanks and walked away. About a minute after leaving that location, I saw a high-rise building with a sign that read, something to the effect, "Baptist residency." I was hopeful as I thought that must be church related. I had learned by now not to hang my hat on many church people, but I needed a place to stay as well as some guidance, and I stopped by to inquire. I told the man I saw, who appeared to be security or the elevator operator, I needed a place to stay. He politely told me that it was a "seniors' home" and pointed me to a Salvation Army a couple of chains away. He said that I would be able to stay there.

My experience with Salvation Army, up to this point, was limited to seeing them collecting money at malls, during the Christmas season. I took the man's advice, and I walked over there. By the time I arrived at the Salvation Army, it had begun to darken. I went inside and told the lady at the desk that I needed a place to stay. She was extremely pleasant and told me she had one bed remaining. It was Number 13, and it was a top bunk. It was as if God had reserved that last bed for me.

I entered the room, placed my traveling bag on the bed and felt very grateful. Immediately, the lady came in with a blanket and linen for the bed. She gave me a quick orientation, and I climbed up on my bunk. I reached inside my bag and pulled out my remaining pancakes from Waffle House. I ate them and drank some water. I then took a shower, climbed up on my bunk, read my Bible and prayed.

Before lying down to sleep, I asked if anyone knew Joy Dempsey's church. A woman told me she goes there and would be happy to go with me. I woke up the following morning and got ready for church. I was dressed in a pair of blue jeans and a brown tweed jacket. The women were most gracious in telling me how great I looked. It was the first time that I was wearing a pair of jeans to church. Actually, I had a few suits, but because I had only just entered the shelter that previous evening, I had not the time to sort them out.

Linda and I left for church, which was on Dale Mabry Highway in Tampa. She paid her bus fare using her 30-day bus pass, and I told the driver I had no money and was asking for a ride. By now, I had become accustomed to asking in faith, believing that God who opened those doors to get me thus far, would continue to be faithful. He obliged without making me feel like, "You poor little thing." I was most grateful and sat down.

When we got to the intersection of Kennedy and Dale Mabry, we had to change bus and get on Bus 36. I approached the driver in a similar fashion, and he agreed to allow me a free ride. Soon, we arrived at Tampa Free International Church. The senior pastor there was Joy Dempsey. We arrived in the middle of the first service and stayed for the second, which began at about 10:30 a.m.

Praise and worship began, and I was totally engrossed in the worship. Soon, they called for those needing prayer. I quickly went to the altar.

There were a few men and women, along with Brother Dempsey, Joy Dempsey's father-in-law, at the altar. A woman asked me what I wanted her to pray about. I told her that God sent me there to see Pastor Joy Dempsey. Pastor Joy Dempsey was not present at that moment, but she came out shortly after. It was the first time I was seeing her in person, and I was not sure what I thought of her. I was now living at the Salvation Army shelter and had more important things to think about. In any event, the woman told me that Pastor Joy would not be able to see me, personally, but I should listen to the message when she came to preach, and God would speak to me by way of the message. I was very disappointed, but I went back to my seat after she was finished praying. The service continued and I continued to worship God.

Eventually, Pastor Joy, as she was affectionately referred to at *her* church, came to deliver the message. God spoke clearly to me by way of the message. I felt reassured and wonderful. God was still on the case, and he said it was going to be fine. It was time to return to Salvation Army at Florida and Henderson Avenues. I did not feel inclined to ask for a free ride on the bus back home. I reasoned, "God sent me here. I am with God's people. Surely, I can get five dollars to pay my fare back home." By now, I had learned I could not depend on people who say they are God's, but I was hopeful.

I went to Brother Dempsey and asked him if I could get five dollars to pay my fare back to Salvation Army. I chose to ask Brother Dempsey because, in observing, he seemed to be very visible as one who held an important role in the church. To my utter bewilderment and utter surprise, he looked at me and then he asked, "How did you get here?"

I told him, "God got me here by giving me favor for free rides on the bus." With what appeared to be ridicule and sarcasm, he told me, "Let God get you back home," and he walked away. I was not daunted, however, and I decided to ask another brother, whose name I do not remember. He told me to wait a minute, and I waited. In about five minutes, he was back with five dollars. He gave it to me and told me, "God bless you."

The following week was uneventful. I was learning the way of living and surviving at a shelter. It was not easy, but it was doable. I remembered—as Linda volunteered to me that I could get a phone for ten dollars—that as I walked out of the house at West Palm Beach, God had told me I would have a cell phone in two weeks. At that time, it seemed so far out of reach because I was so far down, but as Linda told me about being able to get a phone at Walmart and the ability to get minutes for the phone without a "plan," hope rekindled in me. Before I was homeless, I always had a plan for my cell phone—costing in the range of fifty-nine and seventy-nine dollars per month. I knew nothing of getting a phone without a *plan*, but now I was being schooled in a whole new way as to how I could live a less encumbered life.

Each day, Monday to Friday I went to the computer lab at Metropolitan Services on Florida Avenue. There, I searched for and applied for jobs. Metro, as we referred to it, was a fully staffed establishment catering to the homeless and poor in the general Tampa area. They had a food bank, and provided you could prove that you had a kitchen, they gave you all the food you wanted. They also had a thrift store, and if you fell into any of the categories listed above, after speaking with one of their counselors, you could get a voucher, once per month, to the thrift store for free clothing of your choice. They had phones, and a person could call anywhere in the United States for free. It provided many essential services for those in need while treating you with love and dignity.

The computer lab had phones and a fax machine exclusively for the purpose of assisting individuals needing their services for searching for a job to be able to do so. There were generally two trained persons in the lab, assisting with resumes as well as sharpening the computer skills of those less familiar with modern devices. Each person was allowed one hour per visit to the lab, but if there was no one waiting, a person was allowed to remain on a computer as long as he or she wished.

In anticipation of getting a job, I called my sister, Marva, in Philly, and asked to borrow some money. Of course, she turned me down when I needed bus fare from Orlando to Tampa. I believe, however, that we all deserve a second chance. I was happy to report that I had made it to Tampa, to show that I had forgotten the past—and, yes, to get a loan to prepare for my job interview. I asked my sister for a fifty-dollar loan, and she obliged. I purchased some hair products, a cell phone at Walmart for ten dollars, and I was getting established.

Approximately two weeks after arriving in Tampa, I had a cell phone, just as God had told me I would. I also received an e-mail from a temp agency asking me to give them a call. Within a few days of that e-mail, I met with Linda and Kevin for an interview and received a temporary six-week placement at a law firm Downtown Tampa on Kennedy Boulevard.

When I made it known that I had a job offer, Homeless Recovery directed me to an organization that outfitted the less fortunate and help them to prepare by showing up at interviews, looking as professionals—complete with someone to assist in picking out the suits that are suitable for you, there are rows of suits, handbags, jewelry, shoes and other accessories as well as designer make-up—lipsticks, rouges, etc. Generally, they gave two suits on a visit to an individual, but since I was small, they said that I could have five suits. I left that place, on that day, with two large shopping bags containing everything I needed for the job. The suits were beautiful, and I knew that it was God who opened those doors and provided for me, yet again.

On Friday, February 9, 2010, I reported to Gray law firm and began my temporary job. I rather enjoyed the position. It was fulfilling. I learned some new things, kept busy and earned some well-needed cash. After approximately two weeks at the Salvation Army shelter, I was able to move to the Salvation Army Women's House. In order to live there, you need to have a job. It provided me some level of privacy with my own small room. We had to sign in and sign out; chores were assigned each week, and it costs anywhere from fifty to ninety-six dollars per week, depending on your salary. There was also a director, a manager and a house mother named Ms. G. I liked Ms. G. There was something about her that I thought was earnest. Micki, the manager, was okay too. She was a bit brusque and reminded me of my early teenage days when I was a bit of a tomboy, I thought. In the end, however, I became extremely disappointed in her.

The temporary position ended somewhere around March 25, 2010. At the end, I had repaid my sister that loan, purchased lots of dresses and shoes and continued attending Tampa Free International church. It was the Saturday before Easter Sunday 2010 when I stood before my metal locker, in my small room, at the Salvation Army Women's House and heard the voice of God say, "Wear that pair of jeans to church tomorrow." I had worn a pair of jeans to church before when I needed to, but this was going to be Easter Sunday, and everyone was going to be dressed in her Sunday best. Furthermore, I had many beautiful dresses that I had bought. It seemed a bit strange that God was making this request of me. I was not entirely sure, though, that it was, indeed, my Heavenly Father, although it sounded a lot like him, and so I stood there looking at the pair of jeans and wondered why my Father wanted me to wear a pair of jeans and not one of my beautiful dresses. I again heard the unmistakable clear voice of God, as if in a command, telling me to wear the jeans. I replied, "Okay, Lord, I will." I pulled out the pair of jeans, matched it with a blouse and a pair of shoes, went to bed and waited for Sunday.

As I walked toward and through the large open dining area of the women's house, I saw a few of my housemates staring at me. Generally, they commented by telling me how nice I looked, but now they were wondering, I thought, based on their quizzical stares, *Why in Jesus' name I would be wearing a pair of jeans to church on Easter Sunday?* They knew I was a Christian, and, indeed, I had my Bible so there was no mistaking where I was headed. I signed out and left. I walked down to Marion bus station and got on a bus.

I arrived at Tampa Free International Church, as usual, and worshipped as was customary. The service proceeded—singing, prayers, announcements, collecting of tithes and offerings, etc., and now it was time for Pastor Joy to preach. She began by putting a table on the platform. The table was set with knives and forks. She had a number of people sitting around the round table as if dining. She began to preach, and I listened intently, as always, and took notes. She said that someone was going to meet her Boaz—alluding to Ruth marrying Boaz in the Book of *Ruth* in the Old Testament—today, and he's going to take her to have a meal. I wondered who she might be referring to. My mind and thoughts were not in that direction.

You see, while I was working on that temporary job at the law firm in Tampa, I heard the voice of God say that the lawyer, with whom I worked, was going to take a fancy to me, and I should allow it. He was the owner of the law firm. I was amazed by that too, but the very next day, as I sat in the little room where I worked, the gentleman, in a most uncanny way "moved," it could be said, his office in that little room and took up residence there. He then made no pretensions about how he felt about me. It was a very awkward moment for me, as the women, in the office, clearly saw through his actions.

Believing this to be the will of God, based on what God told me prior to it happening, I did not rebuff his overtures. There was no outward display of intimacy, but there was no doubt about the fact that the gentleman both fancied and favored me. On a few occasions, he asked me to remain and finish up some needed work, and, though, we were alone at the office, we simply worked, after which he gave me a ride home. He said that he wanted to train me to become a lawyer, and, to that end, he gave me much challenging and interesting work.

As my temporary assignment, at the firm, was drawing to an end, he called me into his office and asked me what I would do next. I told him I did not know, and he simply smiled. I had the feeling he intended to extend my temporary stay, although he did not say that. A week later, the temp agency got me an interview at a large law firm; however, I did not tell him until the appointed time. I think he was displeased about that. A few days later, he remarked that maybe I wanted to work at a "large" law firm. I gathered he concluded and was suggesting that I did not want to remain at his small firm. It was a wonderful company, and I had no such feeling as to a preference for small or large. I was simply trying to secure a job when that one was over. After leaving the firm, I had few conversations with the gentleman, by phone, and then he somewhat faded away.

In any event, on that Easter Sunday, I left Tampa Free International Church at approximately 1:30 p.m. and made my way to a bus stop on Dale Mabry, on which Tampa Free International was located. I was standing there for about ten to fifteen minutes, and I decided to eat an apple I had. Upon finishing the apple, I heard a voice say, "Sit down." I knew it was God's voice, and I sat down.

Just as I sat down, I heard an audible voice behind me say, "The bus is not coming." I turned around to look and saw a man sitting in a beige Mercedes Benz car. I replied, "Yes, it's coming, but today they run on the hour." I continued, "I will take a ride to the corner of Kennedy." I got up and went into the car. As we drove south on Dale Mabry and chatted about the state of the economy, which was my introductory comments, and as the gentleman, who was clearly most informed, eloquent and well learned, explained to me in a clear, concise and knowledgeable way why things were the way they were, I was most impressed and thought, *Indeed, he must be a friend of my former boss.* The same classy approach was very evident.

The real reason I entered the car was because my former boss and I had a few heated conversations on the phone since my departure from the law firm. I somehow, naively, thought he had sent one of his friends to get me to make amends. As we turned east on Kennedy Boulevard, and the gentleman began to read me as if I were a book, I began to feel a bit uneasy. I had never told the things he was telling me to my former boss, and I wondered who this person might be. A few minutes later, he pulled up at Panera Bread in the Bayshore area of Tampa. We got out of the car and headed for the restaurant. He ordered a meal, after asking me how hungry I was. The truth is that I was quite hungry, which is part of the reason I was eating the apple earlier.

Just about five minutes after meeting the gentleman, I felt extremely safe and comfortable with him. Even so, I was not about to admit to a total stranger that I was indeed very hungry. I do not recall what my answer was. Based on the fact that he ordered a salad as the main course leads me to think I may have told him I was not hungry. Now, I do not want you go off thinking I lied. There are some things you do not admit to a total stranger, and besides, I really do not remember what my response was.

We sat outdoors, at the front of the restaurant, and ate. I was, of course, curious and was asking many questions. I immediately mentioned the friendship I had with my former boss and asked if he knew him. When he told me no, I was very disappointed and even said so. If he was deterred by this revelation, he did not let on. He was quite a gentleman, and I put away my disappointment and decided to make the most of the afternoon.

There was something extraordinary about this man. He did not appear, in any way, to be like any person I have ever met. He was not just a gentleman. He was a *gentleman*. He was gentle, sweet, warm and caring. Apart from the things he said, in the car, on the way to the restaurant, which did not take the form of questions but rather statements that I concluded were facts about me, he was unobtrusive. He reminded me, at the moment he matter-of-factly stated those things, of the woman in the Bible whom Jesus met at the well who ran to her village to tell her village folk, "Come see a man who told me everything I ever did."

As we sat eating and my curiosity gave way to my almost non-stop chatter, I looked at this most wonderful, extremely out-of-this-world person sitting there and said, "Tell me about yourself." He told me he was a math professor at Florida State University (FSU). It was not hard to believe. It was very much on display by way of demeanor, as well as speech, that he was indeed an intellectual, a very sophisticated and intelligent man. He mentioned something about being married a long time ago, when I asked him, "How is it possible that a person of your stature and status can be unattached?" Something betrayed the "married a long time ago" statement, which caused me not to believe that account. He, however, immediately followed that up by telling me that he was looking for a strong Jamaican woman, and he seemed to have found her.

We finished our meal and walked hand-in-hand back to the car. As we approached the car, he quickly moved ahead of me to open the door. We hugged after which I sat down, and he closed the door very gently.

We were now driving through the exclusive Bay Shore neighborhood, and I saw a restaurant with a sign advertising pate. It was the first time I recall seeing that word, and I asked my new-found companion the meaning of the word. He explained to me what it was in terms of food and what it consisted of. I realized then that he knew a lot about fine dining as well.

We drove to a park in Bayshore, directly across from Davies Island, separated by a body of water. We sat down and talked while we looked across at Davies Island. I told him that the lawyer I spoke of lived on Davies Island. He said it was okay. I began to realize that talking about the lawyer was improper. I turned to my new companion and said, "I cannot believe I am sitting here with a most warm and wonderful man and here I am talking about this lawyer." I do not recall his response to that, but I decided that I would refrain from such speech.

It felt wonderful sitting by the bay talking to this most incredible person whom I was getting to be better acquainted with. While we were at the restaurant, I said to him, "Talk to me." He said he did not know what to say, but I should ask him *anything* I wanted to know, and he would tell me.

Now, here we were at the park. I did not know what else I wanted to ask so we sat at the edge of the water and hugged each other. It was an amazing moment. It not only felt entirely special, it felt supernatural as well—so supernatural that I turned to look at him as I asked, "Are you an angel?" I did not mean it in the sense of a really good-hearted human that we often refer to as angels. I saw something in the gentleman, which, in my view, defied everything I knew about humans on earth. He was way too gentle, too sweet and too special—a purity I had not known before. His reply to my question was, "I wish."

We were there for a good while, and I asked him if he would like to drive me to Davies Island. I had heard so much about Davies Island. I had never been there. Now that we were so close to it, I did not want to pass up the opportunity. My friend said yes. A few minutes later, we were off.

Now that we were at Davies Island, I was a bit surprised. It was okay, but it was not the place I conjured up in my mind. He showed me Derrick Jeter's multi-million dollar waterfront mansion that was still under construction. There was also a large house that he pointed to and told me he knew the person who owned it. He said he attended a party there once. I wondered which of the houses we saw belonged to my former boss, if any. We drove all around and then I felt that I had had my fill. I suggested to my friend that we could get off the island when he was ready. He said he would take me home. I thanked him for a wonderful afternoon, as he drove me to the Salvation Army Women's House. Before leaving the car, we hugged, and he gave me his phone number.

I approached the door of the women's house and pressed the buzzer. Someone buzzed me in. I entered and made my way up the stairs feeling very excited. I entered the landing at the top of the stairs and Mercedes, a housemate, was sitting there. She was looking directly down at where the car stopped. She looked at me in a manner which, in my view, communicated *I saw*. Not caring what she thought, I proceeded happily to my room. It was a new day.

Mercedes was a Spanish woman of about 60 years old. The first day I entered the women's house, she gave me a warm welcome. She also invited me to her room. She had an opulent-looking bed with wood-head and footboard. Her room was so decked out; It had every appearance that she loved it there and may have been there for a long time. She seemed quite at home.

I asked her if she was going to be moving from the women's house. She said that she would as soon as she received some money she was expecting. After a few days, we hardly ever spoke. In fact, she became hostile toward me. There was also another woman named Carol, who, on my arrival at the women's house, asked me if I was wearing a wig. I told her I was not, and she appeared quite surprised. Carol and I became good pals for a while. One day, she drove me a far way from where we lived to get my hair permed. I think it was in New Tampa. I offered to put twenty dollars gas in her car, but she told me that ten dollars would be enough.

I ended up paying a Jamaican woman ninety dollars for perming my hair. It was a total disaster, and I regretted going to her. She was so bad at what she did that I wondered how the State of Florida could have given her a license to operate professionally—that may have been the reason she had her salon at her house. She burnt my scalp all over. After the full effect of her inadequacy was realized, a few days later, I had to call and tell her that she did such a poor job that I would not consider her doing my hair again. The ride to her house was the high point of the trip. Carol and I chatted about many things, and I became somewhat fond of her. Another day, she and I were in the washroom, and I told her that I met a gentleman who "rocked my world."

The Monday after meeting my new companion, I thought about him all day. I thought it would be great if I could see him again that day. Maybe, among other things, I wanted to convince myself that this was not just a great vision or the best dream I have ever had. I went to the phone room, in the women's house, and called him. He answered the phone and told me that he was in a meeting with some students from his accounting class, which ended a short time ago. Not wanting to encroach on his time, in light of what he told me, I asked if he would like to take me to dinner that evening. He agreed and asked me to meet him on Kennedy Boulevard, which was a ten-minute walk. I was excited.

I was wearing a cream, linen dress, with embroidery. Its length was about two inches above the knee. It was a designer piece, and it was beautiful. I completed the look with a cream scarf thrown over my shoulders, a black evening purse and black high heel slippers. As I walked across the dining area, some of my house mates told me how wonderful I looked. I thanked them and left.

I made it to Downtown Tampa, and I waited in a Jamaican restaurant for his call. I anticipated every waiting moment, and soon, my phone rang, and he told me where he was at—which was within very close proximity of the Jamaican restaurant that I was waiting at and not on Kennedy Boulevard, as he earlier stated. A few steps outside, there he was sitting in his car. I looked at him, and he appeared even so much more handsome than he seemed a day earlier. I thought to myself, he looked almost like a different person. We hugged, and he drove off in the direction of the expressway. We headed toward St. Petersburg, and, as we chatted, I giggled and felt like I was sixteen all over again.

After a while, we pulled up at a restaurant in Clearwater. It was by the sea. There was a plank leading up a few chains over the water, and I followed him up there. He held me close to him, but I was a bit scared. We stood there in a close embrace for some minutes. The wind off the sea was a bit chilly, making the embrace so much more comforting.

We walked hand in hand as we entered the restaurant. There were many patrons inside, but we did not have to wait long to be seated. As we were moving toward our table, a song with a nice rhythm started playing. He, in a pink Lauren polo shirt and bright dark khaki, looked at me and asked, "Want to dance?" He was already snapping his fingers and rocking to the rhythm. I had never seen anyone so handsome and kingly. I looked at him tenderly and said, "No." I suppose I was just a bit shy.

We ordered New England clam chowder as the appetizer. I went to the ladies' room, and when I returned, it was almost cold. We asked the waiter to change it, and he gracefully accommodated us. I had not had clam chowder since my New York days so it was very good to be having it again in such fine company. We finished our meal, and it was enjoyable.

Ms. G, the house mother, had given me permission to be out past eleven o'clock. Therefore, I was in no rush to get back. I expressed this sentiment to the gentleman, but he said he would get me back by eleven, anyway. I thought, "What a guy."

We drove to a quiet location and watched the stars in the sky and a few planes coming in for landing at the St. Petersburg airport. We chatted and chatted. Soon, he pulled out some wipes and wiped both my hands. I had no idea why he wiped my hands, but this became a regular practice whenever we were together. He took me home, and he left for his home. I called about an hour later, and he said he was safely home. We talked for some minutes and then said goodbye. The following day, Ms. G asked about the restaurant. She said she had been there before and really liked it. It was, indeed, a nice one.

I did not see the gentleman again for about two weeks, though, we spoke, at times, by phone. One Sunday, after leaving Tampa Free International Church, I called him. He asked me where I was. I told him I was at the bus stop where we first met. He said I should remain there, and he would get me there. When he pulled up at the bus stop, we hugged and hugged and hugged, after which I asked, "Where have you been?" He replied that he was attending meetings in Miami. This was the third time we were together, and I felt I had fallen "head over heels" in love with this most wonderful man. We dined again at Panera Bread, after which we drove to the Bayshore Park, sat in the car and chatted. On the drive home, we continued talking. He then looked across at me and said, "That's not *irie*." I recognized that to be a Jamaican expression but did not know to what he alluded. He followed up that sentence by telling me to put a "nice" suit on, on Monday, and go Downtown Tampa and hand out resumes. It had not occurred to me, at that particular moment, that, "That's not irie" and "nice" were closely connected. I took it as a bit of good advice, and on Monday, I dressed in a brown pants suit and set off for Downtown Tampa. It was not the *nicest* suit I had, but it was the one I felt like wearing. It was professional, comfortable and nice.

I walked from one company to the next, handing out resumes. I was doing what he advised. I took a break to call and inform him that, indeed, I was downtown handing out resumes. I believe his response to that was, "Yeah? Okay." I was very pleased that I was actually carrying out an idea, suggestion, advice that *he* gave me. In my private moments, I often reflected and wondered what he meant and what was he saying was "not irie."

After the Sunday of our third meeting, I had not seen the gentleman for a while. From time to time, I called, and we spoke by phone. Something was happening on the inside of me that was quite compelling. I had come to realize that something outside of the ordinary had occurred and continued to occur. Indeed, I have to say it was supernatural, as I discovered that each time I spoke with the gentleman, I was telling him not about me *now*, but rather about things that happened in my life from a child. Nothing was too distant and nothing too private or secret. It was as if I was pouring out my soul to him.

After each *pouring-out* episode, I remembered something else that happened eons of years ago that I needed to tell him about, and I told him the next time we spoke. It never occurred to me that I was telling a somewhat complete stranger the most intimate and sometimes sordid details of my entire life. You could say, I had a revelation that this gentleman was no ordinary human. I simply could not withhold those pieces of information. I had to tell him. It was not a choice. These were things I had not told anyone before, but I felt very comfortable telling him. It was freeing, so to speak, and was met on the other end of the line, with what appeared to be, total love and understanding and words of consolation. I felt like God was here, on earth, in human form and giving me the opportunity to relate to him.

For about a month, I had not spoken to the gentleman. When I called his phone, voicemail took a message. One Sunday, after being thrown out of Tampa Free International Church simply for worshipping God, I tried desperately to reach him but did not. I had been attending Tampa Free International Church since January 2010. Being a worshipper, it appeared my style of worship was not in line with their norms, and one Sunday after church, I was asked to see a member of their staff.

I had interviewed for an administrative position at the church. Naturally, I thought the individual was going to be updating me on the progress they were making in that regard. You can imagine my disappointment and surprise when they told me that I could no longer worship the way I was. One would think I was throwing stones, dancing on their piano or chairs or ripping their cushioned chairs apart. No, no. I simply lifted my hands, prostrated myself in front of the altar, and on one occasion, I went on the podium and joined other worshippers in worship.

When I returned to the Salvation Army Women's House, I sent an e-mail to the woman who relayed Pastor Joy Dempsey's message, telling her that I intended to continue worshipping as usual, since my purpose was to worship for the glory of God, and I did not see how my style of worship was in anyway offensive. Amazingly, when I entered the church that following Sunday, Pastor Joy Dempsey's team was waiting for me in the foyer. They told me I was not allowed to enter the premises anymore. I resisted by telling them it's God's church, and since I did not do anything wrong, I would not leave. They brought out a uniformed police officer, who was on assignment at the church, to threaten me with arrest if I ever "set foot on the premises again." I was beautifully dressed in a lovely black dress that I was wearing for the very first time and never got the opportunity to worship in.

I wanted to hear what the gentleman would say about this matter. When I failed to make contact, I resorted to visiting another church.

It was about nine months since I was thrown out of Tampa Free International Church. I decided that I would return. Surely, I thought, by now they are over their hate, and they have returned to love. I was sorely mistaken. I went and worshipped, as everyone else did, standing in the pews and singing, nothing out of the ordinary. That Sunday went without incident. However, while I sat there, I noticed that Pastor Joy seemed to be staring at me. The following Sunday, shortly after getting to church, and as I sat in my seat, security approached me and said, "Weren't you told not to come back on the premises?" I replied, "I cannot believe that after nine months you still remember that. Is this a church of God or not? Furthermore, what is the wrong that I have done?" They replied, "This is private property. Leave or you will be arrested." I left, and that was the last time I visited Tampa Free International Church.

At the end of May 2010, I still had not spoken to the gentleman. However, one day during that period, as I listened to Moody Radio, I heard a man on one of its programs speaking, and he appeared to be speaking to me. I listened intently, and I heard him talk about a man who would be leaning on a staff at the bridge. There was a huge bridge some chains from where I resided at the women's house. I generally pass under it going or coming from the bus station of just taking a walk downtown.

On this day, as I walked back from the food store with a couple of bags, I saw a gentleman with thick, white hair standing by one of the columns of the bridge leaning on a staff. I approached him and offered him a pack of nuts from one of the bags. I then began a conversation with him. He did not say much. I felt drawn to him in a special way, and I spent some time there with him. After a while, we both sat down on the sidewalk. I talked and talked, and he listened while, ever so often, glancing across at me in a warm and seemingly knowing way. We were there for hours, just the two of us. Sometime later, as a police car approached us, he said, "They're going to tell us we cannot sit here." The police stopped and told us to be careful as to how we put our feet out in the street.

We adjusted our position and continued sitting there. He told me his name was Mr. Lew. Later that evening, I microwaved a couple of boxes of those ready-made meals and took them to him. I did not know if he needed them, but I wanted him to have them. Mr. Lew thanked me. I wished him a good night and went back to the women's house.

From that day, Mr. Lew sat somewhere in the vicinity of the bridge, and I went daily and hung out with him talking about a wide range of issues, including the gentleman I had become so fond of but haven't heard from in some weeks. I always told Mr. Lew of my desires and a hoped for future with the gentleman. One day, Mr. Lew asked me, "What's his name?" I told him, "Roger, but I do not believe that's his name."

Mr. Lew looked across at me in that usual, warm and seemingly knowing manner of his. He was the only true friend I made in Tampa, and his friendship became invaluable to me. He was unassuming, unpretentious, wise, intelligent and decent. I have never heard Mr. Lew use a curse or swear word. I also have never heard him say anything negative about anyone, and he always looked out for me.

Soon, Mr. Lew came to have a group of people around him wherever he was. They gave me a lot of good advice. They, too, were extremely intelligent. They knew just about everything. They did not seem like normal people, and they did not seem to have any concerns about their supposed "homeless" state. They were always well dressed and well behaved. They provided me guidance and friendship. On the occasions when I needed Mr. Lew and he was not readily available, they pointed me to him. Now, this may sound crazy to many, but I have oftentimes thought of Mr. Lew as God manifested in the flesh and those wonderful men and women as angels. Such uncommon set of people, I have never encountered in my life—and to have had them all in one place for as long as I did—unheard of.

I hung out with Mr. Lew and his crowd on weekdays and weekends. On weekdays, we all dined at the five-star *free* restaurant called Trinity that was located on Henderson at Florida Avenue. On Saturdays and Sundays, people showed up, at various times, with all kinds of "good" food. There were no hamburgers and hot dogs. The meals were tasty and showed that much thought and preparation went into making them. They dished the meals and handed them to us with drinks, etc. They did similarly for breakfast, as well. Often, others came and handed out clothing articles. They were new brand-name clothes. I was amazed at the generosity and camaraderie that were displayed during these times. Each one looked out for the other. Others looked out for Mr. Lew, but when I was present, I always wanted to be sure that Mr. Lew was okay.

He was not fussy, and he never made a big deal about anything. At times, when I was in the distance approaching the group, I could see them showing Mr. Lew that I was coming, and he was always happy to see me. I told Mr. Lew anything I needed to discuss or needed help working through, and he provided much wisdom and excellent advice, always. I always did as he advised and always got great results. We talked about the Bible at length. The people with him were most knowledgeable about the Bible, as well. They taught me to understand Biblical things in a way that I had not thought of or seen before. They were all tremendously helpful, always looking out for me and making sure that I was fine. And so, while "Roger" was away from the scene, I developed this most wonderful friendship with Mr. Lew and his friends—many of whom became my good friends, as well.

Between late May and early June 2010, I was listening to Moody Radio, as I always did. It was the only Christian station I was able to find on my clock radio in my room. Again, I heard the same gentleman, whose program I was listening to when he spoke about the man at the bridge with the staff, say, "He's coming to where you are. He's coming local today." Knowing, again, that this word was for me, I got dressed and went downstairs.

I did not see Mr. Lew so I sat on the sidewalk, a stone's throw from Trinity while keeping my attention in that location. Soon, I was joined by a handsome, tall fellow who decided to debate me on the virtues of Christianity versus the Muslim belief. We had a spirited debate, and, in the end, he agreed with me that Christianity was the way for mankind to reconcile to God. I do not know if he was Muslim, and I do not recall what started the conversation.

As we were ending our debate, with my eyes fixed on Trinity, I saw a male, with a movement that seemed supernatural, enter Trinity. It appeared to me that he came in for a landing. Immediately, I was pulled, as if by a force, and I got up and proceeded to sit directly beside him. He went in line for lunch, and I followed. We began talking about the Bible, and we continued all the way through lunch. After lunch, we went outside, and I was about to say goodbye. He said to me, "Don't leave." We went to sit on a small brick wall, some feet from the cafeteria, and there we continued our conversation about God and the Bible.

I noticed at that point that he was wearing a green T-shirt with FSU (Florida State University) on the front. Something clicked at that moment, and I began asking him to tell me about Heaven. He spoke at length about Heaven and other things pertaining to the Bible. We sat on the brick wall, for a long time, as I listened, admiringly, to everything he said. He was more talkative, more outgoing and seemed funnier.

He was shorter and slimmer. His hair was the same as before, exactly the same—baldness, color, cut, appearance. When he was ready to leave, he asked me to walk with him a part of the way. We walked and chatted. Soon, we were standing under a huge tree, with widespread branches, and, there, he took me in his arms and kissed me tenderly. The moment he began kissing me, I recognized he was indeed "Roger," although he was now calling himself Richard. As he continued kissing me, I could hear myself saying, "It is you; it is you," and he replied, "Yes, yes."

It was a moment that could find itself nicely assimilated in the Book of *Songs of Solomon*. I whispered in his ear, "Why didn't you call?" He said that he did not have my number, and he asked me to give it to him again. As we kissed, I could see that while changed, Richard was, indeed, the gentleman who, for a moment, called himself Roger. I declined to give him my number, not really being fully assured, yet, that Richard was Roger.

I went home very happy with my lips feeling as if honey was dripping from them. I was exhilarated at the thought that Roger was back as Richard. When Roger told me that his name was Roger "Fixit," I thought he was not being fully honest. *No one has the name Roger Fixit*, I exclaimed, and now the pieces of the puzzle were coming together. I sat on my small bed in the room and smacked my lips, reliving every wonderful, delightful kiss that Richard placed on them. I also remembered how I had prayed to God for Roger to kiss me. Here, my prayer was answered on his return. I also thought of the awesome goodness of God in actually speaking, by way of the man on Moody Radio, to inform me that Richard would be on location.

The supernatural began to emerge as I came to realize that Richard needed to tell me he was Roger because when he reappeared, he was going to be different in appearance. When I asked Richard where he lived, he told me he was at the Good Samaritan. The Good Samaritan is an inexpensive home for the homeless. It is about a ten-minute walk from the Salvation Army Women's House. Richard had ditched his late model Mercedes Benz car along with his whole persona to one that fitted the homeless community and came, after being away for approximately two months, to join me in that community. The realization of this fact, along with the magnitude of the whole happenings, taught me something about *love* that I never knew. I also realized that on that first day when I asked the gentleman if he was an angel, my question was not far-fetched. Something supernatural was going on here, and it was fascinating.

It was on a Friday when Richard returned. At our parting, he told me to meet him downstairs the women's house at nine o'clock Saturday morning. Naturally, I could not wait for that time to come, and on Saturday morning, I promptly made my way down at the agreed-upon time. Now, to my utter dismay, I did not see Richard.

I waited, and soon, a young man approached me. He did it in such a way that made me know that he knew I was going to be there waiting on Richard. This was getting way too bizarre for me. It now appeared that I was on another planet, though, I knew both my feet were standing on earth in Tampa, Florida. I decided to be patient while thinking that I cannot believe that Richard changed again. I simply did not understand what was going on.

I spoke with the young man for a while, and in my frustration, I went back upstairs to my room. I must have connected something he said to me because as soon as I returned to my room, I went straight to my closet, and it now occurred clearly to me that I needed to take some clothes back to Syms. Syms was a department store that had locations in many states. This one was on Hillsborough Avenue in Tampa. I began to see that this was what "Roger" alluded to when he told me, "That's not irie" and followed that up by telling me to put on a "nice suit."

Here is how the "clothes" situation occurred. While I was working temporarily at the law firm in Tampa, I regularly went to Syms to shop. There were often great discounts, and I love bargains. There were, at times, lovely dresses on sale, and I purchased many. One Saturday, I went to Syms; I needed a couple of nice suits for work and future anticipated interviews. There was a nice pants suit. There was also a nice skirt suit. I looked at the prices, and they were quite expensive, but I liked them, and I decided that I would get them. I brought both to the fitting room and tried them on. They were perfect. I picked up some other things, as well.

When I was finished shopping, I went to the cashier and handed everything to him. He took them, rang them up and then placed them under a plastic. He told me the amount of my bill, and I paid him. I thought it sounded less than my mental calculation, but I did not say anything to him. I took my purchase and left the store. When I arrived home, I took my receipt and carefully went over the number of items and the price for each. To my great surprise, it appeared the pants suit and the skirt suit were not included on the receipt, although he neatly packaged them with the rest of my purchase. At this discovery, I thought of returning to the store to inform them of the error, but I wrestled with the decision. I would be required to take two buses to get there. The more I thought about it, the more it seemed it was too much for me to do. I reasoned, "It was his error, not mine so I did not steal them. After all, it was the cashier who checked, packaged and handed them to me. I should not have to go through all that hassle when it was not my fault." I also thought that if I went back and told them of the error, the cashier might be fired. I decided to keep the suits and not return them to the store.

Now, I was being made to reckon with a decision I made two or three months earlier. Though, I saw nothing wrong with my reasoning as to why I need not return the suits, God saw it totally different, and he was now requiring me to do the right thing. I pulled the suits out of the locker, and, for good measure, I also pulled out a dress that I had once tried to return to the store and was stuck with it because they could not locate it on my receipt, though, I was sure that it should have been on the receipt I took with me when I returned it. I put them in a bag and made my way downstairs to the street. The young man was still there when I returned. I told him that I was taking the clothes back to the store. He seemed to be in agreement, and he followed me down to the Marion bus terminal. We bade each other goodbye.

I went on the bus, and he told me he was going to North Carolina. As I sat on the bus, I wondered what I would say to the store manager. I wondered if he or she would call the police and try to convince them that I had stolen the things. Though, I had been shopping at Syms for many, many years—New York and Florida, I was now living in a shelter and any such accusation would cause the cops to think my homeless condition matched the profile of shoplifting. I knew I was innocent, but what would they think? I also thought of the possibility of being asked to identify the cashier.

As I changed from the Number One bus to Number Thirty-four at Hillsborough and Florida Avenues, I heard God say clearly, "Don't worry. It's going to be alright. Just tell them what happened. Nothing is going to happen to you." I felt a bit of the pressure lifting, but thoughts, nonetheless, lingered; thoughts of my family being contacted to come to my defense was one of the most troublesome. The bus rode down Hillsborough, making one stop after the other, and as it inched closer, I thought, "It's time to face the music. I am innocent; it's their fault, and God said it's going to be okay." With that thought, I consoled myself. I stepped into the store and asked to see the manager. He appeared from the back of the store. He was very well dressed, in a dark suit that fitted him well. I recognized that I had seen him in the store before. I walked up to him and told him, "Sometime ago I purchased these suits here. Upon arriving home, I checked the receipt and discovered that they were not on it. I wanted to return to the store, but I did not want the cashier to be fired. I wore them a couple of times. God told me to return them to the store." He thanked me and told me no one will be fired. I thanked him for understanding, wished him a good day and thanked God profusely for protecting me, again, from what might have been. I returned to the women's house.

The next day, Sunday, at approximately 10:00 a.m., I went downstairs. It was customary for them to serve delicious, healthy meals in a yard, just across the street from where I lived. I went with a view of enjoying a plate. I was standing on line, and I was approached by another young man. This one was again quite handsome, of African descent, very personable and of a quiet demeanor.

I tried to avoid him, but the more I tried to avoid him, the more intentional he seemed in his mission, which I knew not what it was. I was hoping to see Richard, but now, in just two days, I had seen two men who appeared to have been sent to me. I stepped out of the line, and he came where I was and encouraged me to get back on. I wanted to lash out at him for coming into my sphere and creating more confusion, but I could not. I simply started crying and asked, "God, what is going on? It seems lately, everyday a different man is coming to me. I do not understand. What have I done to deserve this?"

The young man asked me why I was crying, and I tried to explain to him what I had just said to my Father in Heaven. He was very understanding, and he went and got us both a plate of food. I thanked him, and we ate. When we were finished eating, he prayed for me and pronounced a blessing over me. At the end of the blessing, he said, "Angela, do not just take charge, take over." He then told me to follow him.

I needed the prayer, and I really needed a blessing. The fact that he blessed me, was mild mannered and seemed so intent on carrying out his mission, made me think that he was, indeed, another angel so after asking, "Where are we going?" and he replied, "The library," I decided to follow him.

We arrived at the John F. Germany public library Downtown Tampa. We sat outside at the east wing and chatted for a while. He told me that when I pray, I should pray in the Spirit along with other godly insights. After about forty-five minutes, he excused himself, telling me that he would be back shortly. He went inside the main area of the library.

A short while later he returned, and we continued our conversation. I felt that he was waiting for a particular moment. I was right. This anticipated moment came when he told me, "Let us go inside the library."

I had no idea what we were going in there to do, but we entered the main floor, and he simply walked ahead of me and then stepped aside as if removing himself from further involvement. I looked, and there was Richard standing there. I was elated. I must have been the happiest person on the planet at that moment. There he was; he had returned, again. That moment not only made my weekend, it made my life. I do not remember if I screamed in my joy and utter excitement, but I do remember that, in moments, I was in his arms, and we were hugging and kissing as if we were the only two persons there. A short while later, we went for a walk, and we were together until late that evening when he escorted me home to the women's house, bid me goodnight and left.

From that moment, Richard and I became inseparable. Except for the evenings when we reluctantly parted to go to our separate abode, we were always together. Each day, he came by the building, and I met him downstairs. We went to a number of places, including the library, Metro, the park, riding the buses to supermarkets, hanging out on park benches and so on. We spent our time together speaking, almost exclusively, about our Father in Heaven.

We both enjoyed the talks tremendously. We discussed many Bible truths as he taught me more and more about who God really is. The more I heard, the more I wanted to hear. I was like a sponge. I felt an insatiable thirst. I had spent years listening to all things Bible, and here was a gentleman who, I could see, loves God and knows much about him. When he said, "Father" or "My Father" or "Our Father," I knew, immediately, that he *truly* knows him and that he *truly* has an intimate relationship with him. There was such resonance and love. I had the feeling that he was not just speaking about someone in Heaven, but there is a close bond, and God, indeed, is *his* father.

After listening to the personal, affectionate manner in which he spoke about God, his vast and seemingly personal knowledge about all things God, the universe, things in the universe and how they work, I came to the conclusion that he was, in fact, Jesus, walking here on earth among us. His knowledge and intellect are way beyond anyone's I have ever read or heard. He knows everything, and he speaks of them in ways that says, I know; I created them. And, with all that knowledge and understanding, he is totally unpretentious. He is gentle, loving, kind, long suffering and selfless. He is always giving of himself, always wanting to give and always making sure that I am always totally fine.

When our conversations took a departure from our Father, he told me about things I could combine to make great edibles, and when I tried them, they were unbelievably delightful; for example, Spanish onions with cheese and biscuits and almonds and chocolate to name a few. Richard referred to many things that we, "humans," use as "paint." By this, he meant they are bad for us.

We continued to spend quality time together, and I continued to be totally blown away by his wealth of knowledge. I once told him he was like a bottomless pit of information. His demeanor continued to be "other worldly," totally different than anyone's on earth. He is easy to talk to, talk with and love. Soon, all I wanted and desired was to be with him all day, every day.

We spent an average of eight to ten hours together daily; we talked and totally enjoyed each other's company, and, yet, I felt the need for more. For the first time in my life, I felt truly loved by someone, other than my parents. He truly loves me, and it is a pure love. He showed up on time each day; if he did not show up when he said he would, I became concerned, but, in minutes, he generally appeared.

One day, he told me to meet him at the intersection of Florida and Hillsborough Avenues, at a particular time. I was having a less than perfect day and felt that when I saw him that would all change. I jumped through many hoops to get there and expected him to be there when I showed up. It took a while for me to get a bus, and I was a bit late. When I arrived at the location, I did not see him, and I felt quite disappointed. I do not know from whence he appeared, but I blinked my eyes, and in the time I blinked and looked, there he was. I was so glad to see him, and we hugged and hugged and kissed, as had become the norm for us.

I was convinced, after seeing and experiencing so many supernatural occurrences, that this most wonderful of men, this gentleman who calls himself Richard, was Jesus. One day I told him, "I'm going to tell people that you are Jesus." He said to me, "Sure, if you really believe that, go ahead."

That night, I told Micki, the manager at the women's house, that, "I have met Jesus, and he's in Tampa." She wanted to know how I came to that conclusion. I related some of my experiences to her. She asked me, "Doesn't the Bible say he will come back to Mount Olivet?" I told her, "Yes, but I'm convinced that he's in Tampa."

She went to the computer and did a "search." We both read that he would come back to Mount Olivet, as per our understanding of what we read. I was still sure that he was in Tampa and that I saw him each day. One day, my beloved friend, Mr. Lew, said to me that he believed Jesus was in Tampa walking around and nobody recognized him. I told him I agreed. "Nobody but you and I," I said.

Nearing the weekend of July 4, 2010, Richard and I had an argument, brought on by me. The reason was that I had never used food stamp. Food stamp is assistance given to the poor by the United States government to assist them in purchasing more healthy foods. Because I was homeless, I was forced to apply for it. I was thankful for it because, since being in Tampa, it was primarily what fed me. However, I was not comfortable with the idea, and I wanted to get off it.

This day of the argument, Richard and I were together, and I told him that our Father told me to ask him for whatever I need. I followed that up by saying, "I need to get off food stamp." He said that if that was our Father's way of providing for me, at the time, I should be thankful, and I should not worry about it. I began protesting by telling him that God can do better than food stamp. I then crushed the food stamp card. When I did that, he became very angry, as I have never seen him before. He stormed off and walked away.

As he walked down the street, at a fast pace, I ran behind him. He kept saying, "Stop following me," but I continued following, saying, "You're worth it, you're worth it." He left the main road and walked off into a road off the beaten path, and I kept following him. After a while, he came back to the main road, and we ended up at a bus stop in the area. He drank some water from a bottle and then handed it to me. I drank. Soon, the bus came, and we both got on, heading in the direction of the women's house and the Marion bus terminal. He kept telling me to go home. I traveled past the women's house, which was approximately a five-minute walk from the bus terminal.

Shortly after arriving home, there was a knock on my door, and I was told that two men were there to see me. I told the person, who knocked on my door, that I was not expecting anyone. Eventually, I came out and was directed to a conference room where they were waiting, along with Micki. When I inquired as to what they needed, they told me that Micki called them and told them that I told her Jesus was in Tampa, and she was concerned for my sanity. I told them that Micki did not have to believe me, but I knew what I was experiencing and believed every bit of it. They told me that they were from Mental Health Clinic (MHC) and were there to Baker Act me. They said an ambulance would be there shortly to get me so I should pack my bag. Quite disappointed, I rose from where I was sitting, and I looked at Micki and thought she was a traitior.

There were two male attendants in the ambulance, and they were most kind. The moment I went through the doors at MHC, I immediately recognized that it was different from the other times I was "Baker Acted" in West Palm Beach. I was given a comfortable seat, and the staff was most personable and friendly. While I sat in the waiting room thinking about the events of the day, a man came and sat in a seat beside me. He greeted me, told me his name was Kevin, and he told me that God sent him to tell me that he loves me and God also gave him Isaiah 12 for me. I thanked him, and I quickly pulled out my Bible and read Isaiah 12. After reading it, I was consoled. I realized that God had, indeed, sent him, and it was going to be fine both with Richard and the current spate of things.

I was assigned a large room with two other women. They were quite wonderful. All the patients at MHC gathered each day in a room to talk about our aspirations. When they asked me about mine, I told them of my love for Jesus and that I want to win millions of souls for Jesus. I actually said, "I want to populate Heaven and depopulate hell by the millions." The people that were there were ninety-nine percent young people. They were warm, funny and accommodating. They all appeared quite sane to me, which led me to believe that they, too, were angels, largely there to keep me entertained. We were a happy and a lively bunch. Daily, as they came and went, I was sorry to see them go.

MHC offered me medication, which I refused. Everyone else lined up, took their "meds" and appeared to enjoy getting them. Each day, I met with the doctors and told them about Jesus. I also told them I would not take any medication. I said, "I know that Jesus is real. I believe I met him in Tampa. Accordingly, no one is going to medicate me for my beliefs."

They said that the law required them to have me see a judge. A date was set for this hearing to take place. A lawyer was provided for me. A judge came to MHC along with the requisite court clerks, and court was in session. In the end, the judge agreed with me. No one could force me to take medication that I did not want to take, and no one can hold me in confinement. I am well able to live a normal life and take care of myself. God had used this opportunity to once and for all free me of the "Baker Act" demon that was trying to control my life. *No one, according to the judge's order, could ever Baker Act me again.* I had won that battle. Let me, please, correct that statement. God had won that battle for me. After court, I was at MHC for another couple of days. In total, I was there for approximately a week. Rather than feeling like a hospital, it felt like a vacation at a lovely retreat. I met many wonderful men and women and thoroughly enjoyed myself. I also met a tall Italian male by the name of William. We called him Will for short. He came a few days after I was there and left a day before I did.

After seeing so many supernatural occurrences, I asked God to let me see something, of the things I had been experiencing, happen before my very eyes. Two days before I left MHC, I was moved from the left side of the building to the right side, close to a window. There were two other females in this room. One day, I was looking out the window, and I saw a white Caucasian male walking toward his vehicle. Just before he entered the vehicle, in the blink of an eye, he became an Asian—a Japanese or Chinese. I was amazed. I smiled and thought, *Awesome God.* I realized that the only reason for moving me to that room was so that God could show me what I asked him to do.

About two days later, I was discharged at approximately 9:00 p.m. They told me that they do not usually discharge patients that late, but I was an exception. I think they were testing me because I had spoken so much about *my* God. Now, I believe they wanted to see if I would protest the late discharge. I did not. I had no idea where MHC was located, and I did not know where to go in order to get out of there. Believing, however, *rather* knowing that God cannot fail and will never leave me or forsake me, I asked them which way to turn. They showed me, and I was off. I walked a long way until I happened upon a bus stop. After a long wait, a bus came, and I asked if it was going Downtown Tampa. I entered the bus with great joy in my heart and began telling everyone on the bus that Jesus loves him or her before settling down to find a seat. I, eventually, reached Marion bus terminal.

I had sworn not to return to the women's house to live. Accordingly, I went to the temporary shelter at Salvation Army. They told me they had no available bed. I went across to the women's house, and Micki was there. She told me that Richard stopped by and asked her to hold my room. She also told me that he asked her to tell me that he was now at New Beginnings.

I went to my room, pulled out a few toiletries out of my locker, told Micki I did not need the room and left. It was approaching midnight, and I had no idea where I was going. I had no money, but I knew I was no longer staying there. I reasoned, "If I cannot be allowed my beliefs, as per my experiences with Jesus, I want no part of this place." As I headed out of there, a number of my housemates, who were not sleeping at the time, came running after me saying, "Angela, come back. Where are you going?" I said, "Bye," almost tearfully, as I headed for the exit. I went down to Marion bus station in the hope of getting a bus to New Beginnings. When I arrived at Marion, there was an older lady whom I met at MHC on my first night there, but I never saw her again during my stay. Now, here she was, well dressed and waiting, as if she knew I was coming and was waiting on me. I approached her and said, "Hi." She greeted me warmly and asked where I was going. I told her that I was trying to get to New Beginnings but did not know where it was. She said it was late, and the buses had stopped running for the night. She invited me to come and sit beside her on a bench. I thought she was probably going to be renting a hotel room, and I sat and waited patiently as the night passed on.

Eventually, a cop came and told us that we could not stay there. I said to her, "Aren't you going to rent a room?" She said, "Let's go down the road." We walked until we saw a bench in front of a building and there she sat, and I, again, sat beside her. We sat there for about two hours. Security came and told us that we could not stay there, and we moved on again. Next, we walked on until we saw a place with a concrete pavement, and she said, "Come." I thought, *Are we going to sleep here?* She lied down on the concrete and fell soundly asleep. I sat there for a while, and, soon, I lied down beside her. I twisted and turned all night on the cold concrete. I told her I had never slept on concrete before. She said that she had. I probably got a couple of hours sleep. When I awoke, it was very early in the morning. She was still asleep. I lied there and patiently waited for her to wake up. Eventually, she did. We walked to a food truck, and she bought us some coffee.

She then handed me a jacket to put on. It was a nice white jacket, and I foolishly thought that we were going somewhere. She got on the Number Thirty bus headed for the airport, and I got on with her. The bus arrived at the airport, and we both sat in our seats. I knew that she was waiting to see what I was going to do. The bus left and headed back to Marion station. We rode all the way back to Marion station. The bus headed for the airport again, and we were again on our way to the airport. When the bus arrived at its airport stop, we both remained in our seats. This time, she looked at me, and I said, "Are we going somewhere?" I do not remember what her response was. The bus again headed for Marion, and we were both on it. Halfway into the journey back, she asked me for the white jacket that she had given me to put on. She took the jacket and left the bus, and I never saw her again. I continued on the bus to Marion.

As I was getting off the bus at Marion, the African young man, who weeks ago led me to Richard at the library, was coming on the bus. He said to me, "Don't get off." I stayed on the bus, and we rode to a café on Kennedy Boulevard where they served food. We ate and then we rode the bus to FSU. I was getting a bit concerned since I had no clue where I would sleep that night, but I felt somewhat comforted because I had begun to realize that he was a key liaison. We took another bus and then got off. While waiting for another, he said, "Angela, you're going home with me." When the bus stopped, we were at New Beginnings. I was thrilled and began inquiring about Richard. I was told that he was at the *other* New Beginnings. This was a smaller complex that housed women and men, and there was a much larger one that housed men alone.

I spent two days there without seeing Richard. On the third day, I went, along with others, to Homeless Recovery in order to get my rent paid at the shelter. I told Beatle, the owner of the complex, that I was not eligible for further assistance because I exhausted my eligibility while at the Salvation Army shelter, when I first arrived in Tampa. He, nonetheless, thought I should go, and he provided me the requisite letter.

I boarded the van, along with others, and we went to Homeless Recovery. I stood on line for a moment and then decided that it was a total waste of time. I stepped out of the line, and I spent the time chatting with people on the sidewalk. At some point, the van left and returned to New Beginnings without me. I had no money and did not know where to turn or what to do. Soon, I saw a young man, whom I had met before while being out with Richard. He stopped to speak with me. He asked me if I had seen Richard, and I said no. He told me that he was going there and invited me to join him.

We began walking, and I walked for over three hours before arriving at the New Beginnings where I was staying. The young man stopped at that location with me, and we had some food to eat, after which I changed my clothes. A little while later, I was called into Beetle's office and told that I could not stay there because I did not get the housing assistance I needed to pay for my stay there. They were kind enough, however, to give me a number to another homeless shelter. I called the number and discovered that it was a place called Homeless Helping Homeless.

After all this had taken place, the young man, with whom I walked from Homeless Recovery, was now ready to move on to the other New Beginnings complex where Richard was, and we walked on.

Approximately forty-five minutes to an hour later, we arrived there. He asked me to wait outside while he went to locate Richard. In a few minutes, Richard came out. The issue I had with having to go to yet another shelter, that I had no concept of what would be expected of me there, paled into the background as I jumped up into Richard's arms. It was the first time I was seeing him since leaving MHC. It was wonderful to be reunited with him again. I recalled that a day after I was admitted at MHC, a man of about thirty-five to forty years old had approached me and said to me, "You are right—he was Jesus, but he went back to Heaven, and this is the Holy Spirit." I never saw the man before, and I never saw him again. I attributed that statement to God sending yet another angel to let me know that, indeed, I was *not* crazy as Micki had led those men to believe. I was again with Richard, and I continued to believe that, indeed, he was Jesus or as the man now told me, he was the Holy Spirit manifested in flesh.

Richard and I sat at a picnic table, out in the yard, at his New Beginnings. We talked about many things. There was a large tree, across from us, that had a running plant going from the root all the way up. As it approached midway on the tree, it opened up into two distinct parts and then back into one. He looked at the tree and said to me, "They are trying to separate us, but just like that plant going up that tree, we will separate for a little while and then we will be back together for all time."

That was a profound moment, as I looked at the plant and reflected on the impact of his statement. He then said, "Our life is writing an epic." He then changed "epic" to "saga." We had a brief debate as to the distinction between the two. He also said that when we got together, meaning sharing a home, he would sometimes go outside for moments by himself. He asked me not to think those moments had anything to do with me. Rather, he said, they were times to *ponder* and reflect on our Father. At one point during these conversations, I asked him, "Do you think I am prideful?" He replied, "Any woman who would wear a pair of pants that many sizes bigger that her fit, doesn't have to worry about that." It was a stark and hilarious moment.

A few days before I was made to go to MHC, Richard and I had discussions about not being too encumbered. He said, "It should be that if God should say 'go', we should be able to do so with basically just a backpack." On the basis of that, I went home and emptied my closet of all the nice clothes I had purchased while working at Gray law firm. There were approximately fourteen pairs of shoes, twenty dresses, pants, blouses, pocket books, mohair scarves and suits. I placed them a table in the dining area for my fellow housemates to take. They went like hot bread. The next time I looked out, I saw a lady looking at a couple pairs of shorts that remained. There were still a few things that I held on to. The following day, when I saw Richard, I proudly told him that I had given away almost everything. He told me not to give away anymore. That evening, however, after getting home, I heard a voice say, "Give everything away." I thought the voice to be God's and so I obeyed. I took out a black evening purse and gave it to Ms. G, the house mother. She told me that she was going on a cruise in two weeks, and she would take it along. Next, I put the remaining dresses, etc., in the only suitcase I had, and I dragged it up Florida Avenue to the Metropolitan Services thrift store, and, there, I did away with all my worldly goods.

When I arrived at New Beginnings, I literally had one suit of clothes—the one I had on. I told a woman there, who called herself the Rose of Sharon, that I needed something to put on. She gave me that pair of jeans and a blouse. I changed into them, not really caring what they looked like. The truth be told, I had more important things to think about that day. The lady that gave me the outfit was a size twelve. I was, at that time, a size four. It was this pair of pants that Richard alluded to in answering my question. It was indeed a poignant moment, as it now occurred to me that I did not spend the time to look at my appearance before going to see the love of my life. I thought, "Thank God his love for me is not about the clothes I wear." He had seen me, though, in some rather fine outfits before I gave everything away, and each time, he approved.

We spent a few hours at the picnic table talking. As evening drew closer, and it began to get dark, I now turned the conversation to the new place I had to go to. He turned and said to me, "Don't worry; you may like it a lot better than the others; I think it's going to be real nice." It's been a while since I had been to a "nice" place. Actually, since leaving the house in West Palm Beach, I had not actually had a nice place to live, and I was hoping that this would actually be as Richard had said. It began to get dark, and he said to me, "Go ahead and call them. They might even come and get you." I said to him in amazement, "Come and get me, do you really think so?" He said, "Yes."

I had learned by then that whatever Richard told me always happened the way he said it would, and whatever he said he would do, he did. Hence, whatever he told me, I believed. I dialed the number and someone answered. His name was Jerome. I explained that I needed a place to stay, was given their number, and would he please send someone to get me. To my great surprise and pleasure, he said yes and asked where I was. Richard took the phone and provided directions. Jerome said in approximately forty-five minutes someone would be there.

When the ride arrived, instead of being grateful, my first reaction was "That's it?" I was not expecting a top-of-the-line vehicle, but I was not prepared for the beaten up red pick-up that came. Richard, in his gentle, sweet, diplomatic way coaxed me into the vehicle.

Now, here I was in my oversized pair of jeans, in the beaten up vehicle, off to a place I had no idea where or what I would find there. I bade Richard goodbye, and he stepped up to the vehicle, opened the door and closed it after me. I waved and looked back until I could see him no more. I then turned to the gentleman and asked his name. He said he was Mr. Andrews. I asked him if he would please stop at the other New Beginnings so that I could pick up my stuff. He agreed. I then asked, "Could you not come with a better vehicle?" I thought he might have said something like, "The nerve of you. Here we are doing you a great favor, and you're complaining about the vehicle?" Instead, he took the time to explain to me that all the other vehicles were out at the time I called. He was not at all upset.

We stopped at Beatle's New Beginnings. I retrieved my things, and we were now officially on our way to what would become my new home.

Realizing, Mr. Andrews was a decent man, I began asking him about this place called Homeless Helping Homeless. By the time he finished telling me, we were at the gate of the facility. We drove through a gate into the yard, and I was directed to the office.

Jerome was still there when I arrived. He was a tall, handsome and young man, with a pleasant smile. He gave me a form to fill out, which I did and gave back to him. He gave me a bit of orientation, including a glimpse into the fact that he knew the Bible and enjoyed talking about it. We chatted for a bit about the Bible and then he accompanied me to the women's house. When I arrived there, I was pleasantly surprised. Just as Richard hinted, the place was indeed nice. There were three bedrooms, a living room, a dining room with a fire place, kitchen, washroom and a large front porch. The bedrooms had nice wood bunk beds with comfortable mattresses. The living room was comfortable, well-furnished and nicely decorated, as was the rest of the house. It looked more like a well-kept home rather than a home for homeless women. I liked it the moment I stepped in. I said, "Thank you God. You answered my prayer."

I was told that the people who stayed there panhandled. The organization gave them buckets labeled with its mission statement. Each day, the organization drove the individuals to various locations around Tampa. Motorists, pedestrians and others read the mission statement and placed a contribution in the buckets. The buckets were designed in a way that once the money was put in them, it could not be taken out until the individual returned to the organization. A senior representative of Homeless Helping Homeless opened the bucket in the presence of the individual, counted the money and returned fifty percent of the amount to the person who collected it. That person in turn paid ten dollars for each night's rent and food. There were others who sold bottled water and various types of drinks that were provided by the organization. The arrangement was the same—fifty percent organization, fifty percent to the seller.

I was told that I would *not* be allowed to do any panhandling or selling. Instead, I would be required to clean the men's house and the office complex as a trade-off for my living expenses. I never thought I would be good at panhandling or selling anything so I was grateful for the role I was assigned. I started the very next morning and continued for approximately two months. It was particularly beneficial to me because once I was finished with my duties, Mr. Keith, the person to whom I reported, gave me the rest of the day off, and it allowed me time to spend with Richard.

One day, as I swept the men's house, I stopped to reflect and thought, "Here I am sweeping floors and feeling like a princess, while I was living in a mansion and felt like nothing." I was having a great time at Homeless Helping Homeless. The women—Ms. Casey, Ms. Joy, Linda and others were a jovial, good-spirited, warm and friendly set. We all got along extremely well. The men were okay too. We did not interact much with them. When we had an occasion to work together, such as once when we panhandled at the Buccaneers NFL game at the Buccaneers stadium in Tampa, it was a great experience and lots of fun. They were very protective of me, and we collected lots of money.

On a particular day, while I was sweeping the front yard of the office building, William, whom I had met at MHC, came through the gate and greeted me by saying, "Hello Angela." I could not believe my eyes. The very tall William, whom I noted earlier was at least a six-footer, was now no taller than I was. I looked at him, marveled to myself, and thought, "Yeah, Richard was as tall when I met him at first too." Will looked exactly the same, only so much shorter. I also thought to myself, "I knew you guys were angels." Will spent about a month at Homeless Helping Homeless. He regularly told me how clean I kept the place and that I was doing a great job.

Mr. Parker, the proprietor, was wonderful, as well, although, on occasions, we disagreed on various issues. We had spirited debates regarding rules governing the organization. Sometimes, he agreed with me by saying, "Okay Ms. Angela, I'm going to change that." I believe that the men and women, whom I interacted with, were *all* angels. They just did not exhibit the normal traits of humans—the ones I had spent all my life dealing with. They were happy. Many knew the Bible extremely well as if they studied it all, and they quoted passages of it from memory when they needed to substantiate a discussion we were having that necessitated that part of the Bible. They were very intelligent, full of life, free, contented and never took themselves seriously.

When I was having issues, they consoled and comforted me. Jimmy told me where in the Bible to read, depending on what was happening at a particular time. It was also Jimmy who told me that God still wants me to observe the Sabbath. I checked the information with Richard, and he confirmed that, yes, the Sabbath (Saturday) should be observed. Since then, I have been observing the Sabbath. It was refreshing and wonderful interacting with the majority of them. I met men and women at differing times as I went about Tampa. They talked to me about the Bible, asked me questions about it, and they debated me on it—all in good fun, and I learned much at those times, as well. The only person I had that level of proof—that they were angels—for, however, was Will who went from six feet plus in height to just over approximately five feet in about two weeks.

After two months of scrubbing toilets and sweeping floors, I had had enough and wanted out of the cleaning chores. One morning, with tears in my eyes, I told Mr. Parker and Mr. Keith that something died in me as it relates to cleaning the property, and I could no longer do it. They did not appear surprised when I told them that. They simply said that I could do panhandling if I chose, and they would get someone else for cleaning. I agreed to try panhandling.

I was given a bucket and assigned to the corner of Floribraska and Tampa Avenues. This location was about a two-minute walk from the office. I was amazed at how easy it was and how willing people were to give. They gave me amounts ranging from one dollar to five dollars. We were given the option to decide how long we wanted to panhandle each day, but we had to make at least twenty dollars. The idea being that after the organization got its fifty percent, we would have ten dollars to pay our rent for that night. I did extremely well at this, and I was really loving it. I knew that God was giving me favor in this regard too.

People were giving eagerly, and I thanked and blessed them. Even little kids, traveling in the rear seat of their parents' vehicles, oftentimes called for me to come and get their dollar bills. I took the money, smiled at them and thanked and blessed them. I was taking in large sums daily. Soon, it went around to the others that I was taking in the most money each day. Mr. Parker told me that he tried that corner before with others and they brought in nothing. He said that was why that location was still available. Everyone was amazed and was happy that I was doing so well at panhandling.

Each day, when I thought I had collected enough, I returned to the office. My average time spent collecting each day was three hours. My obligation met, I went off to meet Richard at an arranged location, and we hung out for the rest of the day. At other times, I went to hang out with Mr. Lew and his friends. I was having a truly wonderful time at Homeless Helping Homeless. I got along with everyone—Mr. Parker, Jerome, Mr. Keith, Ms. Casey, Joy, Jimmy and the others. I felt that they really liked me, and the feeling was a mutual one. We discussed the Bible at length, and I learned a lot from them. Jimmy and Jerome were particularly versed in the Bible. I was amazed at the way Jimmy could recite passages of the Bible and the correct references for them. It was as though he had an audio Bible inside him. Once, Mr. Parker told me to come up with an idea for anything I would like to do, and he would fund it. I thought of his offer but could not think of anything at that time.

After approximately two months of my being at Homeless Helping Homeless, a woman named Serena came to the organization. She said that she was Jamaican. I did not particularly care for her. It appeared from my observation of her that she was a troublemaker, and her purpose was to make me, a Jamaican, look bad. I was not exactly sure why she thought her acting out, in the ways she did, would reflect negatively on me, but the more I observed her the more I was convinced, and I did all I could to avoid her. I succeeded for a while.

One day, I came to the office, and she handed me four lovely blouses. Homeless Helping Homeless regularly received donations of clothes, food, etc., on a regular basis. The clothes were plenty and needed sorting. On that day, she was assigned to sort the clothes; she saw the tops and thought they would be nice on me. They were quite nice and I thanked her. I now felt a level of obligation to be civil or nice to her and that was what I forced myself to do.

It was customary for me to go to the park or by the waterfront Downtown Tampa, by myself, just to go and gather my thoughts and watch the boats sail on the river, when Richard was not there on the Sabbath or on some Sundays. On this Sunday, I was leaving to go downtown, and she asked to accompany me. Though, I told her no, she insisted and came along anyway.

For much of the way, I walked ahead of her and even ignored her while we were down at the river. Never one to be deterred easily, she entertained herself with a couple's pair of German Shepherd dogs. When it was time for me to leave, she suddenly stopped playing with the dogs just as easily and suddenly as she began. Trek, trek, trek, she came behind me up Tampa Avenue. She began asking questions about many things, and I began responding, clearly showing my disapproval and displeasure. We returned to the women's house at Homeless Helping Homeless, and I proceeded to make some dinner. She asked me to make enough for her too, but that was where I drew the line. I told her no way, and I meant it.

Life continued as usual. I got dressed in the evenings and went to meet Richard, who at this time was employed at the Springs thrift store, a shelter for women, and took the bus each day to see me. Almost without fail, when I left each evening, Serena was at the house or met me on the way out and told me how nice I looked. I thanked her and went on my way.

It was never the same after Serena arrived at Homeless Helping Homeless. The atmosphere was not as joyful and pleasant as before. On the surface, she appeared to be a nice person, but one got the feeling that there was something else going on under that exterior.

She encouraged me to file for bankruptcy. She told me she had recently done it. She accompanied me to get some of the requisite forms.

She promised that she would assist me in completing the forms, But once I had the forms and sought her assistance, she pretended that she did not know what to do. Thankfully, I had some legal training, which came in quite handy.

One day, she and I were in the backyard of the house at Homeless

Helping Homeless. She made some unsolicited, unexpected and mean-spirited comments about Richard. I promptly put her in her place, as the saying goes, and left.

She was, at times, helpful. The challenge was to know if there were ulterior motives and finding out what they were. Once, I was trying to get a place so that I could move out of Homeless Helping Homeless, and she wanted us to get the place together. I decided against it. Another time, she wanted us to purchase a car that Homeless Helping Homeless was selling for one thousand five hundred dollars and move to Lakeland. I told her no on that too.

The mood at Homeless Helping Homeless was changing not only because of Serena's arrival, but also as a result of other women who were now coming and going. The first two months, there were the same four to six women at the house, but after Serena's arrival, it became more of a constant coming and going. The same four to six women were there, but each day there would be one or two short termers. They were fascinating characters, though. You could not help but like them. They were odd in a very likeable way.

I recall Linda who said that she was once a professional singer. She had an air about her that suggested plausibility. One day, she sat down to tell me her life's story. I cannot recall all the details, but except for the fact that I was never a professional singer, one could say it was *my* story. Her account of her life was eerily similar to mine.

There was another woman, who spent a night in my room, whom I did not recall ever seeing, yet she told me, "Angela, while you were at the Salvation Army Women's House, you had your own room. Now, we are in the same room." Since I did not know what she was talking about, I thought to myself that she was crazy.

There was also Jojo, whom I first met at the Salvation Army shelter when I first arrived in Tampa. At that time, she told me that she was a nurse. She said that she had to leave her house in a rush. The cops told her she had to leave immediately, and she was able to grab seventy-five panties before leaving, and that was all she left her house with. She came to Homeless Helping Homeless for a couple days but left because she could not successfully collect money with the bucket.

There was Tammy. She came in the very night I did. She shared her food with me that night. We got along well, initially. She sold sheet sets at Homeless Helping Homeless and did well doing so. After a while, she started drinking and acting quite strangely. She knew I was a Christian, and had no problems with me or my faith. We shared the same room, but we had different bunks. One day, totally unprovoked, she used a number of profanities to me. Mr. Parker was not impressed and told her to apologize. He also told her that behavior would not be tolerated. There was Ms. Gayle. One day, while Richard and I were hugging and sharing one of our private moments in the street, a lady came up and handed me a flower. Months later, when she arrived at Homeless Helping Homeless, she reminded me of that day and told me that she gave me the flower. She too turned out to be quite a character. When she was sober, she was kind, helpful and wonderful. When she drank, which was often, she was a totally different person—just aching to give everybody a hard time. She became the administrative secretary to Mr. Parker and did a good job of it. One day, during the 2010 Christmas season, she handed me two boxes of hand-made Christmas cards along with lots of postage stamps and told me to send them to everyone I knew. Another day, she gave me lots of lovely earrings, many of which I still wear.

With the different personalities entering and going, Mr. Keith decided to get a stern, stricter house mother. One Friday evening, a woman arrived. She was so large that she looked like a bouncer. The very moment she arrived, she lied on me. I do not recall all the details; however, I became quite furious, and I used the BS word. I had not used words like that in many years and was not pleased that I was forced into that position. I was also at the point of quitting the bucket collection. Though, I was very successful at it, I felt I could no longer do it. I discussed it with Mr. Lew, and he agreed with me. I made my intention known to Mr. Keith and Mr. Parker. They encouraged me to continue. However, I told them I could not. They said I had enough credits for the weekend, but my credits would run out the following Monday. That Monday, they waited for my decision, and I simply told them I would not do it anymore.

Serena, the Jamaican, had by now left for Good Samaritan women's house. She said that she was upset about the way they treated me that Friday, and she was concerned that they might treat her the same way, and she would not tolerate it. She returned to Homeless Helping Homeless to tell me that she had secured a bed at Good Samaritan for me and would pay the ten dollars per night. She had paid forty dollars in advance. I told her that she should not have done that, but I thanked her. I moved to Good Samaritan women's house in early October 2010. I had never experienced depression. I heard the word but had no concept of what it was. My first night at Good Samaritan, I decided not to share the room that Serena was in, though, there was an unoccupied bed above her. I opted for a bed in another room. Almost immediately after stepping into that room, I felt something on the inside of me being drawn into a dark hole. It was a most disturbing feeling and one I had *never* experienced before. I rebuked it, and it let up, but it immediately returned.

I thought to myself, *This must be depression, but why?* This was the fourth women's house I was living in since arriving in Tampa. As with Homeless Helping Homeless, this house was nicely furnished and homey. I climbed up on my bunk, prayed, read the Bible and tried to sleep, but I was unable to do so. It was a difficult night, but as morning approached, I began to feel better. That feeling left and never bothered me again.

Upon my arrival at Good Samaritan, Serena began acting even more strangely, and I saw some ugly, disturbing traits and behavior coming from her. I tried avoiding her at every turn, but the more I avoided her, the worse she acted. It was as if she was waiting for me to leave Homeless Helping Homeless so she could have her way with me, and she tried to, but I did not allow her. It was a relief to be able to leave each day for Homeless Helping Homeless. You see, I no longer liked the Homeless Helping Homeless women's house, but I certainly had no problems with the rest of the folk there. I also liked the office staff and Mr. Parker, and they liked and respected me. Serena, on the other hand, could not stand them.

Mr. Parker of Homeless Helping Homeless had started up a new business venture licensing cars. He invited Ms. Gayle, Michael and I to work in that business. It was interesting. I learned many things about tracking the history of vehicles. It was also wonderful to get dressed each morning and report to work. It also afforded me the opportunity to be among some of the people that I liked at Homeless Helping Homeless. It was a two-minute walk from Good Samaritan. The first two weeks of working there was a success. I realized that, indeed, whatsoever I did, God prospered.

We were paid based on the number of cars we processed, and I made some money. I did not tell Serena about this. Serena had, at this point, ticked me off almost completely. One day, while we were at home at Good Samaritan, Richard called me to say that he was on the bus and would be there in fifteen minutes. I was excited and was getting dressed. She interrupted my mood and pace by telling me to tell Richard that he should not come. She went on to say that I should not say yes whenever he says he's coming to see me; sometimes I should say no. Richard and I had been dating for nearly a year. We had spent practically all our time together, and we were totally enjoying each other. I met Serena only two months earlier, did not much like her and did not trust her at all, yet she thought I would adhere to her advice over what I knew and came to love about Richard.

After being at the women's house at Good Samaritan for nearly two weeks, a young woman named Jonie came to live there. She was in my room. She behaved, at times, like she was the best Tampa had to offer. From time to time, she fussed about this or that but never directed her fussing at me so I went about my business, trying not to be bothered by her.

One night, Juliette, the house mother, decided to have a meeting with the occupants of the house. Serena was not present; she was gone from the premises. Juliette wanted everyone to air her grievance. The meeting went well, and she encouraged everyone to keep respecting each other. At that moment, Jonie blurted out that I sang loudly, and it disturbed her. The other women countered by saying that it was not true. They said the times when I sang, I was not loud, and they did not have a problem.

Juliette said that I should cease singing. I told her that others talked on their cell phones, talked with each other, played their radios, played the television, while I enjoyed humming songs or singing softly. I told her it was unfair. I had a right to live as the others were, without that type of pressure. She said that if I did not stop talking she would call the police. The moment that threat was off her lips, she was on the phone to the police.

Two policemen showed up. They told me that if I decided to "behave" I could stay. I told them that since I did not consider singing within the parameters I did it, to be "misbehaving," and since I would not allow myself to be treated as a child, I would leave. I packed my backpack, said goodnight and went through the door. I went directly across the street to Good Samaritan—the living quarters for men and women. John, the owner, was there. I explained to him what had happened. He said he would go and speak to Juliette. I told him it would be of no use because I did not want to be there anymore. By now, I was not just tired of Serena, but I was also tired of Juliette and her condescending way of speaking to me, though, I never complained before, and now, too, was Jonie. I had had my fill.

John told me that there was a room upstairs where four women are usually accommodated. For the longest time, he said, only one has been there. It was not as comfortable, by way of furnishing, as the women's house, but it was okay. I readily accepted and went upstairs. Roomie, as I would later affectionately call her, was there when I arrived. She briefed me on how things operated there, and I quickly settled in, wondering what Richard would say about the fact that I had changed shelter yet again. Principle, I thought to myself, is something I have always lived by. The fact that I am homeless is no reason to throw it away. And, as I went from place to place, shelter to shelter, I had that understanding that Jesus was with me, and he was *not* going to leave me simply because I changed a shelter and neither was Richard.

Indeed, the hand of God was constantly seen as God continued to amaze me in ways I could not fathom. I continued to do well at Mr. Parker's office. During the days, I spoke with Richard by phone, and I eagerly awaited his arrival by bus in the evenings. Being with Richard was by far the best part of my days. We continued having great conversations and were enjoying each other's company immensely. I longed to be home with him. I wanted to be with him permanently. I began to pray about that, and, soon, we began having that conversation. God was moving in other mighty ways.

While at work, during the days at Mr. Parker's, if I felt that I wanted Greek salad, Greek salad arrived in abundance. If I wanted home-made yogurts, they arrived from Publix supermarket in abundance. Whatever I desired or asked for, they showed up in abundance. It appeared that Mr. Parker realized that God was favoring us by showering us with the many niceties that he sent our way each day. While I was in the office working, and not being aware of what was going on outside, Mr. Parker generally came to the door and said, "Come, Ms. Angela, take some yogurts, etc., and take some home and put in your fridge, as well." There was no shortage of anything. Designer and brand name clothes were in abundance too.

One day, I told myself that I could use four new pairs of nice jeans to add to my wardrobe. That day, true to form, four lovely pairs of jeans arrived with other clothes. They were my exact size and taste.

In early January 2011, I asked Mr. Parker for some time off from the job, and Richard and I rode the buses to a few areas looking for a place to call home. We took notes as we went to the different places. One day, as we sat on a bench under a tree in the yard of a Baptist church, we looked in *The Tampa Tribune*, and there was an apartment listed for rent. Richard called and inquired, and we were told we could see it. The following day, we met the owner at the address and viewed it. It was a lovely two-bedroom apartment on the first floor. We both liked it, and we took it. On February 7, 2011, we moved into the apartment, and it became our first official home.

Richard was even more wonderful as my mate. He went to the supermarket. He cleaned, and he dedicated his time to detoxing and restoring me. He purchased everything—things I had not even thought of—he got lanolin for my feet, green tea leaves oil for my hair, natural herbal lotions for my skin, many various types of teas, organic fruits and vegetables—everything.

Richard lovingly prepared all our meals, and I came to realize that he was also an excellent cook. I did not prepare a single meal. He was totally committed, devoted and totally wonderful. I had not heard of or seen a man so amazing. We went to the library often, and we brought home many books. We read and read and talked and talked. We had no television and no Internet, but we did not miss them for even a moment. We filled each other as we continued to talk about our Father in Heaven and all things relating to God.

We learned more about each other, and I found that Richard was more wonderful than I earlier experienced. One day, I was walking in the hallway, somewhere in the vicinity of the living room, and Richard met me there, hugged me and said, "Welcome home!" That, too, was very special for me. He went on to say that our Father had chosen me. He also said, among other things, that he enjoyed being with me because he could place a book about our Father on our coffee table, talk about our Father at length, knowing that I would enjoy it. He had, that day, purchased a book titled, *Know the Bible in 30 Days*, by J. Stephen Lang. He continued by saying that he did not know of anyone else who would so enjoy the things of God with him.

I was sure that God had sanctioned our sharing a home. Richard insisted on *no* sex. We hugged, and we kissed as usual, but intercourse was off limits. One day, while at home, I saw a vision. It was so real; I felt like it was actually happening to us. I was dressed in a white dress with an elaborate train. Richard was dressed in a white suit, resembling a riding suit. We did not appear to be standing on earth. Rather, we were somewhere with the appearance of being out in space. There were two strings of white crepe paper plaited and hanging with a large white bell in the center. I approached from the right of the bell. As I came to stand under the bell, two white doves flew in and sat on each of my shoulders. Richard then appeared from the left, and as he came and stood in front of me under the bell, two white doves appeared and sat on each of his shoulders. Two additional doves came and sat on the string of paper on either side of the bell. I did not see any other form of life apart from Richard, me and the doves. I felt, at that moment, that the Holy Spirit had married us.

I had some spiritual struggles, though. After about two months of setting up our home, and happily residing there, I began having a battle with a force that became so prevalent in my mind that wanted me to move out. Richard kept telling me that it was our Father's will for us to be there together. One moment I felt fine—an hour or two, maybe. After a while, it returned, forcing me again to have to run to Richard for consolation and cover. It was very strong, dark and persistent.

One day, Richard went out and purchased two red and white coolers. Richard said that since we were no longer homeless, he thought it was a good idea for us to prepare sandwiches and drinks to take Downtown Tampa and give to those who were still homeless. The devil now wanted me to think that Richard bought the coolers to make a point—a point so offensive that in the devil's view, I should move out. On another occasion, I went to the hairdresser to get a haircut. When I returned home, I opened my closet, and there was a note from Richard that read, "HONEY BUNCHES." The devil tried to convince me that he placed that note there because he wanted me to move out. Richard was patient, loving, kind and understanding as I battled, each day, that demon that wanted to turn our life upside down. One evening, as we sat on our couch, Richard said to me, "Honey, do not think that anything you do or say will be a burden to me."

I was almost relegated to a child, constantly needing affirmation and that was what Richard provided. He constantly and promptly provided any affirmation that was required while pouring out his love on me. There were times, as this presence continued, when I wondered if I might become a burden to him. When I tried to tell him of my concerns, he listened in silence. At times, when I was about to say something, just before I said it, he said, "Shhhh." Amazingly, when I did not say it and thought about it, I later saw how stupid a thing it was and was glad he kept me from uttering it. That happened time and time again, and I no longer wondered how he knew. I only knew that he did, and he continues today to caution me in that way.

Now, when he says, "Shhhh," when I'm about to speak, for the most part, I do not. There have been times when I felt the need to and proceeded against that caution and felt quite stupid after. Thankfully, Richard doesn't judge. Another day, as my need for affirmation continued, Richard, again, lovingly said, "Honey, I want you to know if you were somewhere else, I would be there. Wherever you are, that's where I will be."

Richard suggested that I go on a fast for as long as I could endure. I did and fasted for five days without eating or drinking. On the morning of day five, as he fixed breakfast, he placed a bowl of healthy delicious-looking strawberries on the counter and said, "There, Honey you can eat if you wish." I declined.

Later that day, I went to visit Mr. Lew and his friends. One said to me, "What's wrong with you?" I said, "What do you mean?" He said, "Your face looks different." I told him, "I have been fasting." He said, "How long?" I said, "Five days." He said somewhat in a shriek, "Five days!!"

I realized at that point that I needed to break the fast. I went home that evening and told Richard that I would have dinner. After that fast, I began to feel a change—a positive one. I started feeling stronger. I was now speaking to what was pressing in on me. I began telling the devil, "God placed us here, and I am going nowhere."

Richard said that I should start taking ownership of our home. He told me to fill the place with my presence, and I did as he said. I began to remember that while I was at the Salvation Army Women's House in April 2010, about two weeks after taking up residence there, I had felt a similar force—just as tormenting but more forceful—telling me to go back to

West Palm Beach. I had to go down in serious prayer in that tiny room. I asked God to please speak again so that I would be sure that I am standing on *His* solid ground.

I was listening to Moody Radio one day after praying that prayer, and I heard Tony Evans, in a sermon, speaking directly to my situation. He said that God had moved me from an abusive situation, and now demons are tormenting me, wanting me to go back. "God says you must *not* go back," he intoned.

As I went to church services, God allowed one person after another to tell me *not* to go back. As that episode came back to me, I realized, without a doubt, that Satan was at it again. I began to pray more directly, and God began to respond more directly. Richard also told me, when we first met, that I should not end my prayers with "Amen" when I prayed. He said that since Amen-Rah was an Egyptian god, using the word Amen at the end of my prayers, was canceling out my prayers. It was as if I was praying to the Egyptian god and not to *our Father*. Since putting that advice in practice and since I started ending my prayers with, "Thank you, Father, for hearing my prayer and thank you for the answers, in Jesus name," I have noticed that my prayers were being answered promptly and that after each prayer, God *always* spoke directly to *anything* I asked. He told me when, how, where, etc., and the results were always as he said they would be.

I moved a bit away from getting affirmation from Richard to getting confirmations from God, and, indeed, God began to speak quietly and profoundly, many times daily, and as was customary, I noted what God told me. I read and reread what Richard told me, but more importantly, I read, reread and reread what God had said. I digested them and meditated on them. I was hearing God confirm what Richard had been saying, and, now, we were all on the same page. I read the Bible daily—many chapters. I prayed, for the most part, three times daily. I took notes of what God was saying each day, and I stood on the word of God. Indeed, I discovered that: *The weapons of our warfare are not carnal but mighty through God to the pulling down of strongholds*. It began to get better—a lot better.

One day in August 2011, as I lied on the carpet in our bedroom reading the Bible and pondering some things, I heard the voice of our Father telling me that he wanted Richard and I to move to the country of Jamaica. I did not say anything to Richard at that time. Too many things were happening, and I wanted to be sure it was, indeed, our Father. I decided to ask for confirmation.

A few days later, as I was lying at the same place in our bedroom, our Father began to speak. He not only told me he wanted us to go to Jamaica, but he went on to elaborate as to why he wanted us to go. I decided to tell Richard.

One evening, as Richard sat reading in the living room, I asked him if he would like to live in Jamaica. He said maybe we could go for a visit. He would think about it. I believe it was in October 2011 when Richard announced to me that we were going to Jamaica. I now asked him, "Why do not we go for a visit first?" He said, "Why go and come back only to waste all that money. We'll just make one thing and go." I was amazed.

When I thought he may have forgotten about it, here he spoke, and when he did, his decision was made, and it was final. He is a lot like that. One night, as we sat on our couch at the apartment in Tampa, he looked across at me and said, "Honey, it's inevitable that we get married." I thought, "Wow, great!"

Well, after a few months of not knowing whether I should be making plans for a wedding, I decided to broach the subject by asking, "Honey, you said we are going to be getting married, when?" Richard was standing in the kitchen, and he calmly looked at me and said, "You Jamaicans are so hasty; it will happen."

I began to make plans for our going to Jamaica. There weren't many plans to make. We had decided to ship a few things, including our stacked washer and dryer, a couple of sentimental things, including our globe, a small table and a table lamp.

Less than a month after we moved into our apartment in Tampa, Richard went to the library and came back with a big, black bag. He handed it to me and told me to open it. When I looked inside, there was a large blue globe with a gold-looking stand. I asked, "Why did you hand it to me?" He said, "It's for you. Are you not familiar with a guy's way of telling a girl he wants to give her the world?" I felt a bit sheepish for not being familiar, but I knew it was classic Richard, expressing his love in the unique ways I have begun to learn that he expresses it, and I was touched to the core of my being. It was a tender and beautiful moment, and I said, "I'm sorry I was not familiar. Thank you so much. That is very sweet, and I am so touched." By the time I was finished making my acceptance speech, we were in each other's arms hugging and kissing.

Another day, Richard went to the supermarket to pick up a few things. I took the opportunity to lie in bed for a bit. He returned with a very nice round wood table with a lamp. The wood on top of the table has the appearance of yellow marble, and the lamp is a good match with a gold shade seeming to be made of silk. Again, I was touched by Richard's sweetness and love, and he placed them on my side of the bed. I told him how nice they looked. He soon decided that they were a bit high for there, and we moved them to the sitting room. We decided to sell the rest of furniture. In the end, we gave it all to the Springs, after selling the dresser and chest to my niece who resides in Tampa. We booked our tickets, and I called some of my siblings to inform them that I was returning, along with Richard, to Jamaica for a while. The reception was lukewarm.

# CHAPTER XII

# OUR MOVE TO JAMAICA

On January 31, 2012, we landed at Norman Manley International Airport in Kingston, Jamaica. We picked up a car we had reserved and drove directly to St. Thomas, and we rented an apartment, by the sea, for three days. We went into Morant Bay a few times. At the end of the initial three days, we took to the road discovering—and in my case—rediscovering some of Jamaica.

We drove to Portland, and we visited Reach Falls—a lovely place off the beaten path. We also visited Port Antonio, and we stopped at a few beaches along the way. When night fell, we checked into a room in a motel, by the sea, in Portland. We were quite adventurous. We drove up a hilly terrain and across a road leading through the mountains of Portland. The road was so narrow that two cars would not be able to pass on it. Fortunately for us, there were no other cars.

The following day, we drove through St. Mary into Ocho Rios. We stopped and visited the Ocho Rios market. We picked up a few things, and we were again on our way. We spent a night in Trelawny and another in Montego Bay. Soon, we were in Negril. We visited some sites in Negril, and as evening beckoned, we decided to drive along the coast into Mandeville, an affluent town in the Parish of Manchester. It sits approximately three thousand feet above sea level and boasts a spring-like temperature all year. My brother, Carlton, suggested it, and we thought we would check it out.

We arrived in Mandeville on a Sunday night. We checked into a lovely guest house for the night. The following day, we purchased a copy of the *Jamaican Gleaner* and looked over the listings of places to rent.

We decided to drive around for a bit. As we approached an apartment complex, a man, who was driving a Volvo, stopped by us. Richard told him that we were looking for a place to rent. He was a real estate agent and told us he had a few places that we could look at.

He drove us to a large one-bedroom apartment on a hill. It was quite lovely, and we decided to take it. It was not being rented furnished, but, at our request, the agent decided to furnish it for us. We spent a couple of nights at the Golf View Hotel, in Mandeville, while the apartment was being set up. On February 9, 2012, we moved into our first home in Jamaica.

It was wonderful. As had become the norm, Richard took to the kitchen, making us delicious meals and continued to make delicious snacks. We were now having sugar loaf pineapples, lettuce, cottage cheese and mayonnaise salad on a regular basis. He also made local Jamaican goat stew. We became great fans of East Indian mangoes.

In the mornings, Richard blended many fruits together—oranges, avocados, mangoes, bananas, papayas, etc., to create the most wonderful and delightful drinks we have ever had. We oftentimes went out exploring the outskirts of Mandeville on foot. We began to enjoy many organic fruits and vegetables. Richard also continued to search for the best products available for us to use. He now added Shea Butter to the repertoire. I had not heard of Shea Butter before, but he found it in Jamaica, and I do like it very much, especially when Jojoba Oil is added to it. Richard told me it is prevalent in Africa. Richard is always looking for the best natural products, so it's always exciting when he introduces me to something new. I had a few experiences at that apartment. One morning before waking up, I dreamed that there was a pink and white loveseat in a corner beside my closet, and a young woman was standing in the living room hiding behind another woman. In reality, there was a brown floral loveseat, of the same shape, in the exact location as the one in the dream. That very day, a young woman showed up outside my kitchen window wearing a sweater-like knitted blouse. The material from which her blouse was made exactly resembled the pink and white couch I saw in the dream. She asked me for some clothes. I asked her, "Why?" She said that she got wet in the rain and wanted a change of clothes. I wondered why she did not go straight home to get a change of clothes.

We were not exactly on the beaten path. You had to come looking for us. I ran a few thoughts over in my mind, and I was very reluctant to give her my clothes. She stood outside our kitchen window pleading. I consulted with Richard as to his thoughts regarding her request. He said that I should give it to her if there was anything I had that could fit her. I gave her a blouse and a pair of jeans. Richard also gave her one thousand five hundred Jamaican Dollars. After she left, the dream came storming in my head, and I began regretting that I gave her my clothes. Richard calmed me down by telling me, "It's okay." I do not know what that dream meant, and we never saw the young woman again.

In February 2013, Richard and I returned to Tampa for a week. On our return to Mandeville, we started saving for a car. In preparation, we went to a few car lots and scouted. The prices for cars in Jamaica amazed me. I wondered how can there be so many cars on the roads in Jamaica at such astronomical prices.

In October 2013, I was listening to a local Christian television station called PFM. It is owned by a church headquartered in Jamaica, and they have live services on Sunday mornings, which I frequently listened to and liked. As I listened on that Sunday morning, I heard a female, who went to the podium to give an exhortation, proclaim, "Little is much when God is in it. I do not know what you're trying to get, but God wants you to know that little is much when God is in it." I received that word as ours.

A few days later, I heard God say to me, "One day in the coming week, go to a lot off the main highway and look for the car." I asked Richard if he was agreeable to go looking for a car in the coming week. He said that we needed over a million Jamaican Dollars to get anything decent. I said to Richard, "I am putting my faith out there in believing that our Father will find us a nice one." We did not know of a particular lot along the highway. I told Richard that while we were going to the airport, I thought I saw one going in the direction of Kingston.

We called a taxi and asked the driver to take us out on the highway going to Kingston. As we sped along the highway, Richard was looking at one side, and I was looking at the other. We were about two miles on our way, and I heard Richard say, "I believe I saw a lot. I saw a lot." I quickly asked the driver to stop and turn back. We got to the lot, and we began looking. Richard asked me if I saw any car that I liked. Referring to a red Mitsubishi Galant, I replied, "This is the only one I like." It was stylish, in great condition and "loaded." He test drove it and said he liked the feel of it. He also looked great driving it. We asked the salesman for the price of the car. To our surprise, it was exactly the amount of money that we had saved. We went and got the money and returned to pick up the car. We finally had our car and no longer had to take taxis or rent cars when we needed to go out.

The very day we returned from picking up our car, as I stood at our bathroom door, I heard God say, "You'll be moving in two weeks." I was surprised, very surprised. We had just bought the car with all our savings. We were living in a furnished apartment. We were thinking of moving, but we weren't keen on getting another furnished place. We wanted our own furniture.

Two weeks seemed a relatively short time, in my estimation, but not in God's. He has *never* told me anything that did not happen as he said it would. I had learned to trust him. I went to the Internet and searched for homes that were renting in the area. Richard and I love fruits, and we were hoping to find a place with lots of fruit trees. I found, in the listings, a three-bedroom house advertised on a large lot with "lots" of fruit trees. I wrote it down.

Richard and I were out for a drive that Sunday, and Richard drove into that area. Since we were there, we decided to call the agent. He told us we could see the house on Monday. We asked for directions, and we drove to the address. The gate was locked. Therefore, we were unable to see the backyard. It was a most exclusive neighborhood in Mandeville called Ingleside. We returned home. I was listening to Christian television that evening, and I heard an American pastor talking about an experience he had with a house he bought in an exclusive neighborhood in Texas. He said the house was "run down," but God told him to take it, anyway, and he later sold it for a huge profit. I thought there was a message there for us, though, I had no concept of what the house looked like inside or out.

About six weeks earlier, I had seen that very house, with the awnings all around it, in a dream. That Sunday, I prayed and asked God if we should take it. God said yes. On Monday, we arrived at the house and walked through it with the landlord and his agent. It was a nice house, but it was not well maintained. The backyard was very rough, but there were lots of fruit trees—oranges, grapefruit, apple, tangerine, avocado and bananas. The kitchen was large but not modern. My first instinct was not to take it, but I remembered that God said we should. I also remembered that our Father said we would be moving in two weeks, and I also recalled that pastor relating his experience. Richard likes a nice kitchen because he loves spending time in there. This really was not, and he was not keen at all on getting this place. I went against his protests and gave the agent a deposit, from money we had in my pocketbook.

I moved in on the first day of November 2013. October 30 and 31 were sleepless nights for me. Suddenly, on October 30, as we went to bed, I was struggling to breathe. As the problem became more intense, I was forced to sleep on a couch, in the living room, where a large window was always open. Even being that close to the window, I was struggling to breathe. I placed a small scarf over my nose, and I breathed through my mouth. The following morning I was exhausted, but I was grateful to have made it through a long night. The following day was largely uneventful, but as night came, and we went to bed, the feeling returned. Additionally, there was a burning sensation on my body. I felt like I was being tortured. I did not tell Richard the extent of my suffering. I simply told him I could not breathe, and I was going to sleep on the couch. As I lied there, enduring another harrowing night, it dawned on me that there was an element of spiritual wickedness present in what I was experiencing.

Though, we had until the ninth of November in the apartment, I realized that whatever was transpiring, I could not spend another night there. As I lied there reflecting, our Father broke through and said, "In the morning, pack your things in the car, take the debit card and go to the furniture store and pay for those things. They will take the card, and they will deliver the furniture right away."

I had not told Richard what our Father had said. However, that morning, Richard got up and started putting our small appliances, my pillow and other things in the car. I asked him for the debit card, and he gave it to me without any questions. I realized that he knew what our Father had said, and I did just as our Father instructed.

That morning, I asked our Father to please have a man on the way to our new home cutting someone's lawn so that I could ask him to cut ours. It really needed a cut. I went to the furniture store, after leaving the apartment, and I used the debit card to pay for the furniture. The owner promised to deliver them in two hours. On my way to the house, I saw a man cutting a lawn, not far from our house. I asked him if he could cut ours when he was finished. He said that the mower belonged to the owner of the yard he was cutting. Before he finished speaking, a young man ran from a yard, directly across the street. He said that he overheard the conversation and knew of someone who had a mower for rent, and he could find two guys, immediately, to cut it for me. He used my cell phone to call the owner of the mower.

The arrangements were made right there, and, in less than two hours, two young men were there to cut the grass. While they were cutting, the furniture store made good on its promise to deliver the bedroom set, dining table and chairs, etc. God had given instructions on how I could get out of the apartment that very day so that I would not have to endure another uncertain night. He had also answered my prayer in providing two very dedicated young men who did a most splendid job of cutting the lawn. The electricity at the new place was turned on that very day.

With everything going so well, I decided to leave and update Richard, who was at the apartment. He was very happy to see me when I returned home. Richard is the most wonderful and most honorable person I have ever encountered, and he likes to always do the right thing. Although we signed a year's lease that expired ten months earlier, Richard insisted that we give the landlord a month's notice. I told Richard, "That would be ideal. However, there are extenuating circumstances when we are not able to do what's ideal. It was God who said we should move at the time we are moving; therefore, he will see the process through."

On the basis of that honor, Richard was not keen on leaving before the ninth of November. I had gone ahead and informed the Landlord's agent of our imminent move, which gave him three weeks' notice. The agent immediately tried to put our one-month deposit in jeopardy by mentioning a month's notice. I told him that we would have wanted to do so, but things did not happen in a manner that would have made that possible. He started making a legal argument, which forced me into telling him that if he wanted to be legal about it, "We have been living here for ten months without a lease. You did not give us a new one. Of such, we are under no legal obligations, and we intend to get back our deposit."

He told me he would have to see what management says. God did speak, and he said we *would* get back our deposit, and we should not worry about it. Some more furniture, we had earlier purchased from another store, arrived once I returned home from seeing Richard at the apartment. It may be worth mentioning that it was after that conversation with the agent that I began having those strange experiences at nights. God clearly states in the Bible that if he is for us, no one can be against us. God was clearly showing that, indeed, he was for us. We have always known that. However, it is, at times, imperative for God to allow others to recognize this truth as well.

I spent that night alone at the house sorting out and setting up. On Saturday evening, I drove over to the apartment, and Richard returned to the house with me. On Sunday, he packed our remaining things at the apartment and left for the final time. We handed in the keys at the agent's office, and, in approximately one week, we received our deposit back. God cannot lie, and he never fails.

We had begun to settle in at Bahamia Close, Ingleside, Mandeville. Richard did not want us to take the place. Nevertheless, the fact that it was now our home gave him reason enough to want to make it the very best. It was another leased property, but Richard went out and purchased all the requisite tools. Day after day, he labored for hours out in the yard. He plucked up crab grass, moved buckets of stones and rocks, dug down and built up areas, limbed and trimmed trees and planted shrubs and flowers; he also planted an East Indian mango tree. He purchased grass seeds and spread throughout, where needed. He painstakingly pulled out pieces of broken bottles, barbed wire and other debris buried in the soil. After two months, a complete transformation had taken place. The property had gone from a rough and tumble place to one that anyone would be happy to call home. Richard went out and purchased wood and other materials and screened the complete house, wherever louvers were, so that flies, mosquitoes and lizards could not get in.

The house consisted of three bedrooms, two bathrooms, a living room, a washroom, storeroom, a small library, a front porch and a garage, and it sat on an acre of land. We had some of the best avocados there that we have ever eaten. There was also a fruit tree called Ugly. Its fruits resembled grapefruits, but they are much larger. It makes a most refreshing juice, and Richard really enjoyed it. While he worked in the yard, I often brought him a glass of cold Ugly juice, and so we began to settle in our new home.

It had been one year and ten months that we had been living in Jamaica, and, though, we had been enjoying it, Richard, in keeping with Jamaica's immigration rules, had to return to America every six months and re-enter Jamaica. He received three months upon entering the country; we then went to PICA (Passport, Immigration, Citizenship, Agency), paid a fee and received another three months.

It had begun to become a drag on us. It felt like not being able to put your bags down, let your hair down and just relax. It had the feeling of constantly anticipating the alarm clock going off. It was also hard to see Richard leave for the days he was gone. In August 2013, he returned from the United States. After three months, we again went to PICA. This time, however, they said he would receive no further extensions. It meant he would leave in February 2014 with some level of uncertainty as to what the future held. Richard said, "They are trying to separate us, and our Father wants us together."

One night, I was lying in bed waiting for Richard to join. He emerged from the computer and announced that we would get married. We discussed it at length and decided that we would have a private ceremony. On December 23, 2013, Richard and I got married under a large apple tree in our backyard. There were two witnesses, along with the officiating minister. It was a beautiful ceremony and a most beautiful and tender moment. I wore a white linen gown, and he wore a white short-sleeve shirt with a pair of khaki pants. On August 26, 2013, God told me that Richard and I would get married before the year ended, and, again, he was right.

Richard returned to the United States on January 27, 2014, for a few days. At that time, he went to the Jamaican consulate to get an official visa so that he could begin the process of residing in Jamaica without having to leave at specified times. The following day, he went shopping at a Walmart store in Miami. To protect his documents, he carried them with him in a special bag to the store. I had gone to the doctor because I had not been feeling well. With Richard away, I wanted to be sure that I had my vitals checked. The doctor ruled out hypertension. Based on his examination, he said that he could not find anything wrong with me. As soon as I returned home, my phone rang, and I hesitated to answer because it was a number I did not recognize. Immediately, my phone rang, again, and I answered. It was Richard informing me that he brought the documents with him shopping, and they were missing. His cell phone was among the documents. He borrowed someone's phone to call me. This happened on a Friday afternoon at 3:00 p.m. He was due to return on Sunday, and I had no idea what to do.

I went down to prayer, and God told me that Richard would find the documents. As a matter of extra caution, I called the US embassy and inquired as to the course of action, should it become necessary.

They gave me a number in Miami to call. When I called Miami, they told me that because it was that late in the day, there was nothing they could do before Monday. Shortly after speaking with the office in Miami, Richard called again to inform me that he went to customer service a second time to check, and the bag was there with everything intact. Richard said that the lady at the desk told him that she had no idea how his bag got there. We were overjoyed that it was found, and we gave all the thanks to God, our Father. He certainly answers prayers and, oftentimes, at lightning speed, depending on the situation.

That Sunday, as I drove from Mandeville to Kingston to get Richard at the airport, I was faced with some unexplained feelings. Whenever the feelings came on, I said, "Father, Jesus, hold me." The moment I said that, the feelings went away. Each time a weird feeling came on, and each time I said that, the feeling immediately went away. I arrived at the airport feeling great, and I was there, on time, to welcome my husband home. "Home," indeed, is the perfect word. It would be the last time that my husband had to involuntarily leave Jamaica.

# CHAPTER XIII

# OUR JOURNEY CONTINUES

On February 16, 2014, as I listened to PFM's live Sunday morning worship, as we always did, I heard a guest speaker from *I Can Ministry* in London, England, proclaiming the Word. The title of the message was *Put Me in The Palace*. He spoke about patterns, principles and predictions. He said that patterns in the Bible produce principles. With a promise from God, you can start making predictions, and when you have a promise from God, you can prophesy into the future. He also spoke of Joseph, Esther, Nehemiah, Daniel and Moses, whom God used to save their people by their associations with palaces. He further stated that God is looking for someone whom he can put on the inside to change situations in societies. Continuing, he said, "If God has chosen you for promotion, there is no force in hell that can prevent you from rising to the top. The next twenty- four hours your life can change dramatically." And then he said, "You're chosen for promotion, and there's nothing the devil can do to stop it."

    I knew that he was speaking to me, though, I did not know what "promotion" entailed. I went out to the back to join Richard, who was sitting there. I looked out across the backyard and the beautiful grass he had sown. The fruit trees seemed happy and were blossoming. I thought, *A transformation, indeed.* Suddenly, I said to Richard, as if without thinking, "We should move." I felt surprised after saying it, but he replied with a calm assurance saying, "You know I do not much like it here. We'll start looking next month."

My husband, who was already so tall in my eyes, grew a lot taller. We had only been there four months, and he had spent those months transforming the place. When I asked him not to work so hard and for so many hours each day, while he was doing it, he replied that he wanted *me* to be able to walk around the yard, barefooted, without the risk of being pricked or being cut by broken glass. Just about the time he accomplished that, I was asking him for us to look for another home. I realized, again, that my Richard has to truly be an angel or Jesus himself. I also realized the grace of God, yet again, and that I was correct in believing that message was truly for me. God brought us to Ingleside for a reason, but he was not done. He was going to move us out of there. During the course of that week, the third week of February, God spoke to me and said, we should go to a *particular city* during the second week of March. I did not tell that to Richard, but about two mornings later, Richard told me that he thought we should take a trip to that city in the coming week. Later that day, God told me we should go on Tuesday. The next day, Richard asked me what day I wanted us to go.

I was only too happy to repeat, "Tuesday."

I realized that God was strategically calling the shots. God also told me that he was going ahead of us; we were going to have a lovely time on the way to that place, that *he* was going to find us a lovely place there, and that by the time we returned to Mandeville, we would have a "very nice place." He also said that we would move by Easter. At the moment, it all seemed so far-fetched, but I had learned to believe when God spoke and to trust him.

On March 11, 2014, Richard and I left on our trip to that city. Indeed, we had a lovely time on the way there. It was the first time that he and I were traveling that road, though we had briefly passed through that city during our first week on the island. We bought mangoes and ate them when we arrived there. Upon arrival, we checked into a two-bedroom apartment, by the sea. We swam in their private cove in the sea, and later, we made a few phone calls to realtors in the area. One agent had a place that we could look at immediately, and we went off to view it that evening.

It was a lovely place overlooking the Caribbean Sea with a very large pool, and we liked it very much. Its beauty was astounding. On our return that evening, we dined at an Italian restaurant.

# CHAPTER XIV

# THE UNFOLDING OF THE END IN JAMAICA

While we were preparing to leave Tampa, Florida, for the island of Jamaica in 2012, God told me, "Always read Psalm 91; read it every night before you go to bed, when you get there because people are going to be jealous of you." When we arrived in Jamaica, God told me that we should purchase all our food items in the supermarkets. He said that we should not purchase any food item from individuals. God said, "The supermarkets have set themselves up as places that provide food for everyone. If they do not do right by you, I will deal with them. Do not be afraid to buy anything in the supermarkets to eat." I did not tell Richard the extent of what our Father said. I always assumed that he knew. I did tell him that our Father said that we should buy things in the supermarket. Richard liked to support the *little man trying for himself*. I discouraged him whenever he tried to shop at a stall or go to a farmer's market. He did anyway.

The local news report in Jamaica often reported that praedial larceny was a problem in Jamaica. I informed Richard of that. I went on to say that such behavior could cause individuals to take drastic actions to protect their farm products, and if animals or produce are stolen, they do not fall under the purview of the government. Hence, one could unwittingly be harmed by purchasing products that are not inspected. Richard was not phased by what I told him. He purchased most things at the supermarket, but he continued to buy from the individual stalls. Whenever he purchased fruits and vegetables from the stalls and offered me, I refused.

When I shopped at the supermarkets, I often noticed that the cashiers behaved as if they were carrying on some type of rituals with my purchases. I remembered what God had told me, and I totally ignored whatever they might be trying to accomplish. I proceeded to purchase the goods, pay my bill and leave. I did not allow myself to be intimidated. I continued to go shopping once per week.

After a while, it occurred to me that I have always left home, traveled to and arrived at the supermarket feeling great. However, once I arrived at the supermarket, I began feeling ill. It was a strange sensation that made me feel like I would pass out. Whenever I felt it, I always quote verses from the Bible and asked Jesus to please cover me. Jesus did cover me, and I never passed out, but the feelings always alerted me to the presence of spiritual wickedness in the supermarkets and that someone there was trying to affect my life with witchcraft or some other Satanic force of darkness. I did not know anyone at the supermarket. I simply went there to shop. However, I am God's child, and I know that the darkness recognizes the light whenever the light shows up.

The Bible states in Ephesians 6:10-13 (KJV):

> *[10] Finally, my brethren, be strong in the Lord, and in the power of his might.*
>
> *[11] Put on the whole armour of God, that ye may be able to stand against the wiles of the devil.*
>
> *[12] For we wrestle not against flesh and blood, but against principalities, against powers, against the rulers of the darkness of this world, against spiritual wickedness in high places.*
>
> *[13] Wherefore take unto you the whole armour of God, that ye may be able to withstand in the evil day, and having done all, to stand.*

I began to realize that the massaging of my food items at the checkout counter was their way of allowing their demons to activate and work through them.

I wondered, "Why me?"

While Richard and I lived in our Tampa apartment, one day, he said to me, "Honey, it's not you; when they come at you, it is Jesus they are attacking. They can see Jesus the moment they look in your eyes." Remembering what our Father and Richard told me, I was not daunted. I purchased small bottles of olive oil, blessed them myself and anointed myself each day, by making a small sign of the Cross on my forehead. If anywhere ached, I anointed there too, and when I did, the ache went away.

On a Monday morning, in January 2016, God told me that he was going to deal with Jamaica for all the bad things many of the people did to Richard and me. I did not know what form God's "deal with" would take.

Later that morning, I went to the supermarket that I had been shopping at, on a regular basis, for the last six months. When I got there, I noticed that a lot of produce and other things were in carts in different areas in the store. It was a sloppy mess. I asked, "What's going on?" I was told that their refrigerators broke down—not one refrigerator—*all* the refrigerators. I wondered if God had started dealing with them.

# CHAPTER XV

# LEAVING JAMAICA WAS THE BEST THING

In June 2015, I told Richard that our Father told me that we were going to be returning to the United States soon. He asked me, "What city did he say that we should go to?" I told him, "He did not say, but when he does, I will tell you." Shortly thereafter, our Father told me that we were going back to the United States and that we would leave Jamaica before October 2016. God said that we should go to Manhattan, New York. I told Richard that we were going to be going to Manhattan, New York. I began looking at homes in Manhattan. The prices were amazing, but I thought, God said Manhattan; God knew how he would provide for our home in Manhattan.

> The Bible says, *Write the vision, and make it plain upon tables, that he may run that readeth it.*
> (Habakkuk 2:2-KJV)

I typed in large print what I was expecting God to do for us in Manhattan. Based on the prices of houses I saw, I asked God for millions to purchase the house for cash, on the Upper East Side of Manhattan. I also asked God for money to pay the taxes each year, to invest, put in the bank and purchase other things so that we would never be without and that we would always have abundance. God promised me that he would provide.

While in Jamaica, whenever I *acted up* with Richard, he generally said to me, "I am going to leave." I always replied, "Yes, leave." He would then say to me, "You need me." I generally replied, "No, I do not." He followed up by saying, "That's what you think." Since I was never serious, I did not proceed with further rebuttals. He knew we were both jesting with each other.

Sometime about mid-July 2016, Richard and I had a disagreement. He said to me, "I am going to leave." I replied, "Yes, leave." He said, "You need me." I said, "No, I do not." Richard was, at this time, standing in the kitchen while I was standing in the dining room facing him, and he looked up to Heaven and said, "Father, you heard her say that she does not need me. I am coming home."

A few days later, Richard began complaining of pain in his back. He went to see two chiropractors. His condition seemed to worsen. Richard also began experiencing a slight pain in his left hip in July. It too was progressively getting more painful. He went to the doctor to be treated for that pain too. The doctor prescribed Morphine. Soon, his right hand started feeling numb. He went to the doctor for that, as well, and returned with more Morphine.

I asked him, "Did the doctor not recommend any tests?" He told me that the doctor did. I asked him if he did the tests. He said no. I asked, "Why not?" He said that he would do them the following week. A few days later, he went and had some x-rays done. He went to the doctor afterwards to get the test results. When he returned home, I asked him what the doctor said. He told me that he was not going to tell me. "At least not yet," he said. Richard continued taking Morphine, and he took lots of them to alleviate the pain.

On Sunday, August 14, 2016, I was sitting in our TV room watching television. Richard beckoned my attention. I stepped across to our bedroom where he was on the computer. He showed me his face and told me that it was twitching. I told him, "Let's go to a doctor in the United States. We need to know what's going on." He insisted that we visit the local hospital in St. Ann's Bay, in the Ocho Rios area. We had gone to that hospital, on a few occasions, and I was not impressed with the level of attention given to emergency care.

I told Richard, "You know the way things are there. Please let's go to America." He insisted on going there, and so we got in the car and headed for the hospital. I was driving. It was dark. They had done some changes on the road since I last traveled that way. I did not understand the turns, and I did not see any posted signs. Richard said, "Pull over, and I will drive." I told him, "You are in no position to drive. I will pull over when we get to a gas station." About a mile down the road, there was a gas station, and I pulled into it.

God always provides for us. When we pulled into the gas station, there was a car parked with a young man and a young woman sitting in the front of the car. It was not a taxi. I felt that they were there for us, and so I went over and asked them if they would please take us to the St. Ann's Bay Hospital. They said that they would, and they drove us to the hospital. When we arrived at the hospital, I gave them some money. The driver asked me if I wanted him to come back for me. I said, "Yes, but it might be very late." He said, "It doesn't matter how late it is. Here is my number; call me."

At approximately 1:30 a.m., after a couple of x-rays, the emergency room doctor decided that he would admit Richard. Richard was given a bed among many other men. His bed was close to the nurses' station. I had taken a *just-in-case* bag with a few things. I left that bag with Richard, along with a few bottles of water. When Richard was settled in, I decided to leave.

I called the driver of the car that had taken us to the hospital. It was about 2:15 a.m. I said, "I know it's very late. Are you sleeping? He just got admitted." The young man replied, "Don't worry about it. We will be there in about fifteen minutes." He and the young lady were there in exactly fifteen minutes. We left the hospital to go to my home. We drove along the way where we earlier traveled to the hospital. As we approached the gas station where I parked our car, I asked, "Can I pick up my car and drive behind you? I do not know the way very well." The driver consulted with the young woman seated beside him in the front of the car, and she said, "Sure." We pulled up at the gas station at about 3:00 a.m.

There was a red pick-up truck parked beside my car. There were a male and a female, supposedly, selling scallions from the back of the pick-up truck, at that early hour of the morning. As I approached my car, the lady and the man who were sitting by their pick-up truck, almost in unison, said to me, "You left the car door open on the driver's side." I said, "I did?" They said, "Yes." I thanked them and went into the car and drove off.

In my concern for Richard's well-being, I did not realize that I did not close the front door on the driver's side of our car. I believe that the lady and the gentleman who were sitting by it were angels sent by God to protect our car.

I followed the car that picked me up at the hospital all the way home. Just before I arrived at my gate, I blew the horn and went in front of them. They drove behind me for about a minute. When I arrived home, I opened the gate, drove in and parked the car in the area where it was kept. I went back to the gate and thanked the young man and the young woman, profusely, for their dedication and kindness. I gave them some more money. They told me to go inside the house, and if everything was okay on the inside, I should call them on the phone. I did as I was instructed, and I called and informed them that all was well. They wished me a good night, and they were gone.

The following morning was Monday, August 15, 2016. When I arrived at the hospital, Richard needed some medication, which the hospital did not have available to them. I left the hospital to go and fill the prescription at an outside pharmacy. On my return to the hospital, I noticed that Richard could use some additional personal items. I made the decision to return home and get some additional things for him.

As soon as I went outside the hospital gate, I got a taxi to Ocho Rios. Once I got to Ocho Rios, there was another taxi there ready to take me home. I continued to be amazed at the ease with which I could get a taxi when I needed one. It had every appearance that they were exclusively at my disposal, and I was most thankful to God. Emotionally, I was taxed. God knew that I needed the physical help, and he provided it. A car took me home, and the driver asked me what time I would be ready to go back. I told him, and he was there to get me at that time. He took me to Ocho Rios. The moment I came out of his car, there was another taxi ready to go, and that one took me to St. Ann's Bay.

The hospital is in St. Ann's Bay, but it is not close to any main road. At St. Ann's Bay, I needed another taxi to take me to the hospital. There was one sitting idly by, and I sat in it. Soon, three women and two men, including the driver came into the car. They asked me, how I was doing. I told them about the goodness of God. They began telling me how wonderful I was and that God was going to do something marvelous for me on that day. I had never seen them before. They were a merry and happy bunch. They drove me to the hospital, wished me well and left. It was the first time I ever saw them, and it was the last.

When I returned to the men's ward, where Richard was admitted, I asked the attending doctor when the scan for Richard would be done. He told me that he was having a bit of difficulty getting one done. The center in Kingston was having some difficulties with their scheduling due to computer issues, he told me. I asked him if there were any other centers. I was told that there was one in Mandeville and another in Montego Bay. I volunteered to make the calls, and a female doctor provided me with the numbers. It took me many, many calls before I was able to contact anyone at those imaging centers. I finally got through and was told that the earliest that Richard could get an IT scan would be in two weeks.

I went over to Richard's bed and reported the information to him. He told me that was unacceptable. I agreed. He also told me that earlier that Monday morning, before I arrived, he was drinking from one of the bottles of water that I had left him. Some of the water spilled on him. A bit later, one of the nurses came over to his bed and accused him of urinating on himself. He told her that he was trying to drink some water and some of it spilled. He said that she yelled at him, berated him and even told him that he was lying.

He said that he wanted to be discharged. I asked Richard if he was ready to see a doctor in America. He told me yes. I went to have a private consultation with the doctor assigned to Richard. I told him that my husband's situation was not getting better and that a scan could not be had before two weeks. I informed him that I would like him to please discharge my husband so that we could go back to the United States for medical care. He signed the relevant documents. Richard got dressed, with my help, and we were ready to leave.

When we left the men's ward at St. Ann's Bay Hospital, Richard was hopping on one leg. He was unable to use his right arm, and one side of his face had the appearance of a mild stroke; yet, not one of the nurses offered to assist him in getting out of the ward or out of the hospital. There were approximately six nurses at the nurses' station as Richard limped by. The physician, who signed Richard's discharge, asked the nurses at the station, "Cannot one of you help him with a wheel chair?" They all turned their heads away from the doctor and from Richard. Richard then said to the doctor, "It is okay. I will try to manage." Richard and I slowly made our way to a gate at the side of the hospital. There were three taxis there. We chartered one to take us home. When we got home, the taxi driver saw our car and said, "If you guys are selling that car, I want to buy it." He gave me his phone number so that we could contact him should we decide to sell the car. After getting home, I started packing my suitcases. I also started emptying Richard's closet and drawers and began packing some things for him. A bit later he asked, "What's that?" I said, "I packed some things for you." He used his good hand to pull some things out, telling me that he did not need to take all of that. Afterwards, I pleaded with him to take the things that I had packed for him, and he agreed to take most of it.

Later that night, we sat in our living room and talked. Without saying anything to Richard, I went on the phone and began checking on the availability of flights from Kingston to New York and to Florida. I wanted to go to New York. Richard wanted to return to Florida. When I had a few flight availability options, I told him of them. He said that I should not book any, and he told me that I had done well. He also said that he wanted to go to the Tampa General Hospital.

At about ten o'clock that night, Monday, August 16, 2016, Richard said to me, "This is going to be my last night in this house and nobody seems to care." I knew that was his way of telling me that he was ready to return to America. I thought about his statement, as I lied in bed that night, and mused, "You are always 'classic Richard.' Getting out of here will be the best thing for us."

Tuesday morning, I woke up very early, made some breakfast and made sure everything was in order around the house. I ensured that the toilets, face basins and baths in all the bathrooms were clean. I knew that we were never going to return there, but I wanted everything to be in order, even under the circumstances. At about five o'clock that morning, I woke Richard. He had a hard time getting up. I assisted him. I assisted him with everything that morning, including having something to eat and getting dressed.

Richard said that we should leave the house at about nine o'clock. At approximately eight o'clock, I placed a call to the taxi driver, who had driven us from the hospital a day earlier, and asked if he would take us to the airport. I told him that we would like to leave the house at approximately nine o'clock. He said that he would be there in about an hour. He arrived at about nine-thirty that morning. The traffic was heavy, he said.

Although Richard was barely able to walk, Richard insisted on carrying my luggage. I begged him, "Honey, please, let me do it." He still took a few smaller bags up to the road where the taxi was parked. We got in the car, the driver made sure that everything was fine, and we were off to the Montego Bay airport in Jamaica.

# CHAPTER
# XVI

# GOD'S SUPERNATURAL ORCHESTRATION

While in Jamaica, I used two handbags. One was a Gucci hobo handbag that God supernaturally gave me, during the Christmas season of 2010 while I lived in Tampa; the other was a lovely suede bag. I used the Gucci at special times. The suede handbag was the regular knock around. I had been using the suede bag for a long time. However, I wanted to use the Gucci on this trip to return to America. The hobo bag holds a lot more and is, therefore, convenient for travel.

Due to the sudden nature of our departure, I did not have a chance to transfer the contents of the suede bag to the Gucci hobo bag at home. I decided to do so while sitting in the back seat of the taxi, as we traveled to the airport.

Upon arriving at the airport and entering the terminal, I discovered that the suede bag was missing. I called the driver of the taxi and asked if he saw a handbag on the back seat. He told me yes. I asked him how far away he was. He said that he was in Falmouth. I was surprised that he had traveled that far in the time since leaving the airport. I asked him to hold the bag for me. I told him that I would have someone collect it from him in Jamaica. He agreed. It was after my conversation with him ended that I suddenly realized that the car key and all the house keys were in a zipped compartment in the suede bag.

I knew that we were not going to be returning to Jamaica, but I had planned on sending the car key and alarm along with the house keys back to Jamaica by Federal Express. Apparently, God did not want me to have to go through the hassle, knowing what was ahead of us, even though, I had not a clue as to what the future held. I firmly believe that he allowed the events that led to my leaving the keys in the suede bag, in order to save me the time and expense, and I was thankful.

Richard and I proceeded to the airline counter that had the most available flights when I checked the previous night. We purchased our tickets for a flight to Tampa via a connecting flight in Charlotte, North Carolina. After we purchased our tickets, Richard looked at me with a twinkle in his beautiful grey eyes, a twinkle I remembered well but had not seen in a while, and he said, "You did well, Honey; great job!" I replied, "Thank you, Honey."

Apparently, the young lady at the check-in counter did not realize that Richard had a severe disability, though, he limped all the way to the counter, and I did not know that I needed to inform her. She did notice my Bible that I was holding in my hand, and she commented on it. I was very glad that she, at least, recognized the Bible.

Richard and I left the airline check-in counter. Richard limped, and I walked beside him as we slowly made our way to the boarding gate. We went through security and proceeded very slowly along. It was getting close to boarding, and we were not able to move along any faster. Fortunately, a young man, who was working for another airline, came along with a wheel chair. I asked him if he would be kind enough to give my husband a ride to the boarding gate. He was very happy to assist. His appearance was most timely, and I am very grateful to that young man.

As soon as we arrived at the gate, boarding was announced. Because Richard was ill, we were given priority boarding, and we were two of the first ones to enter the aircraft. We took our seats and felt very privileged and honored to be returning to America. Soon, the flight was airborne. Richard ordered sandwiches for us on the plane, and they were most delightful. We looked at each other and commented on the very good quality of the sandwiches. After a few hours, we landed in Charlotte, North Carolina, and, with the help of an airport vehicle that transports the aged and disabled, we made our way to the boarding gate of our connecting flight to Tampa.

As it was raining heavily in Charlotte, our flight to Tampa was delayed for approximately an hour. Soon, the rain abated and we boarded and left. We landed in Tampa just over an hour and a half later. As a result of Richard not being able to walk, our luggage was located with the help of airport personnel, and we received assistance to a taxi from them, as well.

There were two yellow cabs parked outside the airport terminal. The driver of the smaller yellow cab was in front. We attempted to ride with him, but he deferred to the cab driver behind him, whose car was larger, saying that his car could not hold our luggage. We had many pieces of luggage.

Richard and I sat in the back seat of the yellow cab. After some minutes, we pulled up outside the Residence Inn, Downtown Tampa, Florida. We did not have a reservation so I went inside the hotel to see if there were any available rooms. The attendant, at the desk, told me that she had just one room remaining. There was an adjoining hotel, and I decided to see if they had any rooms, just in case the one available room at the Residence Inn was not suitable. The other hotel had no vacancy. I returned to pay for the room at Residence Inn.

I was gone from the taxi less than ten minutes. Richard was sitting in the cab waiting to learn if there was any available room. I did not have a chance to inform him of my progress. Just as I was finished booking the room, Richard and the taxi driver entered the hotel Lobby with our luggage stacked high on the hotel luggage cart. The taxi driver, as if he was in a great rush, took the fare and quickly disappeared.

A moment later, I realized that our laptop computer was missing. It was in the carrying case on the back seat along with a blue and black backpack. They were both at the same place on the back seat where Richard and I sat. When I looked at the luggage cart, the blue and black backpack was among the luggage, but the computer was not. I quickly ran outside to see if I saw the taxi driver. He was gone, and he never returned. Attempts by the hotel to reach him or his company failed. We did not have his name or the number of the cab. As a result, we were not able to identify him or accurately identify his company.

The computer had on its hard drive all the pictures that Richard took of our life in Jamaica. It was a memory bank of the scenes, sights and the life we lived for four years and six months in that country.

There were pictures of us in the pool at one of the homes where we lived, pictures of us on the poolside deck where we spent so many wonderful hours—day and night—gazing on the sea as day folded into night, watching the lights go by on the vast body of water, without being able to see whether it was a cruise ship or some other vessel going by at night. There were birds of varying types and colors, flowers, buildings—everything that interested us. There were also many other pictures of us at different times.

I especially liked the ones that Richard took of us at the poolside at home, as we just simply hung out and chilled in our bathing suits. He was tanned and golden. Indeed, he was handsome. It appears that all those captured memories may now be in the hands of someone, other than Richard or me.

That was Richard's and my first great loss as we returned to America.

# CHAPTER XVII

# THE UNFOLDING OF THE UNEXPECTED THAT ALMOST CRUSHED ME

On the morning of August 18, 2017, Richard and I woke up at the Residence Inn, Downtown Tampa. We readied ourselves in preparation for Richard's visit to Tampa General Hospital's emergency room. Before leaving the hotel, we went down to the Lobby to have some breakfast. Breakfast was complimentary, and it offered a nice buffet option of breakfast meats, fresh fruits, yogurts, nuts, oatmeal porridge, among other choices. We finished our breakfast, and we were now ready to leave for Tampa General Hospital.

The hotel provided us a ride to the hospital. Transportation is part of the complimentary service that Residence Inn provides to its guests, within a two-mile range of its location. It was helpful that Richard did not have to bend to get into the back seat of a taxi. The hotel's van allowed us to step up and sit on high seats, making the pain more tolerable for him.

We arrived at the hospital and went directly to the emergency room. There were not many people waiting when we arrived. As a result, Richard did not have to wait long to be called in. That morning, I developed a throbbing headache, and my blood pressure was very high. Since we were at the emergency room, I decided to see the doctor, as well. Richard was called in first. We were in separate areas. After doing some tests and successfully stabilizing my blood pressure, the doctor told me that they found nothing wrong with me. Now that I was finished, I went in search of Richard. It did not take long for me to locate him. He was anxiously waiting for me. He told me that they were going to admit him.

They had done some scans along with other tests. They told me that the scans revealed that there were lesions on his brain. They said that they also saw a mass on his chest. They decided to do a biopsy to see what was going on in the hip that was hurting so excruciatingly. I was not prepared for the news that I was greeted with, but I decided to speak faith to the situation. I told Richard that he would live and not die to declare the works of the Lord.

Richard was taken to ICU. He was in excruciating pain, and they were giving him many different types of medication. Eventually, it seemed that the pain subsided a bit. At about two o'clock in the morning, I left Richard's bedside. I took a cab to the hotel, which was about two miles away.

The following morning, I headed down to the hotel Lobby for some breakfast. I fixed a plate for Richard, asked for a ride to the hospital and was there in about six minutes after leaving the hotel. When I arrived, Richard was very happy to see me.

That day was Richard's second at Tampa General Hospital. The oncologist, the palliative care group and the doctor assigned as Richard's primary doctor all came to his room. I was told that Richard had cancer. They may have said that it metastasised, that it was stage four, but I did not recall hearing any of that—maybe I did not want to hear. Richard meant so much to me.

Day by day, Richard and I, along with the person who transported him, went down to the radiation room for palliative radiation of his hip and head. This we did for fifteen days. During one of the treatments, they had to terminate the radiation midway because the pain was overly excruciating. After that premature termination, the nurse decided to give him his "pain" medication a few minutes before palliative radiation and that seemed to have helped. Richard received ten treatments to his head and fifteen treatments to his hip. At the completion of these treatments,

Richard received a few sessions of in-room physical therapy.

Richard was eager to be up and going, and a few times he asked me to help him work his right arm that he was unable to use. While he and I did that, we made some progress. Twice, he showed me that he could move his right arm by himself.

Tampa General Hospital was planning to send Richard to a nursing facility for therapy. Richard was not keen on going to a nursing facility at that point. He wanted to come home to the apartment at the Residence Inn, and I wanted him to have his desires.

On Wednesday, September 21, 2016, Richard and I had a very successful day. Richard got out of bed, and, with minimal assistance from me, he went to the bathroom and back. Richard and I were overjoyed. We gave each other high-fives and celebrated his accomplishment. That evening, I left for home after ensuring that Richard had enough to eat, had enough water on his food table, a few M&Ms, which he loved and enough warm blankets, along with the telephone close to him, so that he could reach it with his "good arm" when I called to check in with him.

On Thursday morning, September 22, 2016, at approximately seven o'clock, I was about to go downstairs to the Lobby for breakfast when my cell phone rang. I quickly picked it up and noticed that it was a call from the hospital. On the night Richard was admitted, the attending doctor told me that if the steroids, which he had recommended to keep Richard's head from swelling, had worked negatively, he would have to call me at home. Although, Richard was doing quite well when I left him that evening, I felt unnerved at seeing the hospital's number. I quickly answered the phone. It was the nurse who was assigned to Richard for that day. He was calling to inform me, he said, that, "Your husband fell, but he did not hit his head." I asked him, "How is that possible?"

I said that when I am there, if he gets up to sit at the edge of the bed, the bells and beeps go off. Also, the heart monitor beeps quite loudly when it unplugs. The nurse said that Richard got up to go to the bathroom. The alarm on the bed was off, as was the heart monitor. Halfway to the bathroom, he fell. I asked the nurse where Richard was, he told me that he was sitting in the chair, referring to the recliner in his room. I asked to speak with him, and the nurse handed Richard the phone. I asked, "Are you okay, Honey? What happened?"

Richard said that he wanted to go to the bathroom. He was calling for help, and no one came to assist him. He did not want to have an accident, and he was trying to get to the bathroom. He fell midway between the bathroom and his bed. After he fell, he called out for help, and they all ran away from him.

I hurried through breakfast and made my way to the hospital, as I had done daily for over four weeks. Richard was so glad when I arrived. I believe he thought, after the fall, that I was the only one who truly cared for him. When I arrived at the hospital, Richard could not move at all. The past four weeks that Richard was in the hospital, he always sat up and always walked with assistance from me, the nurses or by using his "good" hand to pull himself up. Now, he had to be moved from bed to stretcher by pulling or dragging the sheet he was lying on and using it to get him across.

I wondered why his nurse had told me, by phone, that he did not hit his head, when it was that very nurse who told me that no one was in the room when Richard fell. I wanted to be doubly sure since I found his remark intriguing. I called the nurse inside the room and asked him, "Was anyone here when my husband fell?" He replied, "No." I asked him, "How do you know that he did not hit his head as you told me when you called?" He did not respond to that question. I asked him to please ask the doctor to do an x-ray on Richard's hip to see if any bones were cracked or broken because the pain had again become excruciating and now Richard could not move at all. A slight touch to the area was causing him to be in agony.

The doctor called to assure me that nothing was wrong with his hip. I asked her, "How can you say that when you cannot see through his skin?" I refused to let up, asking the nurse at every turn to ask the doctor to order an x-ray. The doctor, eventually, relented. The x-ray, I was told, was negative. About an hour after I arrived at the hospital that morning, Richard had started sounding incoherent and had a bit of slurring of speech. I requested that the doctor order a head scan to see if he had hit his head. The doctor again told me that nothing was wrong with his head.

Later that day, the hospital moved Richard to a room on another floor. They said there was a video camera in that room, and he could be monitored. He was moved one floor above where he was, and I was told that was the trauma floor. There was a teenage male patient in the room when Richard arrived there. The boy's parents were there. He was hooked up to a life support system. His parents told me that he was unable to speak. I asked if I could pray for him. They welcomed the prayer, and I prayed for his recovery.

That Thursday night, I left the hospital after nine o'clock. Richard was not comfortable with me leaving. After the fall, the seeming disorientation, not being able to move at all and now moved to a strange environment, he was obviously very nervous. Thursday was a hectic day, and I had no idea what Friday held. I decided to go home and get some sleep, after getting Richard's approval to leave.

The following morning, Friday, before leaving home, I received a call from a social worker at the hospital. She told me that she had a conversation with Richard and that he told her that he wanted to go to the nursing facility. I told her that when I left Richard on Thursday night, he was in no condition to have that conversation with her. I also told her that I was on my way to the hospital and would speak with her when I arrived there.

That Friday morning, as I exited the elevator on the eighth floor at the hospital, I met the mother of the young man who was sharing the room with Richard. She said to me, "Are you Angela?" I said, "Yes." She said, "Girl, as long as the night was, he called for you."

I had no idea that Richard was so traumatized. I hastened my steps and hurried to the room after being told that. I greeted him, and he said, "Please do not ever leave me again." I promised him that I would not. Shortly after I greeted Richard, a nurse greeted me. She introduced herself by telling me her name. She said that she is the nurse for the young man who is sharing the room with my husband. She continued by saying that she was in the room, and she overheard a conversation with my husband and the social worker. She said that the social worker wanted to move "your husband" to a nursing home, and he told her that he was not going to say anything to her until his wife "got here."

I said to her, "How is it that the social worker told me that he told her that he was ready to go to the nursing home?" She said, "I was right across there in that corner, and I heard the conversation, and he never said that."

A bit later, the doctor called me to say that social services would be sending Richard to a nursing home that day. I asked the doctor if she was aware that he was calling for me last night, that he appears to be traumatized, that he's not speaking well, and he is not coherent. She said that she was told that he was calling for me all night.

Richard's nurse on Friday, September 23, 2016, was a man. He told me that he tried to speak with Richard and that he sounded incoherent. I told him that was not always the case, but he fell on Thursday morning on the seventh floor and shortly thereafter he started a downward progression. I also told the male nurse that I asked the doctor to do a head scan, and she had, so far, refused. The male nurse said that he thought one should be done, and he would speak with the doctor. At about five o'clock on the afternoon of Friday, September 23, 2016, Richard was taken downstairs for a head scan. We were not given the result of the head scan.

When he returned to the room, plans were in full motion to have him sent to a nursing home that evening. Richard said that he was not going to a nursing home. After everything I saw the last two days, I did not think that he was in any way, shape or form ready to be discharged. We had no choice, however, and so I spoke with the doctor again and told her that he could not go to a nursing home. He wanted to go home with me to the apartment at the hotel, and I would let him. She said that she was afraid that he would fall at home. I told her that the irony of her statement was that, *He fell here*, in the hospital, with so many bells and whistles and nurses all around.

She responded by saying, "A person can fall anywhere." She agreed to let Richard go home with me.

At about 8:15 p.m. that Friday, two men, the driver of the ambulance and his assistant, came to transport Richard to our temporary home at the hotel. The men pulled Richard from the hospital bed to the stretcher using the sheet he was lying on.

At the hotel, they lifted him directly from the stretcher to the bed. He remained there all night. I woke up a couple of times, during the night, to assist him with going to the bathroom, and he had a restful night. In the morning, I encouraged him to get out of bed. He did not want to, but I continued to coax him. He agreed to lie on a large couch, which I had pulled up close to the bed. It was then that I realized that Richard was really in no position to go to a nursing home or to be at home. Richard belonged in the hospital.

At six o'clock Saturday evening, one day after Richard was discharged, he had eaten nothing. I tried to feed him some soup, but he refused. He wanted to get back into bed; the task was too much for me. I tried but realized that Richard could not sit up, stand up or assist in any way.

I called a friend of Richard's and asked for some help. This was the first time that she was being made aware that Richard was ill and was back in the United States. He had asked me not to tell anyone, and I respected his wishes. Fortunately, she showed up about an hour after I placed the call. She arrived with her daughter. She lived about forty-five minutes away from our location. All three of us tried getting Richard in bed, but it was impossible.

She immediately called 911, and, soon, two men, from the fire department, were there to take Richard back to the hospital. He was readmitted to Tampa General Hospital that Saturday evening. The readmitting doctor ordered another head scan for Richard. He told me that the result showed that Richard's head was just as the scan he took when he entered the hospital initially on August 18, 2016. He said that he was readmitting Richard at the hospital for a few days to see how he progressed.

On day three of the readmission, a lady from social services came to the room and told me that she had found a nursing home for Richard about twenty miles away. I protested, yet again, that he was too ill to be discharged. The social worker said that the doctor told her that there was nothing else they could do at the hospital. Anything that they could do, a nursing home could do the same.

I called the doctor, the same female doctor who had earlier discharged Richard a day after he fell in the hospital. I asked her, "Do you not have any compassion? Do you not see he is in no position to be discharged?"

I was talking with her for some minutes on the hospital phone. Suddenly, a male voice cut into the conversation and said, "This is Michael. It is to time go." At that point, the doctor said that she had to go, and the conversation ended.

I called Medicare and appealed to them. Medicare gave Richard twenty-four hours, at which time they would review his case.

I was on the same hospital phone with the Medicare representative, making the case as to why I thought Richard was in no shape to be discharged. After a few minutes into the conversation with the Medicare person, someone again cut into our conversation and said, "This is Michael. It is time to go." Immediately, as with the doctor, the Medicare personnel said that he had to go, and the conversation ended there. I am still trying to figure out who *Michael* is.

On the morning of Thursday, September 29, 2016, I went to the floor where Richard had been for four days, since being readmitted. I was told that he was transferred to another floor. Hope welled up in me, as I thought that they had seen the virtue of keeping Richard in the hospital for a while longer. I quickly made my way to his new room. After a few wrong turns, I arrived at his room and greeted him.

His nurse came and went. I began asking her questions about Richard's condition. I tried to have Richard eat something, but he refused. I did not know if he could not eat or if he did not want to eat. Later, his doctor came in, and I began telling him that Richard was not eating. I asked him if there was a way that he could get Richard to eat some food. He told me that he was giving me the responsibility of getting Richard to eat some nutritious foods. I told him that I would try.

About an hour later, a lady came into the room and told Richard and I that she had found a nursing home, and they were in the process of discharging him to that home. She said that Medicare had denied the appeal because the doctor at Tampa General Hospital said that there was nothing more they could do. I wondered why they had gone through the trouble of transferring Richard to another floor on another wing of the hospital when they knew that he was going to be discharged two or three hours later.

I resigned myself to the inevitable and believed that Richard did too. Soon, an ambulance arrived to take Richard to the nursing home. The ambulance crew was made up of two females and one male. Richard was taken to the ambulance on a stretcher. Two attendants sat by him. I traveled in the front of the ambulance with the female driver.

In about twenty minutes, we arrived at the nursing facility that would become Richard's new location. Richard was assigned a room, which he shared with another male. I busied myself arranging Richard's clothes and other personal items in the drawers. There was a large window across from Richard's bed. Outside that window, was a large tree with branches spreading all over. I thought it would be nice for Richard to be able to look outside at the tree, a pleasure he did not have at Tampa General Hospital. Richard, a nature lover, paid no attention to what was going on outside. He was too ill, it appears, to focus on anything outside of what was going on with his body.

About an hour after arriving at the nursing facility, an occupational therapist came to Richard's room and performed some basic routines with Richard. He was not able to sit up, but he recognized one finger, three fingers, etcetera. He used his "good" hand to touch his nose with a finger. He did not follow her finger with his eyes, as she moved it in front of his face so she concluded that he needed to get some interaction with the outside.

She decided to get him a wheelchair so that I could take him outside during the days. She asked me what wheelchair I thought would be good for him. She brought one to his room with a very high back, and I told her that would work. She placed it in his bathroom for safekeeping.

I was hoping to take Richard outside in the wheelchair so that he could see the large, beautiful tree that was just outside his window.

Later that day, a registered nurse, at the facility, came to introduce herself to us. She asked me how I would get home. I told her that I intended to take the bus. She offered to give me a ride home that evening, and she promised to drive me home each evening thereafter. I told her that I was staying at a hotel Downtown Tampa. She said that it was not a problem. I thanked her for her generosity, and she drove me home that evening. When she dropped me off at Residence Inn that evening, I had no idea that she was upset with me. We had been speaking the whole drive there from Fletcher's Avenue to East Tyler Street. On arrival, I thanked her, wished her a good night and wished her a safe drive home.

On Friday, when I saw her at the nursing home, she ignored me as if she never met me the day before and drove me home. She was at the nurses' station. I went by and said, "Hello, how are you?" She barely responded, holding her head down. I did not hear her response, but I decided that I would leave her alone.

That Friday morning, the lead occupational therapist visited Richard before my arrival. She returned when she learned that I was in the room with him. She told me that he was in no condition to be discharged from the hospital. She said that he was "high risk" for the services that they provided at the nursing facility. She said that she literally took her hand and pulled a thick mucus from his nose. She said that I had the right to call 911 and ask them to take Richard to a hospital because he was not breathing well.

Richard had left Tampa General Hospital with the same degree of labored breathing along with an oxygen tank. I told the occupational therapist that I fought to have him remain in the hospital, but I had no recourse, when all attempts failed.

While he was at Tampa General Hospital, I stayed with him until six or seven o'clock in the evenings. Now that I was taking the bus, I left at about five o'clock. Richard was agreeable to that. He wanted me to be safe. Although he was suffering, he was keenly sensitive of my well-being. There were times when, due to his pain and suffering, he got upset with me, but his love and concern for me had not changed, and when it mattered, it appeared that there was no amount of pain that could prevent him from displaying it.

When his friend offered to take Richard to a nursing home near her house, after his readmission to Tampa General, she told me, "He loves you so much. All he kept asking me was what is going to happen to Angie?" I loved him too, so much, and he knew it.

# CHAPTER
# XVIII

# THE DEPARTURE I WAS NOT PREPARED FOR

On Saturday, October 1, 2016, while traveling to the nursing home to spend the day with Richard, my phone rang. My heart skipped a beat when the caller said that she was a nurse calling from the nursing home. Her next word seemed an eternity away. I held on, literally, to the bus rail and to my emotions.

She said, "I am calling to tell you that Mr. Miller developed breathing problems and was transferred to Florida Hospital."

I asked her, "Why did not you send him to St. Joseph's Hospital?" She replied, "When we have to send patients to the hospital, we send them to the nearest hospital." I told her thanks for calling. I had never been to St. Joseph's Hospital, but I once overheard a woman talking about taking her sick son there, and she said that they were "very good." I turned to the bus driver and asked, "How do I get to Florida Hospital on Bruce Downs?" She told me to stay on the bus, and she would tell me when to get off. I did as she instructed.

Soon, I was at the hospital grounds. There was a man sitting on the back of a pick-up truck who asked me if I knew where I was going. I told him, "No." He provided me with directions to the emergency room. I got the impression that he was there to assist me in finding my way.

I went through a set of glass doors. There were two people at the desk as I entered, and I inquired of them as to where Richard might be found. As I left where they were, someone, standing in the direction of where I was headed, offered to show me to where he was.

Richard lit up when he saw me, and I was so glad to see that he was again in a hospital. He was on oxygen, but he appeared to be a lot more comfortable than when he was at the nursing home. We hugged.

I kissed his face and told him that God had answered my prayer. I told him that I prayed for him to be in a hospital.

While they were preparing a room for him on the ICU floor, we talked. A few nurses and doctors gathered in his room, and they asked us about Jamaica. Richard told them that we had lived there for the past four and a half years and had returned because of his illness.

The emergency room nurse was most attentive. She kept informing us of the progress they were making with the room and wanted to know if there was anything she could do to make us more comfortable. About two hours later, Transport came to take Richard to his room.

A short time after getting to the room, a doctor came by. He discussed Richard's prognosis with us. Richard asked him to do whatever it takes to save his life. I agreed with Richard. The doctor said that he would assemble a team of the best doctors at the hospital to help Richard.

Soon after the doctor left the room, Richard asked me for something to eat. I fed him some yogurt along with some fresh cut strawberries, red berries and blackberries that I brought him from home, and he ate it all and thanked me. I also brought him some oatmeal porridge, which he wanted to have. His attending nurse in ICU decided that he should not have it because it might cause him some problems swallowing. Richard wanted the porridge, and I wanted to give it to him because I knew that he was hungry. He had, only seconds earlier, eaten the yogurt and the berries without any difficulties. I pointed that out to the nurse. However, she maintained that he should not get the porridge, and she kept a close watch on us. In the end, I was not able to feed him the porridge.

At day's end, before leaving, I checked with Richard as to whether he was warm, thirsty or hungry. He told me that he was hungry. The hospital told me that because he was admitted to that floor just hours before dinner, a food tray was not among the trays at the normal dinner hour for him. I asked the nurse to please see that he gets something to eat. She promised that she would get him some dinner. I left at seven o'clock. When I arrived at the hospital on Sunday morning, Richard had not eaten anything since I fed him the berries and yogurt on Saturday. When I left on Saturday evening, he was speaking. He spoke all day on Saturday. Now, on Sunday, he was barely speaking. He mumbled just one or two words. That was all.

On Monday morning, when I arrived at the hospital, the cardiologist told me that he did a test and Richard's heart was strong. I was hopeful. A short time later, I spoke with the head of the oncologist department.

He said that he visited Richard that morning, and Richard was weak. As a result, he did not think that Richard was doing well. I told him that the cardiologist told me that he did a test that morning, and his heart was strong. He said, that may be the case, but because there was something down there blocking his breathing, it was making it difficult for him. I told the oncologist that Richard had not eaten since I fed him a small morsel of yogurt and berries, shortly after admission on Saturday. I also told him that Richard was not speaking and that he kept groaning. I went on to say that since he already received his pain medication, I believed that he was groaning because he was hungry.

The oncologist said that he had recommended a test that morning to see which type of feeding tube would be better suited for Richard. Shortly after speaking with the oncologist, the lady that performed the feeding tube test came by the room to tell me that Richard could have the tube down his nose. She said that she had given the result to the doctor. I asked her about the discomfort and possible danger of the tube going down his nose. She said that it would be very safe. I again spoke with the doctor, and he told me that he had ordered the tube. It seemed like an eternity for the process to get to the point where Richard would get the feeding tube.

The nurse who prevented me from feeding Richard the porridge on Saturday, when he was admitted, was the same nurse assigned to Richard on that Monday. She seemed to be doing everything to prevent him from getting fed, and this led me to believe that she appeared to have had some hatred for him.

I placed a call to the nurse manager, who promptly came up, and in a few minutes the team was there to put the tube in and to perform the x-ray to be sure that it was properly positioned in his stomach. After that was done, the next step was to get the liquid food and the pump that would drip the liquid through the tube into his stomach.

The assigned nurse had the liquid food in her possession, but she was refusing to set up the pump. She gave one excuse after another to delay the process. I called the nurse manager again, and she came right up. The nurse manager went and got the pump and stood there until the nurse on duty set it up and got it dripping.

The nurse manager then asked me if everything was fine. I told her, "Thanks, as fine as it could be under the circumstances." She told me that she was leaving to go back to her office, but I should call her if there were any issues. I thanked her again for her kindness and her prompt response.

The assigned nurse said that if Richard's body rejected the tube and food, they would have to remove it. She said that if rejection was going to take place, it would happen in about four hours. Since it was evident to me that she was against Richard, I decided to wait until that time had elapsed before leaving the hospital to go home. At this point, Richard was not speaking at all. I gave him a hug and told him that I love him and that I was leaving. He lied there with the tube in and his eyes closed.

That was Monday, October 3, 2016.

While we were still living in Jamaica, I had been asking Richard to please let us return to America to live. He was not willing to leave, when I wanted us to. However, God had told me that Richard and I would return to America *together*. We did on August 17, 2016.

On Monday morning, as I made my way to the hospital, the gentleman who was sitting on the back of the pick-up truck on Saturday when Richard was admitted and who directed me to the emergency room, greeted me in a familiar way. I did not think that I knew him, but he reminded me that he was the person who directed me on Saturday morning to the emergency room. I apologized and told him that I had a lot on my mind. It appeared, on Monday evening, that I came out of the hospital another way than I had the previous two days. I was not sure where to get the bus, and he directed me.

I was at the bus stop in deep thoughts. A woman came up to me and greeted me. She said that she was a nurse and that she was working at the hospital. She said that she lived in New York, but she was now living in Florida. She said that she preferred Florida. It is warm.

I told her that I preferred New York. She said that I should go back to New York. I told her that I was hoping to do so when my husband got better.

I had told the doctors at Tampa General Hospital, when I discovered that they were only administering palliative radiation to Richard, that I wanted to take him to New York for chemo treatments. I had gone ahead and scheduled an appointment at Mount Sinai hospital in New York. I was still hoping that Richard would get strong enough so that we would be able to do so.

The woman at the bus stop indicated to me that the bus was coming. She wished me well and said that she was going inside to begin work. I said goodbye, and in about a minute the bus pulled up at my stop. I went on the bus.

After getting home on Monday evening, I called the nurses' station at the ICU at Florida Hospital. It was about nine o'clock. I identified myself and asked how Mr. Miller was doing. The nurse told me that he was stable and was resting. I went off to sleep.

I woke up on Tuesday, October 4, 2016, and I began preparing to go to the hospital. Shortly, thereafter, my phone rang. It was a doctor at Florida Hospital. He called to ask me to hurry and get to the hospital. He said that Richard was placed on life support.

I was hurrying, but in less than twenty minutes another call came from the doctor. He told me to get there *now*. I called a taxi and hurried downstairs. The taxi was already in front of the hotel when I got there. I got in and asked the driver to please take me to Florida Hospital on Bruce Downs, as fast as he could. I told him that my husband was in the hospital, and the doctor called to tell me that I had to get there now. He sped up.

My world was turning upside down. I began crying in the cab. I heard myself saying, "This is not happening. Richard has to live. Oh, God, please let Richard live."

We pulled up at the hospital. I inquired as to where Richard was. The doctor had provided me a room number, and I asked to be directed there.

When I stepped in, Richard was hooked up to a large machine with some tubes attached to his body. There was a large tube in his mouth. The machine was pumping, and his chest was going up and down. There were four men and two women in white coats standing by Richard's bed when

I entered the room. They were looking at him while a nurse was busy putting medication in the machine that was pumping. They left shortly after I arrived.

I stepped over to Richard and put my head on his chest. I heard his heart beating. This was something I had done so many times during our times together. Through the years, when Richard was lying on his back, I generally lied beside him and put my head on his chest and listened to his heart beat. It was so comforting to me. I wanted to hear his heart beat another time.

I was crying uncontrollably, and I asked God, "Why?" I said, "Father, you told me that he would live. You have never lied to me. He has got to live."

The hospital Chaplin came inside the room and sat beside me as I continued to cry. He sat there for a while. I began to feel sick—really, really sick. I did not tell anyone that I was feeling ill. I kept getting up to go and rub Richard's cheeks, hands and chest and sat down again.

Sometime later, the oncologist came in—the doctor, who upon admission, had promised to assemble the best team to attempt to get Richard better. He asked the nurse "How are things going?"

She told him that she was continuing to administer the medicine but his heart rate was remaining within a certain range. The doctor said that Richard had about two hours, and he left the room.

The nurse, the Chaplin and I were the three remaining in the room with Richard.

I called Richard's friend, who had come to the hotel just over a week earlier to attempt to assist me in getting him in bed, after he was prematurely discharged from Tampa General Hospital. I told her that I was at Florida Hospital on Bruce Downs, and Richard was on life support. I completed that call.

I continued to cry, and, while sobbing, I said, "Father, I release Richard to you. If you take him, I am still going to love you, and I will always serve you."

I believed that Richard would have wanted me to say that. Although I was terribly distressed, and I was still hoping that God would work a miracle right there, at that moment, I wanted Richard to hear that, just in case I did not get the miracle that I was hoping for.

It has always made Richard very happy when I behaved in a manner that indicated that our Father was in control.

Shortly after that declaration, the Chaplin told me that he was leaving. He gave me his business card and told me to call if I needed him. Just as he stepped out, Richard's friend stepped in. I was still crying, and she told me that she was sorry.

The doctor returned to tell the nurse to stop administering medicine but not to disconnect the machine. He told me, "Go over and hold the man's hand." I did not tell him that I was feeling ill. I was still hoping for a miracle. I wanted to see Richard wake up and begin to smile and laugh again. I sat and waited.

The nurse, who was attending to Richard, asked me if I wanted to see some information in his file. I said that I was not really interested. Richard's friend said that she wanted to.

The nurse said that on Saturday when Richard was admitted to Florida Hospital, they did a head scan, and there were two tumors in his head. One was 15 centimetres and the other was 16 centimetres.

It was the first time that I was hearing that information. I could not believe it.

I continued to feel ill. I had not much strength or anything else at that moment. Occasionally, I got up, went over to kiss Richard's forehead and or squeezed his hand. Otherwise, I sat on the chair in the room, waiting.

A short while later, the monitor began trending down as if it was counting—45, 44, 43, 42, 41, 40. In some seconds, as the three of us stood there and stared at it, it recorded "0."

The nurse said that he was gone, and I was numb. Richard was pronounced dead at 9:47 a.m. on October 4, 2016. Richard's friend and I stayed in the room for another thirty minutes or so. I kissed him one last time and then we left.

Richard's friend drove me to the nursing home where Richard had been, for two days, before going to Florida Hospital. I collected his belongings. She drove me to the hotel and accompanied me to my suite. We sat and chatted for a while.

I continued to feel ill. I told her that I was feeling ill and needed some time to rest. She left; Richard was gone, and I was all alone.

# CHAPTER XIX

# THE REVEALING OF JESUS

When I arrived in Tampa, Florida, on January 21, 2010, I had no concept of what would unfold. God told me to go there, and I did what he said.

The supernatural life that I have lived these past years has been one that no person, on earth, can ever imagine unless he or she has experienced it for him or herself. I have not listed the totality of my experiences because some are most personal in nature, and others are, in my view, difficult to narrate in a way that can be easily understood.

Some things have been a marvel, even to me, though, I had been at the center of them all.

It has been quite a ride.

When Linda and Kevin interviewed me in January 2010 and provided me a job, for which I was so grateful, knowing that I did not send them an application nor did I upload my resume on the Internet, I did not realize that the supernatural was at work.

I had not realized when I showed up for work at the small law firm on Kennedy Boulevard in Tampa, Florida, on Friday, February 9, 2010, that I was going to be working with Jesus.

On the Monday following Easter Sunday 2010, after Roger Fixit's and my first meeting, when I asked him to take me to dinner, and he asked me to meet him on Kennedy Boulevard, Downtown Tampa, I had wondered why Kennedy Boulevard and not where I lived. It appeared that he was leaving hints all over the place. I just did not get them.

Even when Richard told me that he had only two siblings named Martha and Barbara, which were the exact names that my boss, Tom, at the law firm on Kennedy Boulevard, told me were the names of his only two siblings, I thought it curious, but I did not make the connection, although, I did say to Richard, a few times, that I found it compelling that they both had only two siblings with the very same names.

Tom, Roger Fixit and Richard Miller did things that amazed me, but I never questioned them about those things. It also appeared that they always knew what I was thinking.

When my boss, Tom, on my first day at the law firm and the first time I ever laid eyes on him, stood there, before me, and said "Baker Act," and I was at a loss for words wondering, to myself, how he knew that, I was not aware that he knew all things.

Even when my boss, at the same Tampa law firm, moved the contents of his office into my small space, I did not think anything of it, other than the fact that God had told me that it would happen and I should allow it. I saw the nail prints in Tom's hands, that he was showing to me, and I wondered what it meant. I reminded myself that only Jesus had nail prints in his hands, but I was not expecting Jesus to be at a law firm in Tampa so I moved on, mentally.

One Sunday in April 2010, after I had left the law firm, I had stopped Downtown Tampa, on my way from church to see if I would see my boss at the law firm. He often went into the office on Sundays, he had told me. I stood outside the office on that Sunday and called the office number. A man answered the phone. The voice did not sound like that of my boss. It was a strange unfamiliar rumble of a sound that gave me pause. I responded by saying, "I do not know what you're getting so incensed about." I said a few other words and hung up the phone.

The following Sunday, I went to Tampa Free International Church. I heard Pastor Joy, in her sermon, say, "If only you knew who you were speaking to on the phone." I knew that she was referring to me, but I did not, at the time, comprehend what she was saying.

When you are homeless, you do not think about much more than *when will I have a home again.*

Maslow's hierarchy of needs lists the basic needs of man. The two most fundamental are *safety* and *belonging*. A homeless person, I have learned, on account of my experience, has no assurance of either.

It was on Easter Sunday 2010, on my way home from Tampa Free International Church, where the pastor had preached that day that I would meet my Boaz, when I met Jesus, who at the time called himself Roger Fixit. She had said that someone was going to "*meet her Boaz,*" and he was going to take her to dinner.

When Roger Fixit showed up that day, he took ownership of me in a way that did not suggest that he was a stranger. It was at that moment that the supernatural started being revealed. I knew, regardless of what he said, that he was *not* mortal. I saw immortal dripping off him each time I looked at him. Everything about him defied *everything* that I knew about those living on earth.

Two months later when Roger Fixit became Richard Miller with the same exact hair—baldness, cut and color—though, everything else about him had changed—with his many angels who were making his and their presence known everywhere I went, and despite the fact that the manager at the Salvation Army Women's House failed to believe me when I told her that he was Jesus, I knew what I had been experiencing was real.

With every passing day that Richard Miller and I spent talking about Heaven and all things God, the way that he expressed them to me and the way he talked about *his* Father and *our* Father, I knew that *he* knew *him*. And, I knew that his knowledge of God did not come from reading about him in the Bible.

I had read the Bible from *Genesis* to *Revelation* at least three times by then. I had heard many theologians, pastors and many people of the Christian faith talk about God.

When Richard spoke about God, I knew that he knew God, *personally*. He told me things, with such knowledge and command of that knowledge, about creation and everything in the universe, that made me know that *he* created them.

After Richard and I moved into our apartment in Tampa, Florida, one evening, he stood by the sink in the kitchen and revealed his scourged back to me. His back was totally scourged one moment. The next moment, it was whole and unblemished. He gave me that revelation without saying a thing, and he continued doing what he was doing. He was confirming what he knew that I had already determined. He is Jesus.

At the law firm, when I saw the nail prints in his hand, I had not realized because the phenomenon was new, different, unexpected and not normal. I had thought about it, but I did not allow myself to be obsessed by what I saw. I have now seen and experienced so much that one might say I am no longer a rookie.

I had been with Jesus from February 9, 2010 to October 4, 2017. He came, by introduction, as my boss at the law firm in Tampa, then as Roger Fixit, Richard Miller—my spouse, friend, confidant, and the person with whom I have exclusively spent the best seven years and eight months of my life—until his departure by death.

Richard had no friend that I knew of, except for the lady who came to Richard's and my aid at the hotel in Tampa and who was with me on the day Richard died. She told me on that day, "You did well. He spoke so highly of you. You did all you could have done, and he loved you so much. He said you said that he was Jesus."

I looked at her and said, "Was he?" She looked at me and smiled.

I am beginning to think that she was an angel.

One day, while still in Jamaica, not very long before we left for our return to the United States, I was moving around our living room and the most abnormal thought came to my mind. This was what it said, "I want Richard to die of cancer and rise again from the dead, the way he did when he died on the Cross, so that I can experience what the people of that time experienced." It was *not* my thought. I had no idea where it came from.

Richard did die of cancer in a Florida Hospital on October 4, 2016. I have seen Richard in person many times since his death. He looks different each time. He acts in ways to let me know it is him. I acquiesce and move on. I know that he will return soon again. He lives in Heaven, and he lives on earth.

On my return to New York, in October 2016, while I was in a Midtown, Manhattan hotel, I had a talk with my sister in Philadelphia. She was expressing her sadness and condolence at my loss. I thanked her and then began telling her of some of the awesome experiences I had with Richard and the world I had lived in with him. I told her that I missed him terribly, but I was not very sad because I felt that he was going to return.

I realized that what I was telling her was too much for her to grasp.

She politely said, "That is your reality." I told her, "It really is."

I did not expect her to grasp and relate to things that are truly surreal. Had they not been *my reality*, I would not be able to grasp them either. I simply wanted to share with her, and it was my way of telling her that Richard was Jesus.

I told my eldest brother, in December 2010, during a conversation we were having, that I had been dating Richard for the past ten months. "He is so amazing," I had said. "I know that he is Jesus." My brother made light of it.

On one of two visits to another sister's house, in Jamaica, that Richard and I made, I told her, "Richard is Jesus."

She said, "No way."

I said, "Then who is he?"

She replied, "I do not know, but I know he's not Jesus."

I understood where they all stood. It is inconceivable to conceive *my reality* when you have not lived it.

Because I have lived it, I now want to share it with the whole world.